ESSENTIALS OF
THE LAND OF ISRAEL

In honor of
and in grateful tribute to
beloved sages, teachers, and leaders:
Rabbi Jonathan Sacks, *zt"l,* ✡ **Rabbi Reuven Bulka**, *zt"l,*
masters of Torah, builders of community, champions of kindness.

But the land that you cross over to possess is a land of hills and valleys, which drinks water from the rain of heaven, a land for which the Lord your God cares; the eyes of the Lord your God are always on it, from the beginning of the year to the very end of the year.

Deuteronomy 11:11-12

Essentials of the Land of Israel

A Geographical History

Brandon Marlon

VALLENTINE MITCHELL

LONDON • CHICAGO

First published in 2022 by Vallentine Mitchell

Catalyst House,   814 N. Franklin Street,
720 Centennial Court,   Chicago,
Centennial Park, Elstree WD6 3SY, UK   IL 60610 USA

www.vmbooks.com

British Library Cataloguing in Publication Data:
An entry can be found on request

ISBN 978 1 912676 86 6 (Cloth)
ISBN 978 1 912676 87 3 (Ebook)

Library of Congress Cataloging in Publication Data:
An entry can be found on request

Contents

Acknowledgments

My sincere gratitude extends to the Azrieli Institute of Israel Studies (Concordia University) and in particular to its director, Dr. Csaba Nikolenyi, for generously sponsoring this book, including its cartographic requirements; to Rabbi Ken Spiro for his useful manuscript suggestions; to Bill Nelson for our map-making partnership; and to the Vallentine Mitchell staffers for their assistance in the publication and promotion of this work.

List of Photographs

(All photographs © 2021 Brandon Marlon)

1. Edom Mountains
2. Jerusalem
3. View from Mount Tavor
4. Jezreel Valley
5. Hermon Stream
6. Lake Kinneret (the Sea of Galilee)
7. Mediterranean Sea
8. Negev Desert
9. Forested Judean Hills
10. Herodium (Herodion)
11. Nitzanah
12. Nimrod Fortress
13. Gezer
14. Megiddo
15. Maccabean Tombs

Preface

Essentials of the Land of Israel: A Geographical History was conceived and designed as a companion volume to its predecessor, *Essentials of Jewish History: Jewish Leadership Across 4,000 Years*, and likewise aims to serve as a comprehensive compendium for ready reference. It is a geographical history of the Land of Israel, foregrounding the most significant political and natural features of the landscape (borders; capitals; mountains; valleys; rivers; lakes; seas; deserts; forests) and the major biblical and historical events associated with them. The book's unique value is in its novel constitutive premise and in outlining and assembling all of these discrete features – illustrated by original maps and photographs – in one convenient volume. Earlier versions of certain of its sections were initially and individually published online in *The Jewish Press*, *The Algemeiner*, *The Jerusalem Post*, *The Times of Israel*, or *Israel Rising* (2013–2017), all of which have since been revised and updated.

In the course of examining the most salient geographical features of the Land of Israel, readers will come to learn of its dimensions, urban centers, provinces/regions, topography, geology, hydrology, flora and fauna, natural resources, international and regional trade routes, and indigenous polities, as well as sundry etymologies and etiologies.

Essentials of the Land of Israel is intended as a useful resource regardless of one's educational background. For knowledgeable readers, it offers the advantages of its systematic organization and inclusivity of content. For readers unfamiliar with the Land of Israel or Jewish history prior to encountering this book, it affords a newfound and solid grasp both of the lay of the land and of the numerous momentous events that occurred therein, and it is my hope that this foretaste will stimulate further inquiry into the Land of Israel's many important historical sites and natural assets, including archaeological ruins, national parks, and nature reserves. Toward this end, I refer intrigued readers to the appended Select Bibliography and Further Reading.

Brandon Marlon
Ottawa, 2021

Author's Note

For readers' textual facility, I wish to note particular stylistic conventions employed herein:

Biblical Historicity: Regarding biblical figures, Jewish tradition considers personages and events from Abraham onward to be historical, not allegorical; regarding matters divine and/or miraculous, readers will determine whether Scripture is to be interpreted literally or figuratively.

Hebrew Transliteration: I have opted for the "Sephardic" style of transliteration from Hebrew to English – i.e., the letter H/h (not the letters Ch/ch) for the Hebrew letter ה, and the letters Kh/kh for the Hebrew letters כ or כ (in their initial and medial forms) and ך or ך (in their terminal forms). I have employed a mixed transliteration/transcription system that represents characters and captures sounds and pronunciations – e.g., Haderah, not Hadera – excepting certain alternate transliterations long established – e.g., Hebron, not Hevron; Masada, not Mitzadah.

Numbers: The Associated Press style is used for numerals (i.e., in most cases, words for numbers up to 10).

Toponyms: In most instances, placenames feature either transliterations or translations of their original Hebraic names, usually followed by any alternate modern names in parentheses – e.g., Lake Kinneret (the Sea of Galilee); Salt Sea (Dead Sea).

1

Borders of Israel

Maximal: From the Nile to the Euphrates (SW-NE)

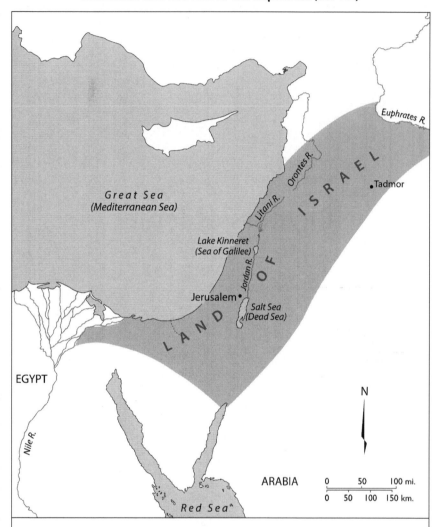

"On that day, the Lord formed a covenant with Abram, saying, 'To your seed I have given this land, from the river of Egypt until the great river, the Euphrates River.'" (*Genesis* 15:18)

"And I will make your boundary from the Red Sea to the sea of the Philistines, and from the desert to the [Euphrates] River." (*Exodus* 23:31)

Minimal: From Dan to Be'ersheva/From Be'ersheva to Dan (N-S/S-N)

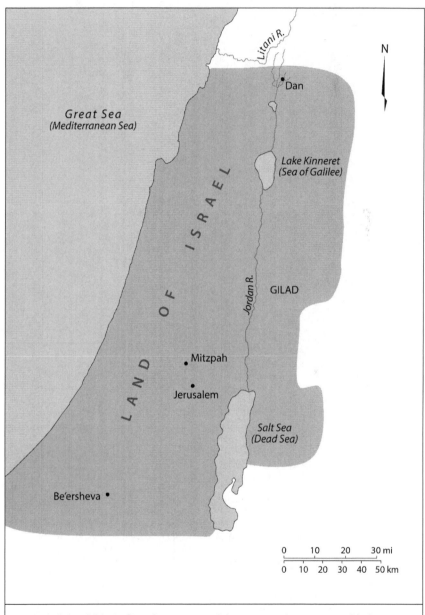

"And all the children of Israel went out, and the congregation was assembled as one man, from Dan to Be'ersheva, as well as the land of Gilad, before the Lord at Mitzpah" (*Judges* 20:1)

Medial #1: The Land of Canaan (W-S-E-N)/The Land of Canaan (S-W-N-E)

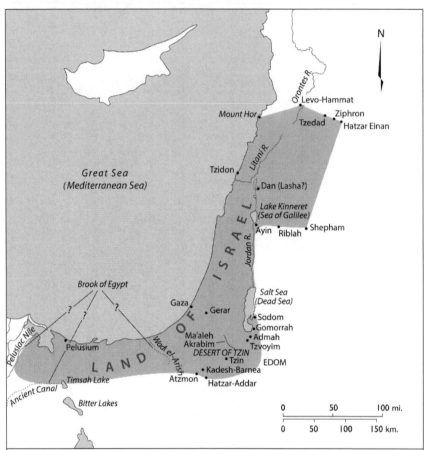

"And the border of the Canaanites was from Tzidon as you come to Gerar, until Gaza, as you come to Sodom and Gomorrah, and Admah and Tzvoyim, until Lasha." (*Genesis* 10:19)

"Your southernmost corner shall be from the desert of Tzin along Edom, and the southern border shall be from the edge of the Salt Sea [Dead Sea] to the east. The border then turns south of Ma'aleh Akrabim, passing toward Tzin, and its ends shall be to the south of Kadesh-Barnea. Then it shall extend to Hatzar-Addar and continue toward Atzmon. The border then turns from Atzmon to the brook of Egypt, and its ends shall be to the sea. The western border: it shall be for you the Great [Mediterranean] Sea and the border, this shall be your western border. This shall be your northern border: From the Great [Mediterranean] Sea turn yourselves toward Mount Hor. From Mount Hor turn to Levo-Hammat, and the ends of the border shall be toward Tzedad. The border shall then extend to Ziphron, and its ends shall be Hatzar Einan; this shall be your northern border. The border descends from Shepham toward Riblah, to the east of Ayin. Then the border descends and hits the eastern shore of Lake Kinneret [the Sea of Galilee]. The border then continues down along the Jordan, and its ends is the Salt Sea [Dead Sea]; this shall be your land according to its borders around." (*Numbers* 34:3-12)

Medial #2: From Levo-Hammat to the Brook of Egypt (NE-SW)

Euphrates R.

Orontes R.

Levo-Hammat

Great Sea
(Mediterranean Sea)

Litani R.

LAND OF ISRAEL

Lake Kinneret
(Sea of Galilee)

Brook of Egypt

Pelusiac
Nile

Jerusalem

Jordan R.

Salt Sea
(Dead Sea)

? ?   ?

N

Timsah
Lake

Wadi el-Arish

Ancient
Canal

Bitter Lakes

EGYPT

Nile R.

| 0 | 50 | 100 mi. |

| 0 | 50 | 100 | 150 km. |

"Now Solomon observed the Feast at that time and all Israel with him, a great assemblage from Levo-Hammat to the brook of Egypt, before the Lord our God, seven days and seven days, [totalling] fourteen days." (*I Kings* 8:65)

Medial #3: From Shihor of Egypt and until Levo-Hammat (SW-NE)

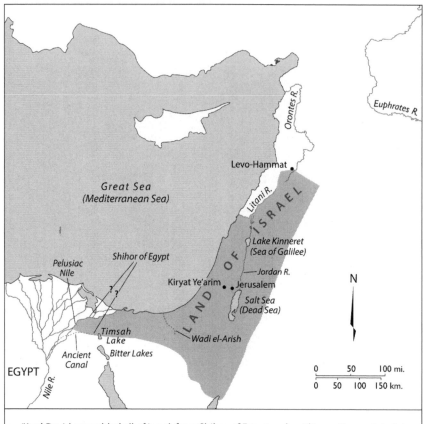

"And David assembled all of Israel, from Shihor of Egypt and until Levo-Hammat, to bring the Ark of God from Kiryat Ye'arim." (*I Chronicles* 13:5)

Medial #4: Ezekiel's Envisioned Borders (N-E-S-W)

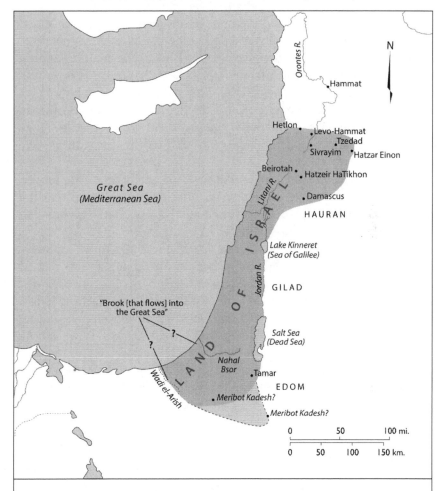

"And this is the border of the land: to the northern side, from the Great [Mediterranean] Sea the way to Hetlon to the road [leading] to Tzedad. Hammat, Beirotah, Sivrayim, which is between the border of Damascus and the border of Hammat; Hatzeir HaTikhon, which is by the border of Hauran. And the border shall be from the sea to Hatzar Einon, the border of Damascus, and in the north northward is the border of Hammat; this is the northern side. And the eastern side is between Hauran and Damascus, between Gilad and the Land of Israel is the Jordan; from the border by the eastern sea shall you measure; this is the eastern side. And the southern side is from Tamar until the water of Meribot Kadesh to the brook [that flows] into the Great [Mediterranean] Sea; this is the southern side. And the western side is the Great [Mediterranean] Sea from the border until opposite Levo-Hammat; this is the western side." (*Ezekiel* 47:15-20)

In the ancient Near East, a triangle of land separated the dominant civilizations of Egypt and Mesopotamia. The Land of Israel famously rested between these centers, a nexus bridging the continents of Asia and Africa. Most of the land was and remains arid desert, and much of it is mountainous.

A series of minor kingdoms to the east and to the south (Ammon, Moab, Edom) abutted the heartland of the Israelite homeland (Cisjordan), as did the southern fringe territories of Midian and Amalek, whose tribes were nomadic or seminomadic. These kingdoms and territories likewise functioned as buffer states between the major empires; sometimes they served as vassals to Hebrew suzerains and other times they were independent.

Definitively delineating the borders of the Land of Israel has proven complex. There are several discrete boundaries given variously in the Tanakh (Hebrew Bible), and disparities existed at any given time between the scriptural and the historical limits.

Scripturally, complications occur due to three territorial extents – maximal, medial, and minimal – derived from eight key textual descriptions. Historically, the boundaries of each of the Israelite or Jewish polities – the United Monarchy of Israel, the kingdoms of Israel and Judah, the Hasmonean kingdom, the Herodian kingdom, the Judean states during the Great Revolt and the Bar Kokhba Revolt, the State of Israel – varied one from another and from one or another scriptural demarcation.

Thus what should be fixed seems flexible. And just as Israel's borders vary, so do the ways of thinking about them. Here, then, is a conspectus of the sundry dimensions of the Promised Land.

Scriptural Borders

Maximal: From the Nile to the Euphrates (SW–NE)

> "*On that day, the Lord formed a covenant with Abram, saying, 'To your seed I have given this land, from the river of Egypt until the great river, the Euphrates River.'*" (*Genesis* 15:18)

These famous bodies of water constitute the widest margins of Israelite territory, the extent of potential expansion and possession. These borders may be conceived as prescribed, ideal, or messianic, for only in King Solomon's era (r. 970–931 BCE) did Jewish sovereignty reach such limits. They may also be considered metaphorical borders, demarcating the region of Israelite influence as opposed to Israelite residence.

This set of borders is sometimes perceived as most significant, not only because of its much larger dimensions but also because it is one of the earliest sets of borders mentioned and appears in the Torah proper as opposed to later books of the Tanakh. This significance is, however, mitigated by the fact that these borders were ephemeral in practical terms.

> "*And I will make your boundary from the Red Sea to the sea of the Philistines, and from the desert to the [Euphrates] River.*" (*Exodus* 23:31)

The latter formulation is a variation on the former, as the northwestern arm of the Red Sea – the Gulf of Suez – roughly aligns with the Pelusiac branch of the Nile River.

Minimal: From Dan to Beersheva/From Beersheva to Dan (N–S/S–N)

> "*And all the children of Israel went out, and the congregation was assembled as one man, from Dan to Beersheva, as well as the land of Gilad, before the Lord at Mitzpah.*" (*Judges* 20:1)

The phrase "from Dan to Beersheva" – or the reverse, which appears twice in *Chronicles* (*I Chronicles* 21:2 and *II Chronicles* 30:5) – is the most common biblical definition of Israel's boundaries, featuring nine times in the Tanakh in the books *Judges*, *I & II Samuel*, *I Kings*, and *I & II Chronicles*. These borders appear later in Scripture and are much circumscribed relative to the original set, and can be conceived as described, actual, or pre-messianic. They may also be considered literal borders, demarcating the region of Israelite residence as opposed to Israelite influence.

The original tribal territory of Dan abutted Philistia in the southwest, wedged between Ephraim and Judah and opposite Benjamin, but as a result of being deprived of a foothold in the northern Shephelah foothills by the Amorite cities, part of the tribe migrated, early in the era of the Judges (c. 1228–1020 BCE), northeastward toward the sources of the Jordan River in the Beit Rehov Valley in Upper Galilee. The part of the tribe remaining in its original tribal territory later came into conflict with its aggressive Philistine neighbors.

Medial #1: The Land of Canaan (W–S–E–N)/The Land of Canaan (S–W–N–E)

> "*And the border of the Canaanites was from Tzidon as you come to Gerar, until Gaza, as you come to Sodom and Gomorrah, and Admah and Tzvoyim, until Lasha.*" (*Genesis* 10:19)

This is the earliest set of borders mentioned in the Tanakh. Technically, it appears in relation to the Canaanites, not the Israelites, and therefore only possesses retrospective pertinence, since the territory originally occupied by the Canaanites was subsequently allotted to the Israelites. In context, these boundaries of the descendants of Canaan, one of four sons of Ham, demarcate the extent to which this people had proliferated in the Levant by the Middle Bronze Age (2100–1550 BCE).

Scripturally, by reassigning the land to the descendants of Israel (Jacob), God is transferring the title from Hamites to Semites (with Scripture as the deed), thereby situating the Israelites at the crossroads of civilizations. With Israel at the epicenter of activity, Israelite ideas such as ethical monotheism, the sanctity of life, and the primacy of justice would more readily disseminate.

Historically, this land transfer can be viewed as part of the recurrent pattern in the ancient Near East of Semitic kinesis – whether migration and settlement, or conquest – westward from Mesopotamia to the Levant and beyond. Over the centuries, Semitic peoples including Akkadians, Hebrews, Amorites, Arameans, Assyrians, and Babylonians partook to some degree in this general trend, a phenomenon best appreciated when considering the relatively crowded confines between the Tigris and the Euphrates rivers, the desire for access to the Mediterranean Sea, the ambition to control desert trade routes, and the irresistible lure of Egyptian lucre.

> *"Your southernmost corner shall be from the desert of Tzin along Edom, and the southern border shall be from the edge of the Salt Sea [Dead Sea] to the east. The border then turns south of Ma'aleh Akrabim, passing toward Tzin, and its ends shall be to the south of Kadesh-Barnea. Then it shall extend to Hatzar-Addar and continue toward Atzmon. The border then turns from Atzmon to the brook of Egypt, and its ends shall be to the sea. The western border: it shall be for you the Great [Mediterranean] Sea and the border, this shall be your western border. This shall be your northern border: From the Great [Mediterranean] Sea turn yourselves toward Mount Hor. From Mount Hor turn to Levo-Hammat, and the ends of the border shall be toward Tzedad. The border shall then extend to Ziphron, and its ends shall be Hatzar Einan; this shall be your northern border. The border descends from Shepham toward Riblah, to the east of Ayin. Then the border descends and hits the eastern shore of Lake Kinneret. The border then continues down along the Jordan, and its ends is the Salt Sea [Dead Sea]; this shall be your land according to its borders around."* (Numbers 34:3-12)

These borders comprise the territory allotted to the nine and a half tribes of Israel that settled in Cisjordan; previously eastern Menasheh and Gad had settled in Transjordan, and Reuven had settled atop the Mishor. While the Tanakh refers to the "half" tribes of Menasheh (i.e., the eastern half and the western half, with the Jordan River as the dividing line), this is an imprecise locution; according to Scripture, only one of the eight clans of the tribe of Menasheh (that of Makhir) settled in Transjordan, along with the Judahite-Menashite warrior Ya'ir and the Menashite warrior Nobah.

The Canaanite borders include the northern Negev Desert, Philistia, Phoenicia, and part of Aram (southwestern Syria); if the "brook of Egypt" is Wadi el-Arish (one of the three possibilities), they also include the Amalekite area of northeastern Sinai. The borders exclude most of Aram, as well as Ammon, Moab, Edom, and Midian (northwestern Arabian Peninsula).

Medial #2: From Levo-Hammat to the Brook of Egypt (NE–SW)

> *"Now Solomon observed the Feast at that time and all Israel with him, a great assemblage from Levo-Hammat to the brook of Egypt, before the Lord our God, seven days and seven days, [totalling] fourteen days."* (*I Kings* 8:65)

These borders appear thrice in Scripture, always in connection with David and Solomon. Hammat (Hama, Syria) lies on the Orontes River, south of the Euphrates River. The toponym Levo-Hammat is identified with the village of Laboueh/Al-Labweh amid the foothills of the Anti-Lebanon Mountains in the Ba'albek District of modern Lebanon.

The fine distinction in diction between "river" (נהר) and "brook"/ "stream" (נחל) has been interpreted by medieval sage Sa'adiah ben Joseph and others to mean that, while the river of Egypt is certainly the Nile, the brook of Egypt is likely Wadi el-Arish, in the northeastern Sinai Peninsula. Other scholars, however, identify the brook of Egypt with the Pelusiac branch of the Nile River (another of the three possibilities), i.e., the easternmost Nilotic arm that divided Egypt from the Land of Israel and the continent of Africa from Western Asia (which silted up toward the close of the ancient period), since it originated in Egypt proper and was a permanent watercourse, whereas Wadi el-Arish runs between the Sinai Peninsula and the Negev Desert (well east of Egypt proper), and is a dry watercourse that floods only every few years and has shallow waters at its estuary, rendering it unsuitable as a well-defined boundary. Either way, this diagonal set of borders is a truncated version of "from the Nile to the Euphrates", though still much more expansive than "from Dan to Be'ersheva".

Medial #3: From Shihor of Egypt and until Levo-Hammat (SW–NE)

> *"And David assembled all of Israel, from Shihor of Egypt and until Levo-Hammat, to bring the Ark of God from Kiryat Ye'arim." (I Chronicles 13:5)*

Medieval sage Solomon Yitzhaki (Rashi) equated the brook of Egypt with Shihor (the last of the three possibilities). In ancient Egyptian, "Shihor" denotes "Waters of Horus" (alternatively, "The Horus Canal"/"Stream of Horus") and refers either to the Pelusiac branch of the Nile River or to the ancient canal/freshwater stream that formerly flowed nearby. An ancient Egyptian text of the 19th Dynasty (*Papyrus Anastasi* III) cites Shihor in connection with papyrus marshes or reed thickets and mentions its salt production and its use as a shipping route. In *Joshua* (13:3), Shihor is cited as the southwestern limit until which Joshua was supposed to possess the land during the period of the Israelite repatriation to the Land of Israel (c. 1273–1245 BCE); *I Chronicles* (13:5) cites it as the southwestern boundary of Israelite residence or influence under King David (r. 1010–970 BCE). If the brook of Egypt and Shihor both refer to the Pelusiac branch of the Nile River, then this set of borders is merely a reversal of "from Levo-Hammat to the brook of Egypt"; if Shihor instead refers to the proximate ancient canal/freshwater stream, then this set of borders presents a distinction without a significant difference. However, irrespective of Shihor's precise identification, if the brook of Egypt refers to Wadi el-Arish – more than 90 miles east of Shihor's potential loci – then these borders not only reverse but expand upon "from Levo-Hammat to the brook of Egypt".

Medial #4: Ezekiel's Envisioned Borders (N–E–S–W)

> *"And this is the border of the land: to the northern side, from the Great [Mediterranean] Sea the way to Hetlon to the road [leading] to Tzedad. Hammat, Beirotah, Sivrayim, which is between the border of Damascus and the border of Hammat; Hatzeir HaTikhon, which is by the border of Hauran. And the border shall be from the sea to Hatzar Einon, the border of Damascus, and in the north northward is the border of Hammat; this is the northern side. And the eastern side is*

between Hauran and Damascus, between Gilad and the Land of Israel is the Jordan; from the border by the eastern sea shall you measure; this is the eastern side. And the southern side is from Tamar until the water of Meribot Kadesh to the brook [that flows] into the Great [Mediterranean] Sea; this is the southern side. And the western side is the Great [Mediterranean] Sea from the border until opposite Levo-Hammat; this is the western side." (*Ezekiel* 47:15-20)

These prophesied borders largely adhere to those of the Land of Canaan detailed in *Numbers* 34. One notable difference is that, due to its ambiguous phrasing, "the brook [that flows] into the Great [Mediterranean] Sea" may not be identical with "the brook of Egypt", leaving open the possibility that the stream intended is perhaps Nahal Bsor and not Wadi el-Arish.

Conceptual Differences

The fine distinction between borders and limits is helpful in elucidating the subject and reconciling our understanding of the maximal, minimal, and medial delineations. Borders denote the actual; limits connote the potential. Limits can exceed borders while borders cannot exceed limits without becoming new, de facto limits. Depending on one's schema, the movement from borders to limits may be a function of Israel's spiritual potency or military prowess (or both). But in pragmatic terms – in terms of national aspirations and civilizational purposes – history serves as a principal cynosure for comprehending, and implementing, Israel's borders.

But which set of historical borders should be considered definitive?

Historical Borders

In King David's era (r. 1010–970 BCE), the Israelites lived with other peoples bordering and interspersed among them. David subdued the Philistines and conquered all of the adjacent minor kingdoms of the Arameans, Ammonites, Moabites, and Edomites, as well as the fringe territory of the Amalekites. This paved the way for his son King Solomon's irenic realm, which during Israel's original golden age possessed the broadest boundaries of any Jewish polity in history:

"And Solomon reigned over all the kingdoms from the [Euphrates] River through the land of the Philistines to the border of Egypt...." (*I Kings* 5:1)

> *"And he reigned over all the kings from the [Euphrates] River and until the land of the Philistines and until the border of Egypt."* (*II Chronicles* 9:26)

This greatest extent achieved during the United Monarchy of Israel (1030–931 BCE) conforms most closely to the borders promised to Abram, "from the Nile to the Euphrates".

After Solomon's decease, his kingdom split into two at the outset of his son Rehoboam's reign: Israel in the north with its successive capitals of Shekhem, Tirtzah, and Samaria (Shomron/Sebaste), and Judah in the south with its capital of Jerusalem. The northern kingdom was the larger of the two, and its borders extended from Dan in the north to Judah in the south, from the Mediterranean Sea in the west through Gilad in Transjordan.

As Judah had previously largely absorbed the tribal territory of Shimon during the era of the Judges (c. 1228–1020 BCE), so too it soon absorbed the tribal territory of Benjamin once the latter tribe agreed to a shared destiny with Judah at the time of the division of the United Monarchy (931 BCE). This gain was offset by the loss of southern Philistia and of a resurgent Edom, the latter shorn during King Yehoram of Judah's rule (r. 851–843 BCE), leaving Judah with only the northern Negev Desert until Edom was reconquered by King Uziyahu of Judah (r. 791–740 BCE).

The Hasmonean kingdom at its apex, under King Yannai Alexander of Judea (r. 103–76 BCE), extended in the south from Rhinokoroura (El-Arish) on the Mediterranean coast to the mountains of Moab (including Kir of Moab, and Tzo'ar south of the Dead Sea); in the east, it included Gilad, Geshur, and Ma'akhah; in the north, Antioch in Syria and most of Galilee down to the Kharmel promontory; in the west, the Mediterranean coast from the Kharmel mountains to Rhinokoroura. It did not include Ashkelon, Akko, Batanea (Bashan), the fortress of Dathema, Rabbat-Ammon (Philadelphia), or the Negev Desert south of Be'ersheva.

The dominion of King Herod the Great of Judea (r. 37–4 BCE) almost equaled that of his Hasmonean predecessors (approx. 5,020 square miles compared to King Yannai Alexander's 5,715 square miles), but featured adjusted borders. It was bereft of the Kharmel promontory and the coastal town of Dor (Dora) in the Sharon Plain, the southeastern Jezreel Valley around Beit She'an (Scythopolis), the Negev Desert, the Aravah Valley, the southern half of Moab (including Kir of Moab, and Tzo'ar south of the Dead Sea), and Raphia (Rafah) and Rhinokoroura along the Mediterranean coast. It retained the Golan (Geshur and Ma'akhah) and gained a sizable region in the northeast including Batanea (Bashan), Trachonitis, and Hauran (Auranitis). Greek cities (*poleis*) established along the littoral and in Transjordan (the Decapolis), however, were largely autonomous. After Herod's decease his dominion was partitioned among his three sons Archelaus, Antipas, and Philip, and was soon mostly administered directly by Roman prefects and procurators.

In the course of the Great Revolt (66–73 CE), Judean zealots managed to liberate Judea, Idumea, southern Samaria, Perea (southern Gilad and the Mishor), most of Galilee, the central Golan, and western Batanea. They were unable to regain, or were deprived the support of, the Negev Desert, the Aravah Valley, the Decapolis, parts of Upper Galilee and the northern Golan (including King Agrippa II's holdings such as Caesarea Philippi), the Sharon Plain, most of northern Samaria, and Gaza. By 70, most of their territory had been reconquered by the Roman legions under Vespasian and Titus, and by 73 the rebellion ended with Masada's fall.

During the Bar Kokhba Revolt (132–135 CE), the last gasp of Jewish statehood before the long bimillennial night of exile, Judean freedom fighters regained the province of Judea (minus the Mediterranean coast), Idumea as far south as Be'ersheva, and southern Samaria. By 134, this statelet was greatly reduced by Emperor Hadrian of Rome's legions to its core of Judea, and by 135 to just its key loci of Jerusalem and Beitar, whose eventual fall signaled the end of the revolt and the beginning of 1,813 years of diasporic wanderings for much of world Jewry.

Modern Borders

The State of Israel revived in 1948 with indeterminate borders to be settled by the outcome of the then ongoing War of Independence (1947–1949). While the Zionist leadership had accepted the United Nations (UNSCOP) partition plan of 1947, giving the nascent Jewish state eastern Galilee, the Sharon Plain, part of western Judea, and most of the Negev Desert from Be'ersheva southward to Eilat on the Red Sea, the Arabs rejected the plan and war ensued. By war's end, Israel possessed almost all of Galilee including the Galilee Panhandle ("The Finger of Galilee"), the Mediterranean coastline from north of Nahariyah down to just north of Gaza, part of western Judea as well as western Jerusalem, and the entire Negev Desert.

The Six-Day War of 1967 closed with Israel gaining the entire Sinai Peninsula and the Gaza Strip, while liberating the Golan, Samaria, and eastern Judea including the Old City of Jerusalem, Hebron, Bethlehem, and Jericho. Israel withdrew from the Sinai Peninsula in 1982, from southern

Lebanon (captured in 1982) in 2000, and from the Gaza Strip in 2005. Its borders now range in the north from the Israeli aspect of Mount Hermon in the northeast down to Metulah then across to Rosh HaNikrah on the Mediterranean coast; in the west, along the littoral from Rosh HaNikrah down to the Gaza Strip; in the south, down to the Gulf of Eilat in the Red Sea; in the east, from the Red Sea up the Jordan Rift Valley and encompassing the western Golan (Geshur and Maʾakhah) northward until Mount Hermon.

Excepting eastern Jerusalem, no part of the liberated provinces of Samaria and eastern Judea – the heartland of the Jewish homeland – has been officially incorporated into the state and thus these regions remain disputed territories. The modern borders also exclude the southwestern area between Rafah and El-Arish (now in Egypt), the Transjordanian highlands and eastern tableland (now in Jordan), and Bashan (now in Syria).

Conclusion

Today Israel's borders are still tenuous owing primarily to the indeterminate destiny of Samaria and eastern Judea, and secondarily to the uncertain future of the Gaza Strip. Today the Jewish polity possesses Dan and the western Golan, Beʾersheva and the entire Negev Desert. But the central provinces of the country – central geographically, historically, biblically, and civilizationally – remain in limbo. Originally the tribal territories of western Menasheh, Ephraim, Benjamin, and eastern Judah, Samaria and eastern Judea are nowadays contested terrain populated by a majority of Arabs with a large minority of Jews. Moreover, almost all of the Transjordanian highlands and eastern tableland has been ceded to Jordan despite the rich biblical and historical Jewish connection to this region.

Dangerous adversaries regularly menace Israel's northern frontier from Lebanon (Phoenicia, where ancient Israel's closest allies formerly dwelt), its northeastern frontier from southwestern Syria (Bashan, once part of the United Monarchy of Israel, the northern Kingdom of Israel, and Herod's kingdom), and from the Gaza Strip (southern Philistia, formerly part of the tribal territory of Judah, the United Monarchy of Israel, and the Hasmonean and Herodian realms). In the absence of amicable neighbors, the possession and control of such liminal areas are yet unsettled.

In area, the State of Israel roughly equates to the divided kingdoms of Israel and Judah; surpasses the Hasmonean and Herodian kingdoms as well as the Jewish polities during the Great Revolt and the Bar Kokhba Revolt; and approximates one quarter of the United Monarchy of Israel.

Edom Mountains

2
Capitals of Israel

Capitals of Israel

Jerusalem is the eternal capital of the Jewish people and of the State of Israel, though it is hardly the only capital the Jews have known. In fact, there were a number of capitals established both before and after the selection of Jerusalem at the close of the 11th century BCE. Some capitals lasted for only a matter of years or decades; others endured centuries. What follows is a précis of their storied history.

1. **Shiloh** – Situated north of Beit El and east of Levonah, in the mountainous territory of Ephraim, Shiloh was the amphictyonic center of tribal Israel and served as the de facto capital for more than two centuries. Shiloh was first settled about 700 years before the era of the Judges (c. 1228–1020 BCE), but had been abandoned before Israelite resettlement and fortification. Here Joshua erected the Tabernacle wherein the Ark of the Testimony (Ark of the Covenant) was housed and here lots were cast to allot the tribal territories and Levitical cities. As the hub of religious worship, Shiloh hosted congregational assemblies, most famously including the annual Tu B'Av festival when Jewish women danced in the surrounding vineyards. Shiloh regularly received devout Israelite pilgrims including Hannah and Elkanah, whose son Samuel was dedicated to the divine service and ministered under Eli the priest in the Tabernacle. Born in nearby Ramah (Ramatayim-Tzophim/Ramatayim/Arimathea) in Ephraim, Samuel received the prophetic call in neighboring Shiloh, which was destroyed circa 1050 BCE after the Battle of Aphek (Pegae/Arethusa/Antipatris) by the victorious Philistines, who captured the Ark. The prophet Ahiyah ben Ahituv was a priestly Shilonite who foretold the advent of King Jeroboam I of Israel, and who later prophesied the demise of that renegade's dynasty. Shilonites were among the Ephraimites who offered oblations in Jerusalem after its destruction by the Babylonians. Shiloh was revived more than once over time, including under Roman rule, and was frequented by Talmudic sages. Jews made pilgrimage to Shiloh to pray at the tomb of Eli until the 14th century. The site, called Seilun in Arabic, features ancient stone tombs and a pool in a rock hollow, and today once again hosts gatherings for prayer and dancing on special occasions.

2. **Givah (Givat Binyamin/Givat Sha'ul)** – The main town in the highlands of the tribal territory of Benjamin and located beside the central road between Judah and Mount Ephraim, Givah ("Hill") is sometimes confused with Geva or Givon, other notable towns in Benjamin. Givah was destroyed by the Israelite tribes during the era

of the Judges (c. 1228–1020 BCE) in a civil war after certain Benjaminites had shockingly gang-raped to death the Judahite concubine of a roving Levite. The town was rebuilt and, because it was perhaps his hometown (his hometown may alternatively have been Givon; the latter was at least his ancestral hometown), served as King Saul's capital, thus as the first capital of the United Monarchy of Israel (1030–931 BCE), and became known thereafter as Givat Sha'ul. During the Great Revolt (66–73 CE), the Roman general Titus encamped at Givah en route to Jerusalem, and his legionaries in time destroyed the site. Givah is identified with Tel el-Ful, three and a half miles north of Jerusalem, where a towered fortress has been excavated. The modern Givat Sha'ul neighborhood in Jerusalem is unrelated to Givah.

3. **Mahanayim** – A site in Transjordan, named Mahanayim ("God's Camp" or "Two Camps") by the patriarch Jacob who had envisioned angels at this locus prior to his crossing of the Yabok River en route to Penu'el. Mahanayim sat on the border between the tribal territories of eastern Menasheh to the north and Gad to the south, and was designated a Levitical city in Gad. After the fateful Israelite defeat and the decease of King Saul at the Battle of Mount Gilboa, following which Saul's cousin and general Avner took Saul's son Ish-Boshet to Mahanayim, the locality became nationally prominent as a refuge for fugitives and embattled monarchs. During the internecine conflict between Ish-Boshet and David, Avner embarked from and returned to Mahanayim as commander of the Israelite army. At the outset of his son Avshalom's rebellion, King David retreated to Mahanayim, where he accepted furniture, wares, and victuals from loyal Giladites. Later, King Solomon appointed his governor Ahinadav ben Iddo to Mahanayim, wherefrom food was provided to Solomon and his household for one month annually. Pharaoh Shishak (Sheshonk) I of Egypt conquered and plundered Mahanayim during his campaign in King Rehoboam of Judah's fifth regnal year (927 BCE). The site's precise location in Gilad is uncertain, though it is probably either the twin site of Tulul adh-Dhahab (al-Garbiya and ash-Sharqiya) by the Yabok River, or else Mahneh (Khirbat Mihna), north of Ajloun.

4. **Hebron (Mamre/Kiryat Arba)** – Originally a Hittite site, and also a key locus along the regional Derekh HaAvot (The Way of the Patriarchs/Ridge Route) connecting Upper Galilee and the Negev Desert, Hebron was where the patriarch Abraham settled by the oaks of Mamre and bought from Ephron the Hittite the Cave of Makhpelah, a double cavern (in Hebrew, *mukhpal* denotes "doubled"/"two-fold")

in which to bury his wife Sarah (Abraham, Isaac, Rivkah, Jacob, and Leah were subsequently buried there as well). During the Exodus from Egypt (c. 1313–1273 BCE), the 12 spies reconnoitered Hebron. The Amorite ruler King Hoham of Hebron was defeated along with his fellow Amorite kings by Joshua in the Battle of Ayalon, and Calev ben Yiphuneh conquered Hebron. The city was later designated a Levitical city and a city of refuge. The Israelite Judge and strongman Samson carried off the doors and doorposts of Gaza's city gates to Hebron. From 1010 BCE, before conquering Jerusalem, King David reigned in Hebron, his first capital, for seven and a half years; here he was twice anointed king, once over Judah then again over all of Israel. David's nephews Yo'av and Avishai slew their foe Avner by Hebron's city gate. Avner, general of Saul's son Ish-Boshet, was entombed in Hebron (along with Ish-Boshet's severed head), as were the Davidic prophets Gad the seer and Nathan. David's son Avshalom began his ill-fated revolt from Hebron, and later King Rehoboam of Judah fortified the city as one of his administrative centers in the Judean Hills. Eventually Hebron was claimed by the Edomites (who had migrated northwest from the Aravah Valley) until the Hasmonean era (167–63 BCE), when Judah Maccabee expelled them and destroyed the city's towers and fortifications. The later Hasmonean ruler and high priest Yohanan Hyrcanus conquered Idumea, thereby reincorporating Hebron into Judea. King Herod the Great of Judea erected the wall surrounding the Cave of Makhpelah (which remains extant). During the Great Revolt (66–73 CE), Zealot leader Shimon bar Giora reclaimed Hebron from the Romans until the Roman commander Cerealis reconquered the city and destroyed it. In the seventh century, Muslim Arabs conquered Hebron, and referred to it by several names: Habra, Habran, Khalil al-Rahman, and al-Khalil. Caliph Omar permitted the Jews to construct a synagogue near the Cave of Makhpelah and a new local graveyard. Hebron is traditionally considered among the four holy cities of the Jews (along with Jerusalem, Tiberias, and Tzfat). Moses ben Maimon (Rambam/Maimonides), Benjamin of Tudela, Petahyah of Regensburg, and Jacob ben Netanel were among the Jewish notables who visited Hebron during the Middle Ages. Ovadiah of Bertinoro was briefly chief rabbi of Hebron. Since the early modern era, many famous sages lived, studied, wrote, and taught in Hebron, including: Elijah de Vidas, Malkiel Ashkenazi, Solomon Adeni, Joseph di Trani, Abraham ben Mordekhai Azulai, Hayyim Joseph David Azulai, Mordekhai Rubio, Judah Bibas, Hezekiah Medini, Nathan Tzvi Finkel, Moses Mordekhai

Epstein, Yehezkel Sarna, and Isaac Hutner. The renowned Slobodka academy was transferred from Lithuania to Hebron in 1925. Arab pogroms against Hebron's Jewish community broke out in 1929 and in 1936; Jews returned to Hebron in the aftermath of the Six-Day War of 1967 and also developed the adjacent community of Kiryat Arba.

5. **Shekhem** – Situated in the fertile valley between Mount Eival and Mount Gerizim, the ancient locus was originally a Canaanite village situated along the regional Derekh HaAvot (The Way of the Patriarchs/Ridge Route) connecting Upper Galilee and the Negev Desert. Upon his arrival in Canaan, the patriarch Abraham beheld God and built an altar here by the terebinth of Moreh. In time the patriarch Jacob encamped before what had developed into a city and purchased an adjacent parcel of land from Hamor the Hivite's sons for 100 silver pieces. Jacob's sons, Shimon and Levi, destroyed the city after its prince, Shekhem, kidnapped and violated their sister Dinah. Jacob buried the foreign idols and earrings of his household under the terebinth of Moreh at Shekhem, and sent his beloved son Joseph from the Hebron Valley to report back on the welfare of his other sons feeding their flock around Shekhem. The city was apportioned to the tribe of Ephraim, in whose northern mountain territory it lay. Joshua assembled the Israelite tribes here and established a covenant with the people to loyally serve the God of Israel, erecting a stone monument under the terebinth of Moreh attesting to the covenant. At Shekhem were laid to rest the exhumed bones of Joseph, in the very plot of land his father Jacob had acquired centuries earlier. In the era of the Judges (c. 1228–1020 BCE), Shekhem became the midpoint of the Land of Israel – exactly 71.5 miles from both Dan in the north and Be'ersheva in the south – and the short-lived kinglet Avimelekh ben Gidon was coronated in Shekhem, whose rebels prompted him to conquer the city, raze its walls, and sow it with salt. King Rehoboam of Judah was coronated and later abjured by the 10 northern tribes of Israel at Shekhem in favor of King Jeroboam I of Israel, whose first capital Shekhem became. In the monarchic period the city featured two-storey abodes, well-designed quarters, and large granaries. Much of the city was destroyed by repeated Assyrian invasions in the eighth and the seventh centuries. Resettlement of the site was transitory until the Hellenistic era (332–167 BCE), during which the Samaritans who rebelled against King Alexander III of Macedon (Alexander the Great) were expelled from Samaria and subsequently regrouped at Shekhem. The Hasmonean ruler and high priest Yohanan Hyrcanus destroyed the Samaritan settlement and

leveled the mound of Shekhem late in his reign (134–104 BCE), and his son King Yannai Alexander of Judea was later defeated by Emperor Demetrius III Eucaerus of Syria in a crushing battle near Shekhem in 89/88 BCE. In 72 CE, Emperor Vespasian of Rome built Neapolis (Nablus) near the ruined Shekhem. During the Middle Ages the site was visited by Jewish travelers such as Benjamin of Tudela. Today the ruins of Shekhem, known in Arabic as Tel el-Balata, lie just over a mile southeast of the modern Arab city of Nablus.

6.   **Penu'el (Peni'el)** – Located in Transjordan south of the Yabok River, Penu'el was where the patriarch Jacob received his new name of Israel after wrestling with a mysterious figure. He called the place Peni'el ("God's Face"), "because I have seen God face to face, yet my life is spared" (*Genesis* 32:31). Local residents later deprived the Israelite Judge Gidon and his fighters of provisions during their campaign against the Midianites, for which reason Gidon later demolished Penu'el's tower and slew the town's male inhabitants. King Jeroboam I of Israel rebuilt Penu'el as his second capital, perhaps to better administer his domains beyond the Jordan River. The site's precise location in Gilad is uncertain, though it is probably either part of the twin site of Tulul adh-Dhahab (al-Garbiya and ash-Sharqiya) by the Yabok River, or else Tel Deir Alla.

7.   **Tirtzah** – A Canaanite town whose king Joshua defeated, Tirtzah was allotted to the tribal territory of western Menasheh. It became the third and final capital of King Jeroboam I of Israel, whose son died in Tirtzah per the prophecy of Ahiyah of Shiloh. It also served as King Basha of Israel's capital for 24 years and as his son King Elah of Israel's capital for two years, until the latter was murdered while drunk in his steward's house by the chariot commander Zimri. The usurper King Zimri of Israel reigned for all of a week in Tirtzah before being burned alive in the royal palace during his rival Omri's conquest of the city. King Omri of Israel reigned for six years from Tirtzah until he transferred his capital to the newly built city of Samaria. The rebel Menahem ben Gadi arose from Tirtzah to infiltrate Samaria, where he slew King Shallum of Israel and took his place on the throne; from Tirtzah, King Menahem of Israel attacked the defiant town of Tiphsah (Thapsacus, or else the village Khurbet Taphsah), whose pregnant women he cruelly ripped open. Tirtzah was likely destroyed along with Samaria by the Assyrians in 722 BCE.

8.   **Samaria (Shomron/Sebaste)** – Founded by King Omri of Israel in his seventh regnal year (878 BCE), Samaria was named after Shemer, who

sold his hill to Omri for two silver talents. Situated on an isolated elevation some seven miles north of Shekhem, the site featured a rectangular acropolis surrounded by ashlar and casemate walls containing the royal palace of Omri, his son Ahab, and the many kings that followed their dynasty. Here King Ahab of Israel built an ivory house for his infamous Phoenician consort Jezebel, and here he met with King Yehoshaphat of Judah to listen to the ominous prophecy of Micaiah ben Yimlah. In Samaria Yehu had the 70 sons of Ahab purged and the temple of Ba'al destroyed; he later found King Ahaziah of Judah hiding from him in Samaria, and soon put him to death. In 785, King Yeho'ash of Israel plundered Jerusalem and hauled the spoils of the Temple and of the royal palace to Samaria. King Pekah of Israel captured 200,000 Judahites and brought them to Samaria, where they were treated mildly then released. Samaria was the capital of the northern kingdom of Israel for almost 160 years until it fell to the invading Assyrians in 722. The city's inhabitants were exiled variously to Hilah, Havor by the Gozan River, and the Median cities ruled by Assyria, and replaced by pagan gentiles from Khutah, Babylon, etc. The Achaemenid Persians retained Samaria as an administrative center within its satrapy, and in the Persian era (539–332 BCE) the local rulers of the Sanballat family clashed with Nehemiah. During the Hellenistic era (332–167 BCE), the Samaritans assassinated Andromachus, governor of Coele-Syria, thereby rebelling against King Alexander III of Macedon (Alexander the Great) who punished them by transforming the city into a Greek colony of 6,000 Macedonians in 331. The Hasmonean ruler and high priest Yohanan Hyrcanus besieged and razed Samaria around 107, but it was restored by the Roman general Pompey the Great. In 25, King Herod the Great of Judea refurbished the city with a colonnaded street, forum, Augustan temple, theater, aqueduct, and new wall with towers and gateways; he renamed the city, now the district capital of the province of Samaria, Sebaste (Greek for "Augusta") as an homage to his patron, Augustus Caesar, which gives the site its modern appellation, Sebastia. It became a colony under Emperor Septimius Severus of Rome. Moreover, the hermetic Jewish preacher John the Baptist is traditionally believed to have been interred here, and the site was a bishopric in the third century CE (and again later during the Crusades); a church and a monastery were also erected in the lower city in the fifth century. In 614, the Sassanid Persians destroyed Samaria. Today Samaria endures as Sebastia National Park under the management of the Israel Nature and Parks Authority.

9. **Jerusalem** – The Eternal City, nestled in the center of the Judean Hills, arose upon two ridges circumscribed by the Hinnom (Ben Hinnom) and the Kidron (Yehoshaphat) Valleys, its residents sustained by the Gihon spring. Originally known by the Canaanites/Amorites as Salem or Jebus and first mentioned in the El-Amarna tablets, the city was a key locus along the regional Derekh HaAvot (The Way of the Patriarchs/Ridge Route) connecting Upper Galilee and the Negev Desert and was once ruled by the priestly King Melkhitzedek, who blessed the patriarch Abraham. During the period of the Israelite repatriation to the Land of Israel (c. 1273–1245 BCE), King Adonitzedek of Jerusalem assembled his fellow Amorite kings to attack Joshua's allies, the Givonites, in the Battle of Ayalon won by the Israelites. Jerusalem, however, remained an independent Canaanite enclave on the border between Benjamin and Judah, allocated to the tribal territory of Benjamin, in which Benjaminites and Jebusites dwelt together. It was soon absorbed into the tribal territory of Judah, however, following its capture by King David in 1003 BCE; thereafter it was known as the City of David or Zion, after the central mount previously known as Mount Moriah. David made Jerusalem his new capital and transferred there from Kiryat Ye'arim (Ba'alei Yehudah) the Ark of the Testimony (Ark of the Covenant), thereby establishing Jerusalem as the ultimate religious and political center of the United Monarchy of Israel (1030–931 BCE). David built a royal palace in the City of David and from King Aravnah the Jebusite he purchased the threshing floor atop Mount Zion, immediately to the north, whereon he erected an altar. Thenceforward Israelites dutifully journeyed to Jerusalem for the three annual pilgrimage festivals ordained in the Torah: Sukkot (Booths/Tabernacles), Pesah (Passover), and Shavuot (Weeks/Pentecost). David's son King Solomon erected the First Temple, replete with bronze pillars named Yakhin and Bo'az, upon Mount Zion, thereafter also known as Temple Mount, in 960; by 948, he had also erected an adjacent royal palace and the Millo (a stepped stone structure or series of terraced platforms supporting houses). Jerusalem remained the capital of the southern Kingdom of Judah, ruled by the Davidic dynasts, after the northern tribes of Israel seceded to form the northern Kingdom of Israel. It was plundered in King Rehoboam of Judah's fifth regnal year (927) by Pharaoh Shishak (Sheshonk) I of Egypt and in 785 by King Yeho'ash of Israel, who dismantled a portion of the city wall. Decades later, King Uziyahu of Judah fortified towers in Jerusalem and had war engines placed atop

the city wall's towers and corners; his son King Yotam built the Temple's upper gate and expanded upon the Ophel wall. In 701, the city was besieged by Emperor Sennacherib of Assyria, but not before King Hezekiah of Judah had fortified the Millo, repaired the city wall, built an additional wall, raised watchtowers, and excavated a rock-cut tunnel channelling water from the Gihon spring into the newly walled Pool of Shiloah (Siloam) within the city walls. Hezekiah's son, King Menasheh of Judah (the longest-serving king in either Judah or Israel), erected an outer wall for the city by the Gihon spring and raised the Ophel bulwark. In 597, Jerusalem was besieged by Emperor Nebuchadrezzar II of Babylonia, who took captive 10,000 elites including King Yehoiakhin of Judah and Ezekiel the prophet; in 586, the Babylonians led by general Nebuzaradan destroyed the city, including the Temple, royal palace, and city walls. After the Cyrus Proclamation of 538, Judahites under Sheshbazzar, Zerubavel, and Yeshua the high priest returned from the Babylonian Captivity and repopulated Jerusalem, erecting an altar of burnt offering then building the Second Temple, completed in 516. During the Persian era (539–332 BCE), Jerusalem served as the provincial capital of Yehud Medinata (a province within the satrapy of Ever-Nahara), and a square-shaped citadel called the Birah (Baris) was erected above the northwest corner of the Temple. During the reign of Emperor Artaxerxes I Longimanus of Persia, the priest Ezra the Scribe led a new cohort of 1,754 Judahite exiles from Persia to Judah and Jerusalem, reintroducing therefrom the Torah and revivifying Jewish spiritual life while his junior counterpart Nehemiah, the Persian-appointed Jewish governor, rebuilt the city wall, built gates for the Birah citadel, and marshaled one-tenth of Judah's Jewish populace to repopulate Jerusalem. After the high priest Yohanan slew his brother Yeshua in the Temple, the Persian general Bagoas (Bagoses) illicitly entered its precincts. The high priest Yaddua welcomed King Alexander III of Macedon (Alexander the Great) to Jerusalem and directed him in offering a sacrifice in the Temple. For much of the next 150 years (301–167 BCE), Jerusalem was fought over by the Ptolemies and the Seleucids; during this precarious period, the high priest Shimon II the Just repaired damage to the Temple, rebuilt Jerusalem's walls which had been razed by Emperor Ptolemy I Soter of Egypt, oversaw the digging of a reservoir, and fortified the city against siege warfare. The Seleucids, however, constructed the Akra citadel south of the Temple to dominate it, as well as a gymnasium west of the Temple. In 169, the Temple was plundered and desecrated under Emperor Antiochus IV Epiphanes (who also slew many Jerusalemites), but was consecrated anew by the Hasmonean hero Judah Maccabee and his brothers in 164 during the Maccabean Rebellion (167–134 BCE), giving rise to the Hanukah festival. Temple Mount was fortified with high walls and strong towers. Shimon Maccabee finally razed the Akra and leveled its hill. Under Hasmonean rule, Jerusalem was once again the capital of the entire Jewish kingdom. In 63, during the Hasmonean fratricidal war, the Roman general Pompey the Great occupied Jerusalem and invaded the Temple. In 40, the Parthians captured Jerusalem and ruled it through the last Hasmonean king, Mattathias Antigonus, until his Roman-backed rival, the future King Herod the Great of Judea, besieged and conquered the city in 37. In 20, Herod began renovating the Second Temple, a relatively modest sanctuary, into a marvelous and elaborate structure atop Temple Mount's enlarged, peristylar esplanade supported by a retaining wall comprised of ashlar stones (of which the Western Wall or Kotel forms a part). At the northwest corner of Temple Mount he reconstructed and refortified the Birah into the robust Antonia fortress, honoring Mark Antony, and also built a theater, an amphitheater or hippodrome, and a monument to himself. He further constructed a new royal palace in the northwestern quarter and erected four great towers named Psephinus, Hippicus, Phasael, and Mariamne (the surviving base of Phasael is today erroneously called the Tower of David). In 41 CE, King Agrippa I of Judea built a third northern wall. The Adiabene royals, converts to Judaism, built royal palaces and pyramidal royal tombs in Jerusalem. In 66, after the Roman procurator Gessius Florus had plundered the Temple, the Great Revolt (66–73 CE) broke out in Jerusalem; after a few years of independence and internecine struggle among the Zealots – and after the surreptitious escape from the city of the sage Yohanan ben Zakkai along with his disciples Joshua ben Hananiah and Eliezer ben Hyrcanus – Jerusalem and the Temple were destroyed by the Romans under Titus in 70. In 135, following the Bar Kokhba Revolt (132–135 CE), Emperor Hadrian of Rome renamed the city, which he had turned into a Roman colony, Aelia Capitolina, and forbade Jews from entering Jerusalem on pain of death. In 312, after the conversion to Christianity of Emperor Constantine I the Great of Rome, Jerusalem became a holy city for Christians. Constantine's mother, Helena, visited the city circa 325, and the Church of the Holy Sepulcher was soon consecrated in 335. Churches and monasteries multiplied in Jerusalem, which attracted pilgrims from near and far. In 438, Empress Aelia Eudocia of Byzantium permitted Jews to pray once again atop Temple Mount. In 614, the Sassanid ruler Shahanshah Khosrow II of Persia briefly occupied the city with the assistance of some 24,000 Jews; in 628, Emperor Heraclius of Byzantium reclaimed Jerusalem for his empire and proscribed Jews from the city. In 637, Jerusalem was conquered by the Muslim Arabs under Caliph Omar, who had a wooden mosque erected atop Temple Mount; this modest structure was replaced in 691 by the Umayyad ruler Caliph Abd al-Malik's Dome of the Rock shrine, reportedly built employing the labor of 10 Jewish families exempted from poll taxes, and the adjacent Al-Aqsa Mosque (repeatedly destroyed by earthquakes and rebuilt until the current structure was constructed by the Fatimids in 1035). Jews were permitted to return to Jerusalem under Arab rule, but the city was neglected and soon conquered by Seljuk Turks in 1077. In 1099, crusaders under Godfrey of Bouillon conquered Jerusalem and established it as the capital of their Latin Kingdom; they also slaughtered tens of thousands of Jerusalem's Jewish and Muslim "infidels". In the 12th century, Jerusalem was visited by the sages Judah HaLevi and Moses ben Maimon (Rambam/Maimonides), and by the itinerant traveler Benjamin of Tudela. In 1187, Sultan Saladin of the Ayyubid Sultanate recaptured Jerusalem for the Muslims. In 1211, hundreds of English and French rabbis repatriated to Jerusalem. In 1260, the city was overrun by the Mongols under Hulagu Khan. In 1267, Moses ben Nahman (Ramban/Nahmanides) came to Jerusalem and reorganized the Jewish community, which was over time replenished by Jewish repatriates to the Land of Israel from Europe, particularly after the Spanish expulsion of 1492, and from Muslim lands. The Mamelukes reconstructed Jerusalem with new edifices and an improved water supply. From 1527–1542, Sultan Suleiman the Magnificent of the Ottoman Empire rebuilt the city walls in irregular quadrangular form with eight gates (Jaffa, Zion, Dung, Lions'/Saint Stephen's, Herod's/Flowers, Damascus, New, and Mercy/Golden), but in general Jerusalem declined severely due to neglect by the Ottoman Turks. Only from 1855 onward were new neighborhoods developed outside the Old City wall, with the help of Jewish benefactors such as Moses Montefiore and Judah Touro. In 1917, General Edmund Allenby occupied Jerusalem for the British after defeating the Ottomans. In spite of the restrictive British Mandate (1923–1948) and of the Arab riots of 1922, 1929, and 1936–1939, Jewish repatriation to Jerusalem increased and

Hebrew University of Jerusalem atop Mount Scopus, founded in 1918, was opened in 1925. In 1948, Jerusalem became the capital of the third Jewish commonwealth, the State of Israel. Following the War of Independence (1947–1949), Israel's government and legislature were transferred from Tel Aviv to Jerusalem, even as Jordan occupied the city's eastern half. In 1967, during the Six-Day War, Israel recaptured the Old City from the Jordanian Arabs and Jews immediately returned to worship at the Western Wall, from which they had been barred by the Arabs for almost 20 years. The Jewish quarter of the Old City, which the Jordanians had demolished, was restored and repopulated. The 50th anniversary of Jerusalem's historic liberation and reunification was celebrated in 2017.

Aside from Jerusalem, all of the capitals of Israel are situated in areas (Judea & Samaria, or Jordan) now predominantly or entirely occupied by Muslim Arab populations. Ceding sovereignty over these seminal historic sites means relinquishing supremely meaningful elements of Jewish national heritage and entrusting them to inimical neighbors whose respect for the sacred sites and regard for the significant antiquities of preceding civilizations cannot be guaranteed. Only under Israeli sovereignty can Jewish heritage ultimately be preserved.

Jerusalem

3
Mountains of Israel

Mountains of Israel

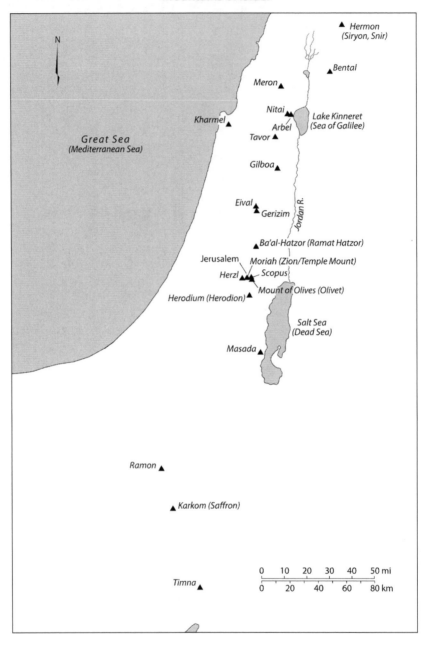

Israel, land and state, is more mountainous than not. Only the quasi-N-shaped network of lowlands – comprising the Sharon and Coastal Plains, the Jezreel Valley, the Hula Valley, the Jordan River Valley, and the Aravah Valley – break up what is otherwise a landscape of hills and heights that constitute the country's central spine. Consequently, the Israelites initially became highlanders, and only later also plainsmen.

Of the three major trade routes – Derekh HaYam (The Way of the Sea/Coastal Highway), Derekh HaAvot (The Way of the Patriarchs/Ridge Route), and the King's Highway (Road to Bashan) – that traversed the Land of Israel, Derekh HaAvot ran along the watershed of the central mountain ridge (through the hill country of Shimon, Judah, Benjamin, Ephraim, and western Menasheh) and the King's Highway ran along the Transjordanian highlands and eastern tableland (through Edom, Moab, Reuven, Gad, and eastern Menasheh).

Over the course of 4,000 years of Jewish history, numerous elevations in Israel have featured in the most significant events within the realm of human affairs. Here is a glance at some of Israel's most prominent summits and their natural and/or historical claims to fame.

1. **Hermon (Siryon, Snir)** – Shared by modern Israel, Syria, and Lebanon, snow-capped Hermon abuts the basalt tableland of Bashan, sending streams and snowmelt year-round down to the headwaters of the Jordan River and into the Hula Valley. Hermon is the southernmost part of the Anti-Lebanon Mountains and its highest peak reaches 9,232 feet above sea level. Known in the Tanakh (Hebrew Bible) for its dews, lions, and cypresses, Hermon was perhaps once the location of a Ba'al shrine, hence its onetime appellation Ba'al-Hermon. Tzidonians of neighboring Phoenicia called it Siryon, while Amorites knew it as Snir. Hivites possessed the mount prior to the period of the Israelite repatriation to the Land of Israel (c. 1273–1245 BCE), following which eastern Menasheh acquired it. Minor temples were erected upon its slopes during the Roman era (63 BCE–313 CE), as was a temple atop its summit. Druze Arabs refer to Hermon as Jebel al-Sheikh ("The Chieftain's Mount") because it has traditionally been where their religious leaders dwell. Today the Snir Stream (Hatzbani) Nature Reserve features the Jordan River's longest tributary.
2. **Bental** – Bental is a dormant volcano in the Golan and is covered with Israeli common oak trees. It reaches 3,842 feet above sea level. The apex features an Israel Defense Forces fort constructed upon a previous

Syrian fort, and offers excellent panoramic views of the Golan, Mount Hermon, and Syria. Kibbutz Merom Golan sits at its base.

3. **Meron** – A mountain that featured a priestly town upon its peak, Meron lies three miles northwest of the mystical city of Tzfat and was often associated in the Talmud with the town of Gush Halav (Gischala) that lies four miles to the north. In 732 BCE, Emperor Tiglat-Pileser III of Assyria conquered Meron in his campaign against the northern Kingdom of Israel. During the Great Revolt (66–73 CE), the Galilean governor Joseph ben Matityahu (Flavius Josephus) fortified Meron against the Romans. The renowned Talmudic sage Shimon bar Yohai (Rashbi) and his son Elazar ben Shimon were buried atop the mount; their graves became a pilgrimage site, and to this day Jews flock to their tombs on Lag BaOmer. A synagogue was erected on Meron during the second or third centuries BCE, and its stately remains lie near the tombs. Hundreds of other tombs lie at the base of the mountain.

4. **Arbel** – Situated in Lower Galilee, Arbel reaches 594 feet above sea level and is distinguished by its high cliffs and early Byzantine synagogue ruins featuring columns and pews that date from the fourth century CE. The synagogue and attached settlement may have been the ancient town of Arbela (perhaps the Beit Arbel mentioned in *Hosea*; the alternate location is atop the opposite peak, Mount Nitai). The mountain is pockmarked with natural caves, some of which were artificially expanded into cave dwellings and interconnected via staircases. In the Hasmonean era (167–63 BCE), the formidable Seleucid (Syrian-Greek) general Bacchides marched (for a second time) against Judah Maccabee and his fighters, encamping at Arbela and capturing it while slaughtering many residents. In the Roman era (63 BCE–313 CE), partisans of the last Hasmonean king, Mattathias Antigonus, revolted in 39 BCE against the future King Herod the Great of Judea and sought refuge in the cliff caves from Herod and his Roman allies, who went to great pains to extract and smoke out the rebels and their families therefrom with fire. In 66 CE, during the early stages of the Great Revolt (66–73 CE), the Galilean governor Joseph ben Matityahu (Flavius Josephus) had walls constructed around the caves in anticipation of the imminent Roman invasion. Jewish priests settled at Arbel following the destruction of the Second Temple. Today the mount hosts four modern villages: Arbel, Kfar Zeitim, Kfar Hittim, and Mitzpah. At the base of the mountain lie the Jewish town of Migdal (Magdala-Tarichaeae) and the Arab village of Hammam.

5. **Nitai** – Named after the local sage Nitai of Arbela, chief justice of the Great Sanhedrin during the reign of the Hasmonean ruler and high priest Yohanan Hyrcanus, the mount lies just west of Mount Arbel and Lake Kinneret (the Sea of Galilee) and north of the city of Tiberias. The sibling peaks of Nitai and Arbel are divided by the Arbel Valley (Nahal Arbel; known in Arabic as Wadi Hammam) and its stream. Nitai's flat summit features a grove of trees and ruins of a walled settlement thought to be the ancient village of Arbela (perhaps the Beit Arbel mentioned in *Hosea*; the alternate location is atop the opposite peak, Mount Arbel). Portions of its slopes are sheer cliffs, and there are also numerous caves and several quarries in the mountainside.

6. **Kharmel** – A mountain range connected to Israel's northernmost Coastal Plain, the Jezreel Valley, and the Mediterranean Sea. Revered as a sacred promontory from ancient times, Kharmel was the site of Phoenician worship of Hadad (Ba'al of Kharmel). The range's highest peak reaches 1,742 feet above sea level. During the period of the Israelite repatriation to the Land of Israel (c. 1273–1245 BCE), Joshua defeated the king of Yokne'am of Kharmel. Allotted to the tribal territory of Asher, Kharmel was most famously the site of Elijah the prophet's triumph over the priests of Ba'al during the reign of King Ahab of Israel (r. 874–853 BCE). Here the Tishbite rid himself of King Ahaziah of Israel's two commanders with their 50-strong companies sent to fetch him. Elijah's Cave lies at the base of the mount and is venerated by Jews, Christians, and Muslims. Elisha the prophet also dwelt amid its treed heights and slopes, which abound in olives, oaks, pines, and laurels. According to Scripture, on Kharmel Elisha was visited by the grieving Shunamite woman, whose deceased son he revived. In the Roman era (63 BCE–313 CE), the then general Vespasian and, later, Emperor Trajan of Rome consulted the oracle Zeus of Kharmel atop the eminence. Tractate *Nidah* of the Talmud cites Kharmel wine – Kharmel is a contraction of "Kherem El" ("God's Vineyard") – and the mountain was beloved for its fruitfulness and its loveliness. Christians worshiped Saint Elias here, and in the 12th century reclusive hermits were drawn to the mountain's numerous grottoes. In 1156 (or else in 1185), the French crusader Count Berthold of Limoges (Berthold of Calabria) founded a hermit colony upon the heights, atop the traditional site of Elisha's Cave (not to be confused with Elijah's Cave); upon Berthold's decease in 1195, the colony that had developed into a monastery was overseen by his successor Saint Brocard. In 1291, the conquering Mamelukes slew the monks and

demolished their monastery. Today the city of Haifa has expanded to cover a sizable portion of the mountain, while the town of Zikhron Ya'akov lies at its southernmost tip and the Druze Arab villages of Isfiya and Daliyat al-Kharmel are nestled amid the central area. The eclectic artists' village of Ein Hod also rests atop Kharmel. A substantial part (almost 15,000 acres) of the range comprises Mount Carmel National Park and Nature Reserve, one of the largest continuous open spaces in Israel.

7. **Tavor** – A lone, dome-shaped mount situated in the Jezreel Valley. Tavor's peak reaches 1,886 feet above sea level and towers over the surrounding plain. During the period of the Israelite repatriation to the Land of Israel (c. 1273–1245 BCE), as a conspicuous landmark visible from a distance, the oak-covered mountain was designated a boundary marker for the tribal territories of Issachar, Zevulun, and Naphtali. In the era of the Judges (c. 1228–1020 BCE), the Israelite general Barak marshaled his forces from the northern tribes against the Canaanite general Sisera; the Israelites descended the slopes with celerity and routed the approaching enemy, whose chariots got bogged down amid muddy conditions. In the Hellenistic era (332–167 BCE), Tavor (known in Greek as Itabyrion/Atabyrium) was a royal fortress and was conquered by Emperor Antiochus III the Great of Syria in 218 BCE during his campaign (the Fourth Syrian War, 219–217) against his regional rival Emperor Ptolemy IV Philopator of Egypt. In 55, the Roman general Aulus Gabinius defeated the Hasmonean prince Alexander, son of Aristobulus II, at the base of Tavor, slaying 10,000 of his men. The Galilean governor Joseph ben Matityahu (Flavius Josephus) fortified the site anew in 67 CE during the Great Revolt (66–73 CE), but after a battle in the plain it was soon surrendered to the Roman general Placidus and his 600 cavalrymen. Later, Christians designated Tavor the locus for the transfiguration of Jewish reformer Jesus of Nazareth; in the Byzantine era (324–638 CE), a basilica was erected atop the peak. Benedictines, Muslim Arabs, and the Knights Hospitaler all subsequently possessed the mount until the Franciscan order claimed it for its monks in 1873. Today the mountain features a Greek Orthodox monastery and a Franciscan basilica, as well as a road and hiking trails ascending in switchback fashion toward the summit. The Israeli Arab village of Daburiyah hangs off the slopes, and the village Kfar Tavor lies nearby in the vale.

8. **Gilboa** – A bow-shaped mountain range southwest of Beit She'an, Gilboa overlooks the Beit She'an Valley and the Harod Valley. Its

highest peak reaches 1,709 feet above sea level. At the base of the mountain ridge lie natural springs (Ein Harod/Ma'ayan Harod, Gan HaShloshah). Here the Philistines were victorious in battle against the Israelites under King Saul, who was killed along with three of his sons, for which the mountain was execrated by David. Today Kibbutz Ma'aleh Gilboa and the Arab village Faqqua rest atop the range, and at the base lie the moshav Gidonah and the kibbutzim Beit Alfa, Hephtzibah, and Nir David.

9. **Eival** – Eival is located just north of Shekhem and reaches 3,084 feet above sea level. Joshua erected upon the mountain an altar of unhewn stones whitewashed with lime, whereon burnt offerings and peace offerings were made; he also inscribed in stone the Torah in the sight of all Israel. In a solemn ceremony, half of the people (the six tribes of Reuven, Gad, Asher, Zevulun, Dan, Naphtali) stood atop Eival to pronounce the curses against those who disobeyed the Torah, whereas the other half atop Gerizim pronounced the blessings upon those who obeyed the Torah, while the priests and the Levites surrounded the Ark of the Testimony (Ark of the Covenant) in the well-watered valley between the mountains. The selection of Eival as the locus of curses might have resulted from the fact that the direction and steepness of slopes affect the vegetative composition and density thereon, and Eival's southern slope is sere compared to Gerizim's northern slope. Ruins and tombs feature on, and at the base of, Eival.

10. **Gerizim** – Sparsely covered with shrubbery and olive groves and possessing many springs at its base, Gerizim is located just south of Shekhem and reaches 2,890 feet above sea level. In a solemn ceremony, half of the people (the six tribes of Shimon, Levi, Judah, Issachar, Joseph, Benjamin) stood atop Gerizim to pronounce the blessings upon those who obeyed the Torah, whereas the other half had stood atop Eival to pronounce the curses against those who disobeyed the Torah, while the priests and the Levites surrounded the Ark of the Testimony (Ark of the Covenant) in the well-watered valley between the mountains. The selection of Gerizim as the locus of blessings might have resulted from the fact that the direction and steepness of slopes affect the vegetative composition and density thereon, and Gerizim's northern slope is lush compared to Eival's southern slope. The Samaritan version of *Deuteronomy* transposes Eival and Gerizim so that the stones inscribed with the Torah and the altar were to be erected upon Gerizim instead. In the Persian era (539–332 BCE), the Samaritans constructed their own temple and altar upon the

mountain's summit, which was in the Hellenistic era (332–167 BCE) converted into a pagan temple to Zeus by Emperor Antiochus IV Epiphanes of Syria and which was later destroyed by the Hasmonean ruler and high priest Yohanan Hyrcanus in 111/110 (the date of this victory, 21 Kislev, was thenceforth celebrated as "the Day of Mount Gerizim"). The Roman prefect Pontius Pilate massacred a large assembly of Samaritans upon the mountain; in 67 CE, during the Great Revolt (66–73 CE), 11,600 Samaritans were massacred by legionaries led by the Roman commander of the fifth legion, Cerealis. According to Samaritan chronicles, following the Bar Kokhba Revolt (132–135 CE) Emperor Hadrian of Rome constructed a pagan shrine to Zeus on Gerizim and there placed the bronze gates of the Temple. The Talmud records a statement by Shimon ben Elazar that Samaritan wines are proscribed due to their use in the worship of a dove idol erected upon Gerizim. In 484, Samaritans revolted against Emperor Zeno of Byzantium and were expelled from Gerizim; a church dedicated to Mary of Nazareth was built on Gerizim, and the Samaritan synagogue was expropriated. In 529, after another Samaritan rebellion, Emperor Justinian of Byzantium erected a defensive wall around the church. Muslims destroyed the church and its wall during the reigns of Caliph al-Mansur and Caliph al-Mamun. Today Samaritans continue to dwell part of the year upon the mountain slopes, pray in the direction of Gerizim, and offer their paschal sacrifices just west of their former temple site (since desecrated by a Muslim graveyard).

11. **Ba'al-Hatzor (Ramat Hatzor)** – According to the *Genesis Apocryphon*, one of the seven original documents of the Dead Sea Scrolls discovered in Cave 1 near Qumran, Ba'al-Hatzor (referred to therein as Ramat Hatzor) is the site between Beit El and Ai where Abraham built an altar and invoked God's name and later, after parting with his nephew Lot, received a divine message: "Look all around you, north and south, east and west. All the land that you see I will give to you and your offspring forever. I will make your offspring like the dust of the earth, so that if anyone could count the dust, then your offspring could be counted. Go, walk through the length and breadth of the land, for I am giving it to you" (*Genesis* 13:14-17). Ba'al-Hatzor reaches 3,333 feet above sea level, sits on the border between the tribal territories of Benjamin and Ephraim, and is the highest mountain in Samaria. Here King David's son Avshalom hosted a sheepshearing feast at which he avenged his sister Tamar, who had been raped by their half-brother Amnon, by having a drunk Amnon assassinated. Ba'al-Hatzor is perhaps also to

be identified with the Mount Azotus mentioned in *I Maccabees* in connection with the decease of the Hasmonean hero Judah Maccabee during the fateful Battle of Elasah.

12. **Moriah (Zion/Temple Mount)** – The holiest mountain in the Land of Israel, located in the epicenter of Jerusalem, on which Abraham was divinely instructed to build an altar and prepare his son Isaac as a sacrifice, on which King David built an altar, and on which King Solomon erected the First Temple in 960 BCE. Before David purchased it, it was the site of King Aravnah the Jebusite's threshing floor. The three pilgrimage festivals of Sukkot (Booths/Tabernacles), Pesah (Passover), and Shavuot (Weeks/Pentecost) annually compelled Israelites to ascend to Moriah and the Temple, where oblations were made by the priesthood on the people's behalf as part of the sacerdotal services. The Babylonians destroyed the Temple in 586, but tens of thousands of Judahites under Sheshbazzar, Zerubavel, and Yeshua the high priest returned from the Babylonian Captivity in 538 and built on Moriah the Second Temple, completed in 516. In the Persian era (539–332 BCE), the high priest Yohanan slew his younger brother Yeshua in the Temple, prompting the Persian general Bagoas (Bagoses) to illicitly enter its precincts. In the Hellenistic era (332–167 BCE), the high priest Yaddua welcomed King Alexander III of Macedon (Alexander the Great) to Jerusalem and directed him in offering a sacrifice in the Temple, and the high priest Shimon II the Just repaired damage to the Temple. In 169, the Temple was plundered and desecrated by the tyrant Emperor Antiochus IV Epiphanes of Syria, but it was consecrated anew by the Hasmonean hero Judah Maccabee and his heroic brothers in 164 during the Maccabean Rebellion (167–134 BCE), giving rise to the Hanukah festival. Temple Mount was then fortified with high walls and strong towers. In 63, during the Hasmonean fratricidal war, the Roman general Pompey the Great occupied Jerusalem and invaded the Temple. In 20, King Herod the Great of Judea began renovating the Second Temple, then a relatively modest sanctuary, into a marvelous and elaborate structure resting upon a Temple Mount enlarged through embanking, its peristylar esplanade supported by a retaining wall comprised of ashlar stones (of which the Western Wall or Kotel forms a part). In 66 CE, after the Roman procurator Gessius Florus had plundered the Temple and the Zealot leader Elazar ben Hananiah had ceased the sacrifices in the Temple on the emperor's behalf, the Great Revolt (66–73 CE) broke out, resulting in the Second Temple's destruction by the Romans under

Titus in 70. Following the Bar Kokhba Revolt (132–135), Emperor Hadrian of Rome renamed Jerusalem, which he had turned into a Roman colony, Aelia Capitolina, and erected a shrine to the pagan god Jupiter Capitolinus atop Temple Mount. In 637, Jerusalem was conquered by the Muslim Arabs under Caliph Omar, who had a wooden mosque erected atop Temple Mount; this modest structure was replaced in 691 by the Umayyad ruler Caliph Abd al-Malik's Dome of the Rock shrine, reportedly built employing the labor of 10 Jewish families exempted from poll taxes, and the adjacent Al-Aqsa Mosque (repeatedly destroyed by earthquakes and rebuilt until the current structure was constructed by the Fatimids in 1035). In 1099, after conquering Jerusalem and establishing the Latin Kingdom, crusaders converted the Muslim edifices atop Temple Mount into a church and a palace, but these were restored to their previous incarnations in 1187 upon the conquest of Jerusalem by Sultan Saladin of the Ayyubid Sultanate. In 1967, Temple Mount was captured by Israeli paratroopers from Jordanian Arabs during the Six-Day War, but Israel ceded control of the esplanade and its sacred edifices to a Muslim Arab religious trust (*waqf*), under whose oversight unauthorized and unsupervised construction and demolition were conducted on the southern end of Temple Mount by means of bulldozers (1996–1999), eventuating in the discarding of unearthed archaeological artifacts, some of which have since been reclaimed with great diligence. Moriah was perhaps named after the Hebrew word for myrrh (*mor*), the aromatic resin burned on the altar for a sweet savor, or else may have referred to the Amorites. The name Zion once referred specifically to the hill below Moriah, formerly a Jebusite stronghold, that became known as the City of David, but the name became synonymous with Moriah already in the biblical era, as evidenced by references in *Psalms* and *Joel* (and later in *I Maccabees*). The modern "Mount Zion" in Jerusalem's upper city (western ridge), where the tomb of King David, the Coenaculum (scene of the Last Supper), the Church of the Dormition of Mary, and a small Holocaust museum are situated, results from a misnomer in the writings of the priestly historian Joseph ben Matityahu (Flavius Josephus).

13. **Mount of Olives (Olivet)** – Divided from Temple Mount and the City of David by the Kidron Valley, the Mount of Olives ridge extends eastward from Jerusalem and includes three peaks. King David worshiped atop the Ascent of Olives, as the site is referred to in the Tanakh (Hebrew Bible). The prophet Ezekiel envisioned the divine

glory standing atop the mount; the prophet Zikharyah prophesied of a day in which God would stand upon the mount and cleave it in two, forming a valley extending east to west, with the upper half moving northward and the lower half moving southward. A Jewish necropolis dating to the First Temple era (960–586 BCE) hangs off the mountain's western slope. During the Second Temple era (516 BCE–70 CE), the Mount of Olives hosted the initial station in the chain of flare beacons between the Land of Israel and Babylonia that relayed information concerning the Jewish calendar, such as the sanctifications of new moons. The site also was then the locus of the burning of the red heifer, and one or two bridges then linked the ridge with Temple Mount. Christians later erected churches and monasteries atop the Mount of Olives to commemorate the places where they believe that Jewish reformer Jesus of Nazareth wept for Jerusalem, prayed with his disciples in the Garden of Gat-Shemanim (Gethsemane) on the night prior to his arrest, and ascended heavenward. When Jews were banned from Temple Mount during the Middle Ages, they circled the Mount of Olives seven times on the Hoshana Rabbah festival. Rock-hewn tombs lie at the western base of the mount, including the Tomb of Pharaoh's Daughter, the Tomb of Avshalom, the Tomb of Zikharyah, and the Tomb of Hezir's Sons. Today the mountain's peaks feature the Augusta Victoria church-hospital complex (commissioned by Kaiser Wilhelm II of Germany and completed in 1914) and the Arab village of At-Tur, a name derived from the ancient Aramaic appellation, Tura Zita. In 1967, the entire ridge was reclaimed from Jordanian Arabs by Israeli troops during the Six-Day War.

14. **Scopus** – Technically one of the three peaks of the Mount of Olives, Scopus reaches 2,684 feet above sea level. According to the priestly historian Joseph ben Matityahu (Flavius Josephus), Scopus was where Yaddua the high priest greeted King Alexander III of Macedon (Alexander the Great) in the Hellenistic era (332–167 BCE). During the Great Revolt (66–73 CE), the Roman governor of Syria, Cestius Gallus, encamped upon Scopus in his assault on Jerusalem; the Roman general Titus later stationed two legions atop Scopus as well, leveling the ground between the mountain and the monuments of King Herod the Great of Judea adjoining the Serpent's Pool. In 1925, Hebrew University of Jerusalem opened atop its apex.

15. **Herzl** – Named after the founder of the political Zionism movement, Theodor Herzl, the western Jerusalem site hosts the annual official state ceremony concluding Yom HaZikaron (Memorial Day) services

for Israel's fallen, as well as the commencement of festivities for Yom HaAtzma'ut (Independence Day). Herzl's unadorned, black granite tomb is situated atop the mount's summit. A who's who of the State of Israel's leaders and dignitaries is interred in the national cemetery, as are worthies of the World Zionist Organization and Herzl family members. Israel's military cemetery covers the mount's northern slopes; Yad Vashem – The World Holocaust Remembrance Center is situated in the western area. The World Zionist Organization is responsible for developing and maintaining the site.

16. **Herodium (Herodion)** – The locus of a fateful battle between the last Hasmonean king, Mattathias Antigonus, and the future King Herod the Great of Judea. After defeating his rival for the throne, Herod in 28 BCE built a partially manmade mountain and fortified estate, named after himself, at the site. Lower Herodium, at the foot of the mount, was an additional palace complex with pools, gardens, and a bathhouse. Herod was buried here, and his mausoleum was finally discovered in 2007. During the Great Revolt (66–73 CE), the Zealots seized the mountain fortress until the Romans recaptured it following the destruction of the Second Temple in Jerusalem in 70. In the Bar Kokhba Revolt (132–135 CE), Herodium was again used as a rebel base by Jewish stalwarts who carved secret tunnels and caves on-site. The biblical town Tekoa and the modern village of the same name are nearby.

17. **Masada** – Originally fortified during the Hasmonean era (167–63 BCE) – either by the ruler and high priest Jonathan Maccabee or by King Yannai Alexander of Judea – the isolated desert stronghold located a mile west of the Salt Sea (Dead Sea) served to protect the family of the future King Herod the Great of Judea during his war against the Hasmonean scion Mattathias Antigonus, who unsuccessfully besieged the bastion. A victorious Herod eventually renovated the site with a remarkable three-tier cliffside palace. A Roman garrison was later installed here but was slain by Sicarii leader Menahem ben Judah and his men in 66 CE during the early stages of the Great Revolt (66–73 CE). Menahem's nephew Elazar ben Ya'ir, after escaping Jerusalem, controlled the site for most of the revolt, during which one of the key Zealot leaders, Shimon bar Giora, also sojourned upon the mountain fortress. The Roman legate Flavius Silva finally conquered Masada in 73, but was deprived of complete victory as the Sicarii defenders had elected to commit mass suicide instead of living as Roman slaves; 960 dead Jews were survived by only two women and

five children who had concealed themselves in underground caverns. The fall of Masada brought the Great Revolt to its tragic and bitter end. In subsequent centuries, the fortress was occupied by Romans, Byzantine Christians, and crusaders. From 1963–1965, excavations were undertaken under the supervision of former Israel Defense Forces chief of staff Yigael Yadin. Today Masada is one of Israel's most frequented historic sites, whose visitors clamber up and down the Roman ramp or winding snake path, or else opt for the modern cable car heading to and from the walled summit.

18. **Karkom (Saffron)** – Rising from the central Negev Desert, Karkom attains 2,778 feet above sea level. The mount was a palaeolithic cult centre amid a plateau featuring 40,000 rock engravings. Religious activity at Karkom is thought to have achieved its acme from 2350–2000 BCE, with the site apparently being abandoned for most of the following millennium (c. 1950–1000 BCE). Equidistant from Kadesh-Barnea and Petra, the peak has even been pegged as an alternate Mount Sinai, though this revisionist theory, which places the Exodus from Egypt (c. 1313–1273 BCE) instead sometime in the Early Bronze Age (3300–2100 BCE), has not been generally accepted by biblical archaeologists or historians.

19. **Ramon** – Situated southwest of the desert town of Mitzpeh Ramon in the southwestern corner of the erosion cirque Makhtesh Ramon, close to the Israeli-Egyptian border, Ramon reaches 3,402 feet above sea level and is the highest mountain in southern Israel. It is part of a cluster of peaks including Mount Romem, Mount Harif, and Mount Loz. Today the summit features an astronomical observatory for serious stargazers.

20. **Timna** – A tabular mountain located in the sandy heart of the Timna Valley that descends toward the Aravah Valley north of Eilat. Some of King Solomon's copper mines lie nearby, as do the tall, red sandstone formations known as Solomon's Pillars and the shrine to the pagan goddess Hathor (built by Pharaoh Seti I of Egypt). West of Mount Timna lie the ancient smelting camps where copper ore nodules were melted for their valuable metal. Between the second and fourth centuries BCE, Roman legionaries of the Legio III Cyrenaica were stationed in the vicinity. The summit of the mount affords breathtaking vistas of the surrounding rock structures, including mushroom hoodoos and natural arches artfully sculpted by wind, humidity, and water erosion. Today part of Timna Park, the mountain is also close to the artificial, recreational Lake Timna and to a reconstructed Tabernacle.

Unlike the seafaring Phoenicians or the riverine Egyptians and Babylonians, the Israelites were largely mountain dwellers immersed in muscular hill country, a geography engendering a lifeway combining shepherding, husbandry, and horticulture. Their lofty heights provided advantageous ground from which to survey their surroundings, defensive barriers against more powerful foes prone to wars of conquest, and high places for sacrificial offerings – both ordained and prohibited – until finally all idolatry was phased out after the Fall of Jerusalem (586 BCE) and all religious worship concentrated in Jerusalem during the Second Temple era (516 BCE–70 CE).

The mountains of Israel are scripturally immortalized in the Tanakh (Hebrew Bible), perhaps nowhere so famously as in *Psalms*:

> When Israel went out of Egypt,
> the house of Jacob from a people of strange language,
> Judah became His sanctuary,
> and Israel His dominion.
>
> The sea saw it and fled;
> Jordan turned back.
> The mountains skipped like rams,
> the little hills like lambs.
>
> What ails you, O sea, that you fled?
> O Jordan, that you turned back?
> O mountains, that you skipped like rams?
> O little hills, like lambs?
>
> Tremble, O earth, at the presence of the Lord,
> at the presence of the God of Jacob,
> who turned the rock into a pool of water,
> the flint into a fountain of waters. (114)

The Hebrew language contains numerous words to describe Israel's elevations, including: *har* (mountain), *givah* (hill), *ramah* (height), *tel* (layered mound), *arayma* (heap/pile/stack), *ma'aleh* (ascent), *pisgah* (summit/peak), etc. Any map of Israel that is two-dimensional is misleading. To understand the land requires one to ascend – giving rise to the time-honored expression, "making aliyah".

View from Mount Tavor

4
Valleys of Israel

Valleys of Israel

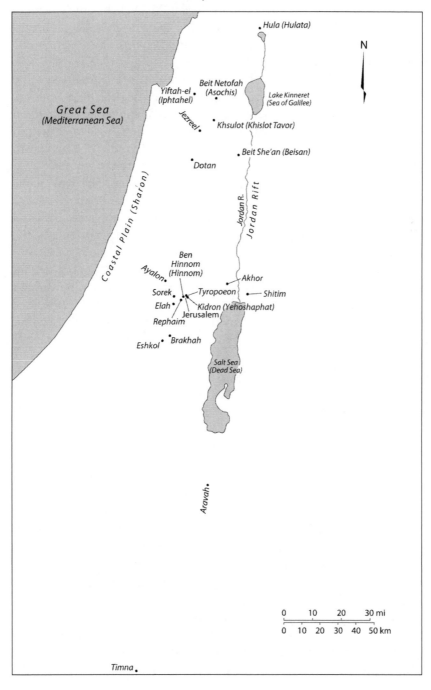

The Land of Israel's quasi-N-shaped network of lowlands – comprising the Coastal Plain, the Jezreel Valley, and the Jordan Rift Valley (which includes the Hula Valley, the Jordan River Valley, and the Aravah Valley) – breaks up what is otherwise a landscape of hills and heights that constitute the country's central spine.

The principal branches of the lowland network contain specific sections that for various reasons – geographical, geological, topographical, or historical – developed something of their own identity (e.g., the Sharon Plain within the upper Coastal Plain; the Valley of Yehoshaphat within the urban Kidron Valley; the Valley of Salt within the upper Aravah Valley, etc.).

Of the three major trade routes – Derekh HaYam (The Way of the Sea/Coastal Highway), Derekh HaAvot (The Way of the Patriarchs/Ridge Route), and the King's Highway (Road to Bashan) – that traversed the Land of Israel, Derekh HaYam ran mostly through valleys, particularly the Coastal Plain, the Jezreel Valley, and the Hula Valley.

Valleys were crucial for travel and transportation routes not only within the Land of Israel by Israelites and other residents, but for overland travelers, pilgrims, merchants, and armies arriving from Phoenicia, Philistia, Egypt, Aram, Assyria, Babylonia, Persia, Greece, Rome, Nabatea, and elsewhere. Flat terrain and the proximity to streams or even lakes made valleys the natural preference for wayfarers wary of the arduous rigors associated with mountain trekking.

Israel's valleys were often named after the major settlement in the vicinity and often served as borders between distinct tribal territories. Here is a précis offering a glimpse at the most geographically and historically significant valleys in Israel.

1. **Hula (Hulata)** – A swampy plain comprising the banks of the Jordan River between Lake Kinneret (the Sea of Galilee) and the later (northeastern) tribal territory of Dan. Its northern section is additionally known as the Beit Rehov Valley. Hula divides the Naphtali Mountains of Upper Galilee to the west from the Golan to the east, and features papyri, reeds, water lilies, water buffaloes, and wild boars, as well as a plethora of migratory birds annually flying to and from Africa. In the 1950s much of the water was drained, but Lake Hula – known in the Talmud as the Sea of Samkho and in the writings of the priestly historian Joseph ben Matityahu (Flavius Josephus) as Lake Semechonitis – endures today in the paradisal wetlands of Lakelet Hula and the Hula Nature Reserve, where flora and fauna continue to

flourish. Much of the reclaimed land is used for farming (grains, fodder, apples, nuts, cotton, vegetables, and bulbs), as well as for the urban development of Kiryat Shmonah.

2. **Yiftah-el (Iphtahel)** – A valley in the territory of Zevulun, serving as part of its tribal border. Yiftah-el has been etymologically and geographically associated with the fortified town of Yodefat, a noted locus where the Galilean governor Joseph ben Matityahu (Flavius Josephus) was besieged by the Romans under Vespasian during the Great Revolt (66–73 CE), and it is likely to be identified with the valley extending westward from Yodefat to Akko. It is essentially the northwestern extension of the Beit Netofah.

3. **Beit Netofah (Asochis)** – A plain in Lower Galilee. It was known for its vetch plant and its high quality clay. Beit Netofah is mentioned in the Mishnah and the priestly historian Joseph ben Matityahu (Flavius Josephus) refers to it in his *Life* as the Valley of Asochis. It is essentially the southeastern extension of the Yiftah-el, between the Yodefat and Tur'an ranges. Today the National Water Carrier's Eshkol reservoir is situated in the western part of the plain.

4. **Khsulot (Khislot Tavor)** – Situated in the tribal territory of Issachar between Mount Tavor and Givat HaMoreh, the narrow valley takes its name from the eponymous town Khsulot, which was later known to the priestly historian Joseph ben Matityahu (Flavius Josephus) as Xaloth and whose name is partially preserved in the Arabic toponym Iksal, a modern town east of Mount Precipice and southeast of Nazareth. In the era of the Judges (c. 1228–1020 BCE), the Khsulot Valley figured prominently in the battle won by the Israelite Judge and prophetess Dvorah and her general Barak against King Yavin of Hatzor and his general Sisera at Mount Tavor, and in the Israelite Judge Gidon's military campaign against the Midianites, who located their base camp within the valley.

5. **Jezreel** – The third largest valley in Israel, which essentially bridges the largest two. Jezreel ("God shall seed") reaches from the Kharmel mountain range to Mount Tavor and contains the Megiddo Valley, with the Harod Valley and the Beit She'an Valley as its eastern extensions toward the Jordan River. Dividing the tribal territory of western Menasheh (Samaria) to the south from Asher, Zevulun, Issachar, and Naphtali (Galilee) to the north, the curving valley runs northwest-southeast and comprises the Kishon River's alluvial plain. It was traversed by the ancient Derekh HaYam (The Way of the Sea/Coastal Highway) international trade route connecting Egypt and

Syria. The area was once dominated by Canaanites, whose iron chariots presented an obstacle to the tribe of Menasheh. After the successful battle won by the Israelite Judge and prophetess Dvorah and her general Barak against King Yavin of Hatzor and his general Sisera at Mount Tavor, the Israelites controlled the plain's peaks. Encamped at Ein Harod (Ma'ayan Harod), the Israelite Judge Gidon later defended the valley against the encroaching Midianites. During the United Monarchy of Israel (1030–931 BCE), the Philistines sought to divide King Saul's realm by advancing through the valley and establishing forward bases at Shunem and at Beit She'an. Saul and the Israelite army encamped by the spring in the valley just prior to their disastrous defeat in battle at the Gilboa mountain range. Still, the Jezreel Valley remained under Israelite control and formed part of King Ish-Boshet's northern kingdom while in the south King David ruled from Hebron in Judah. David soon swept away the Philistine outposts. David's third wife, Ahino'am, was from Jezreel. King Ahab of Israel built defensive walls and watchtowers to fortify the strategic town of Jezreel, his military headquarters, and the fruitful valley also featured Navot's vineyard, seized unjustly by a covetous Ahab. Here a convalescing King Yehoram of Israel, last scion of the Omride dynasty, was slain by the ruthless army commander Yehu ben Yehoshaphat ben Nimshi, who then had the queen mother Jezebel defenestrated and devoured by rabid dogs. The heads of Ahab's 70 sons were sent from Samaria to Jezreel and piled by its gate overnight, and the entire Omride household was promptly extirpated. Subsequently, Jezreel lost its splendor and might have even been sacked by invading Arameans. In 609, King Josiah of Judah died in battle at Megiddo while trying to prevent Pharaoh Neco II of Egypt from passing through the valley to assist Assyria against the Babylonians and the Medes. The valley was in time controlled by the Hasmonean and the Herodian dynasties, which administered its villages and farmlands. Roman legions later occupied and settled in the area, as did crusaders later still. In 1165 CE, the Jewish traveler Benjamin of Tudela visited the valley, stopped in the town of Jezreel, and encountered a Jewish dyer who resided there. Thereafter the district gradually deteriorated into malarial marshes. In 1799, Emperor Napoleon I of France fought the Ottoman Turks at Afula. In 1918, British general Edmund Allenby was bolstered by Australian cavalrymen rapidly crossing the valley during the campaign against the Turks. The plain was drained and resettled in the 1920s. Jezreel is known as Esdraelon in Greek.

6. **Beit She'an (Beisan)** – A valley joining the Jordan Rift Valley with the Harod Valley and the Jezreel Valley. Its land is highly fertile and features numerous springs. Ancient Egyptians controlled the city of Beit She'an and the caravan route that traversed the valley, which was initially allotted to the tribal territory of Issachar but which was soon taken over by western Menasheh. The Philistines encroached inland from the lower Coastal Plain and controlled the area during the reign of King Saul, who died nearby at the Gilboa mountain range in battle against the coastal invaders, who hanged Saul's corpse from the walls of the city of Beit She'an. Later the area was governed by King Solomon's officer Ba'ana ben Ahilud. In the Hellenistic era (332–167 BCE), Emperor Ptolemy II Philadelphus of Egypt stationed Scythian mercenaries in the region, giving rise to an additional name for the city of Beit She'an, Scythopolis. The Hasmonean ruler and high priest Jonathan Maccabee encountered the Seleucid (Syrian-Greek) pretender Diodotus Tryphon at Beit She'an, which the Hasmoneans conquered and refortified. During the Roman era (63 BCE–313 CE), Jews manufactured linen apparel, farmed field crops, and harvested olive plantations in the area. The Talmudic sage Shimon ben Lakish (Reish Lakish) said: "If paradise is situated in the Land of Israel, then Beit She'an is the portal…" (BT *Eiruvin* 19a). The valley supported vineyards, rice fields, and palm trees in the early Muslim era (638–1099 CE) but was devastated by the crusaders during their numerous campaigns. In the 1300s, the sage, physician, and explorer (Estori) Isaac HaParhi moved to Beit She'an from Jerusalem and used it as a home base wherefrom he conducted geographical and historical research, resulting in his masterwork, *Kaftor VaFerah*. In modern times, the Haifa-Damascus railroad line ran through the valley, and the area was settled by Bedouin Arabs from Egypt. Arab marauders used Beit She'an to launch attacks against Jewish residents of the Harod Valley until Jewish tower-and-stockade settlements were established in the vicinity. The area today features several kibbutzim and the Israel Railways line from Beit She'an to Afula and beyond.

7. **Dotan** – A valley at the head of which lies the town of the same name, in the northern section of the tribal territory of western Menasheh (Samaria), northwest of Shekhem and south of Ein Gannim (Jenin), where Joseph's brothers sold him to Ishmaelites traveling from Gilad to Egypt. Later, the prophet Elisha was a resident of Dotan, where he was besieged by Aramean forces that were, according to the biblical account, miraculously blinded and outmatched by fiery horses and chariots defending Elisha.

8. **Akhor** – In this valley near Jericho, Akhan ben Kharmi, who had absconded with forbidden spoils of war, was stoned to death. For his troubling of Israel, the valley was named Akhor ("troubler"). The prophet Hosea envisioned that Akhor would become "a gateway to hope" (2:17) and the prophet Isaiah foretold that it would become an idyllic place for cattle to rest "for my people who have sought me" (65:10). One of the Dead Sea Scrolls, the Copper Scroll, mentions the Akhor Valley as a ruin where a silver chest with vessels was buried.

9. **Coastal Plain (Sharon)** – The low-lying littoral curving along the edge of the Mediterranean Sea, the Coastal Plain is the widest and one of the longest valleys in Israel, beginning at the bottom of the Ladder of Tyre and extending as a widening band from Haifa and the headland of the Kharmel mountain range in the north to Gaza and beyond in the south. Beaches line the western edge of the Coastal Plain, and sand dunes are especially abundant from Jaffa to Gaza. Part of its northern section, from Taninim Stream to the Yarkon River – or from Caesarea (Caesarea Maritima) to Jaffa – is known as the Sharon Plain and was renowned in ancient times for its red and white lilies, anemones, oak forests, pastures, and marshes. The Sharon was part of the tribal territory of Ephraim, and during the United Monarchy of Israel (1030–931 BCE) Shitrai the Sharonite was appointed to supervise King David's herds that pastured in the Sharon. The female persona in *Song of Songs* famously states, "I am a rose of Sharon, a lily of the valleys" (2:1). The area was later conquered by the Assyrians, who built the coastal town of Dor (Dora). The prophet Isaiah lamented that "Sharon is like a desert" (33:9) but prophesied that "Sharon will become a pasture for flocks" (65:10). Later the Persians granted the Sharon Plain to the Tzidonians (Phoenicians). In ancient times, important cities including Akhziv, Akko, Caesarea, Jaffa, Ashdod, Ashkelon, and Gaza were built along the shoreline of the Coastal Plain, and in the modern era these centers were joined by Nahariyah, Haderah, Netanyah, Herzliyah, and Tel Aviv. Jewish settlers drained the malarial swamps of the Coastal Plain in the 1930s and developed the densely populated landscape. Citrus groves were particularly plentiful around Haderah and Jaffa. Today the coastline is a magnet for lovers of sand, sea, and surf.

10. **Ayalon** – A broad valley serving as an ingress to the Judean Hills and mentioned in the El-Amarna letters. In the memorable battle against the Amorites, Joshua bade the moon to stand still over Ayalon. The city of Ayalon, from which the valley derives its name, was initially

allotted to the original (southwestern) tribal territory of Dan, and soon it and its pasture lands were designated a Levitical city; in time the Benjaminites Beriah and Shema became prominent in Ayalon and drove away the Philistines of Gath. The faint and weary Israelites under King Saul and his son Jonathan slew the Philistines on the battlefield at Ayalon and beyond. King Rehoboam of Judah fortified, garrisoned, and provisioned the city of Ayalon as part of a network of fortifications to defend the tribal territories of Judah, Shimon, and Benjamin against the northern kingdom of Israel. The valley was briefly invaded both by Pharaoh Shishak (Sheshonk) I of Egypt during the reign of Rehoboam, and later by the Philistines during the reign of King Ahaz of Judah. The Ayalon features the ancient hot springs at Emmaus-Nicopolis, where the Hasmonean hero Judah Maccabee routed the Seleucids under Nicanor during the Maccabean Rebellion (167–134 BCE) and later where the Talmudic sages Nehunya ben HaKanah and Elazar ben Arakh lived, and which hosted Muslim Arab armies in the seventh century. During the Middle Ages, the crusader fort of Latrun was established. Due to its geostrategic value as an approach to Jerusalem, the valley also witnessed warfare during the British general Edmund Allenby's military campaign against the Ottoman Turks in 1917, and again in 1948 during the War of Independence (1947–1949). The Israel Defense Forces reclaimed the region during the Six-Day War of 1967.

11. **Ben Hinnom (Hinnom)** – A curving valley to the southwest and south of the Old City of Jerusalem, on the original Benjamin-Judah border, formerly infamous for its idolatrous Molekh worship. Named after a certain Hinnom's son, the Ben Hinnom Valley became a notorious site of child sacrifice where the abominable Tophet altar was erected, and for this reason the prophet Jeremiah envisioned that the area would be renamed the Valley of Slaughter, where corpses would be heaped in a gruesome congeries and devoured by predatory birds and wild beasts. As an open morgue and a place of punishment, the valley, whose Hebrew name Gai Ben Hinnom was over time contracted to Gehinnom or Gehenna, became synonymous with perdition. In later Israelite times it became a site for burning refuse. Perhaps in the Roman era (63 BCE–313 CE), a dam with an overlaid road was erected across the valley between (the erroneously named) Mount Zion just outside the Old City and the neighborhood opposite known today as Mishkenot Sha'ananim. In the early modern era, Sultan Suleiman the Magnificent of the Ottoman Empire built a fountain atop the dam, the

Sultan's Pool, extant today. Nowadays the Ben Hinnom Valley is a lovely site where music concerts are held in an amphitheater setting, where random horses roam and graze, and where a youth music center for Jewish and Arab students is situated.

12. **Kidron (Yehoshaphat)** – A valley originating northeast of Jerusalem, then dividing Temple Mount to the west from the Mount of Olives to the east, and finally continuing southeast toward the Salt Sea (Dead Sea). King David crossed the valley in flight from his rebellious son Avshalom. King Solomon set the Kidron as the boundary beyond which the execrating Benjaminite, Shimei ben Geira, could not venture upon penalty of forfeiting his life. King Asa of Judah later burned his grandmother Ma'akhah's idolatrous Asherah image in the Kidron. King Josiah of Judah similarly burned in the valley the Ba'al and Asherah idols that had been introduced in the Temple. The Jewish reformer Jesus of Nazareth often ventured into the Kidron with his disciples to linger in the Garden of Gat-Shemanim (Gethsemane). The central section of the Kidron between Temple Mount and the Mount of Olives is additionally known as the Valley of Yehoshaphat, which is otherwise considered an imprecise (if not metaphorical) locus. The prophet Joel foresaw that, following the Judahite return from the Babylonian Captivity, God would gather the nations and "take them down to the Valley of Yehoshaphat, and I will contend with them there concerning My people and My heritage, Israel, which they scattered among the nations, and My land they divided" (4:1-2). The Beit Zeita Valley, the Tyropoeon Valley, and the Ben Hinnom Valley all converge with the Kidron as it skirts east of Temple Mount and the City of David. In Jerusalem, the Gihon spring issued from the Kidron's western flank, and rock-cut, monumental tombs (e.g., the Tomb of Avshalom, the Tomb of Zikharyah, and the Tomb of Hezir's Sons) were carved out of its eastern flank (the western base of the Mount of Olives), forming a necropolis. Farther to the south, in the Judean Desert, the Christian monastery of Mar Saba features on the Kidron's steep slope as do numerous hermits' caves. The Kidron ("dark") derives its name from its dim stream in winter, or else from its depth or cedars.

13. **Tyropoeon** – A depression running from Jaffa Gate to the Pool of Shiloah (Siloam), the Tyropoeon ("The Valley of the Cheesemakers") formerly divided Jerusalem's upper city and (the erroneously named) Mount Zion to the west from Temple Mount and the lower city to the east. Bridges spanned the valley during the Hasmonean era (167–63 BCE). Over the centuries the valley was filled in with aggregated

detritus. One of the Dead Sea Scrolls, the Copper Scroll, refers to it as the Outer Valley, and Tyropoeon might have been a Greek mistranslation of the Hebrew word for "outer".

14. **Rephaim** – A verdant plain between Jerusalem and Bethlehem, reaching from the Ben Hinnom Valley to the Judean Desert hill now occupied by the Christian monastery Mar Elias. Rephaim was a scene of battle between King David and the Philistines. The Judah-Benjamin border ran across its northern end. Today its section within Jerusalem consists of the German Colony neighborhood and its chic Emek Rephaim Street. Rephaim ("ghosts" or "giants") may have been named after a Transjordanian tribe or clan by this name, dating at least from Abraham's time, that became famous for the tall stature and mighty prowess of its members, and that eventually settled in its namesake valley.

15. **Sorek** – A dry riverbed winding through the Judean Hills and skirting the original (southwestern) tribal territory of Dan as well as Philistia. Here, in one of the central ingresses to and drainage basins of Judah's heights, the Israelite Judge and strongman Samson encountered the charming Philistiness, Delilah, a resident of Sorek. The Philistine city of Ekron and the Israelite city of Beit Shemesh were established along the valley, whose name denotes "choicest vines" and refers as well to "red grapes". The old Jaffa-Jerusalem railway line runs through the valley, whose river nowadays features two large seawater desalination plants.

16. **Elah** – Located in the Shephelah foothills in the tribal territory of Judah, near Azekah and Sokho, the fertile valley is named after its terebinths, though it also features diverse flora and fauna. Here a young slinger, David of Bethlehem, felled the Philistine giant Goliath of Gath in their fateful duel. A seasonal brook whose streambed possesses many smooth stones courses through the valley during the winter after heavy rains.

17. **Brakhah** – King Yehoshaphat of Judah assembled his men in this valley west of Tekoa after three days of despoiling the Ammonites and Moabites; here they blessed God for their good fortune, giving the valley its name ("blessing"). It runs along the main road between Hebron and Jerusalem.

18. **Eshkol** – A fruitful valley in the vicinity of Hebron. Here the 12 Israelite spies severed a bough bearing a cluster (*eshkol*) of grapes requiring two men to carry it back on a pole; they also returned with samples of pomegranates and figs. These specimens attested to the lush

abundance of the Promised Land. The valley might have originally been named after one of the three Amorite brothers who had allied themselves with the patriarch Abraham in his campaign against King Khedarlaomer of Elam.

19. **Jordan Rift** – The longest valley in Israel forms part of the Great Rift Valley/Syrian-African Rift extending from southern Turkey to Mozambique. In prehistoric times, Lake Kinneret (the Sea of Galilee) and the Salt Sea (Dead Sea) formed a single saline lake. The Jordan ("the descender" or "descended from Dan") comprises three terraces and incorporates the Hula Valley, the Jordan River Valley, and the Aravah Valley, and features the meandering Jordan River with its numerous tributaries and fords. Its valley walls, broken only sporadically by tributary gorges, are mostly steep, sheer, and bare. During the period of the Israelite repatriation to the Land of Israel (c. 1273–1245 BCE), the Israelites traversed the valley near Jericho. King Solomon established his brass-foundries in the clay ground of the Jordan Plain between Sukkot and Tzartan. Lions roamed the valley in the biblical era. The Jordan Rift trough also features the Salt Sea, the lowest land point on Earth. The main city situated in the Jordan Rift is Jericho, and today the valley is home to dozens of Jewish agricultural communities as well as a number of Arab villages.

20. **Shitim** – Named after its acacias, Shitim was the Transjordanian site of the Israelites' dalliance with the daughters of Moab and Midian and where they were consequently afflicted by a plague as punishment. Here the future high priest Pinhas, Aaron's grandson, slew the Shimonite prince Zimri ben Salu for fornicating with Cozbi the Moabitess. Thereafter Joshua dispatched scouts from Shitim to spy on Jericho. The prophet Joel envisioned that one day the spring flowing from the Temple in Jerusalem would water the valley.

21. **Aravah** – Biblically, the Aravah ("wilderness"/"steppe"/"plain") referred mostly to the Jordan Rift Valley between Lake Kinneret (the Sea of Galilee) and the Salt Sea (Dead Sea), also known as the Sea of the Aravah, an area known in Arabic as el-Ghor/al-Ghur, but eventually the name Aravah referred solely to the long, deep cleft extending from the Salt Sea southward to the Gulf of Eilat. A section of the Aravah, the barren plain on the Salt Sea's southern shore whose brown soil is flecked with salt, is additionally known as the Valley of Salt; there King David made a name for himself as a warrior-king by slaying 18,000 Arameans (or else Edomites) in battle, and there King Amaziah of Judah later slew another 10,000 Edomites, engendering his

subsequent hubris that proved disastrous. Sand, gravel, and boulders litter the Aravah's arid desert, which features white rock and desert tree species such as acacia and tamarisk. Copper mines were developed in the Aravah at Timna, and especially at Punon (Feinan in Jordan). The desert steppe was often fought over due to its copper resources and to the access it afforded to the Red Sea. The prophet Isaiah envisioned a future time when the Aravah would blossom like the lily and be given the splendor of the Sharon Plain and of the Kharmel mountain range.

22. **Timna** – A semicircular (horseshoe-shaped) plain of sand and stone stretching from the lower Negev Desert to the Aravah Valley north of the Gulf of Eilat. A trio of seasonal streambeds – Nahal Timna, Nahal Nehushtan, and Nahal Mangan – traverse the Timna Valley toward the Aravah. In the center of the valley rises Mount Timna, whose tabular summit affords panoramic views of the surrounding plain and the Edomite Mountains to the east. The valley features natural arches formed by erosion, mushroom-shaped rock outcrops fashioned by desert wind and humidity, hieroglyphic inscriptions and drawings, mine shafts, galleries, and workshops, and the distinctive red sandstone cliff ridges known as Solomon's Pillars. Copper mining and smelting activities took place in the western and central sections of the valley beginning in prehistoric times. Ancient Egyptian expeditions to the valley later developed the area's metallurgic industry, in partnership with local Kenites, Midianites, and Amalekites. A cultic shrine with a rock-cut niche was built in honor of the goddess Hathor during the reign of Pharaoh Seti I of Egypt (c. 1290–1279 BCE), and a sphinx-like head is discernible on a rugged eminence to the east. Roman legionaries of the Legio III Cyrenaica also engaged in copper mining between the second and fourth centuries CE, hauling ore southward to the sizable Be'er Orah furnace. The Timna Valley also features acacias, wild ibex herds, and nocturnal wolf packs. Today the valley, a popular tourism and recreation site, includes an artificial lake, a life-size model of the Tabernacle, and a visitors' center.

As would be expected given the topography of the Land of Israel, the Hebrew language contains numerous words denoting valleys, including: *emek* (valley, dell), *gai* (glen/dale/dingle), *beek'ah* (rift/cleavage), *mishor* (plateau/tableland), *aravah* (wilderness/plain/steppe), *khikar* (plain/pasture/meadow), *shephelah* (lowland), *kenyon* (canyon), *arutz* (gorge/ravine), *agan* (basin), and *apheek* (trough/streambed/riverbed). In addition, many valleys or dry riverbeds that feature seasonal watercourses are generally designated by the term *nahal* (stream/watercourse).

As loci where momentous events occurred, all of the major valleys in Israel appear (some of them scores of times) in the Tanakh (Hebrew Bible) and/or in the post-biblical, historical books *I & II Maccabees* and *The Jewish War* and *Jewish Antiquities*.

While the Land of Israel is primarily hill country, its valleys have always been critical lifelines, places to farm crops and locate flowing water, ingresses to and egresses from every province and district, and battleground sites. For millennia inhabitants and itinerants alike have profited from exploring, traversing, and cultivating the picturesque valleys of Israel, which continue to entice visitants.

Jezreel Valley

5
Rivers of Israel

Rivers of Israel

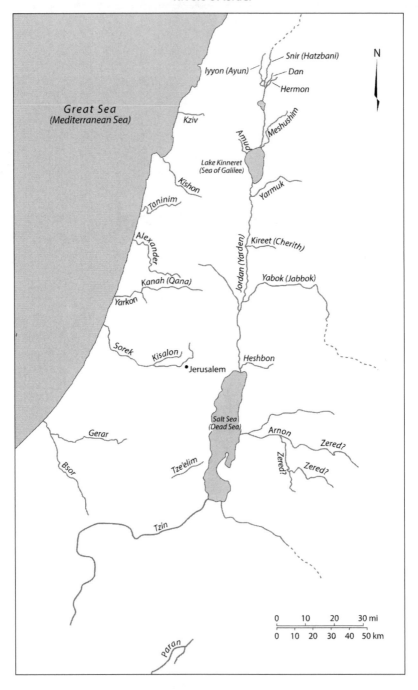

The Land of Israel's numerous rivers sustain life – human, animal, and plant – as they channel through valleys, mountain ranges, and deserts into larger watercourses, lakes, or the sea. The main river in Israel is the famed Jordan, into which many important headwaters and tributaries flow. Most of Israel's watercourses are perennial or intermittent streams with considerably less volume output in seasons other than winter.

From the outset of ancient Near Eastern civilization, rivers served as ready-made borders dividing nations, tribes, and clans, and many important cities, towns, and villages developed alongside them. Good rivers made good neighbors. Such definitional waters were to be shared, and egregious deviations from this principle were grounds for war. Key battles, unsurprisingly, occurred at various rivers, and fording a river signaled the crossing of a threshold, perhaps even a point of no return.

Yet the rivers of Israel played a prominent part as a precious resource not only in the lives and times of the Israelites and their several neighbors, but in the rich ecology and biodiversity of the country. Here is a précis offering a glimpse at the most geographically and historically significant rivers in Israel.

1. **Hermon** – A stream descending from Mount Hermon through the conjunction of the Golan and the Hula Valley, the Hermon courses for over 2 miles along a steep basalt gorge and through the ancient city of Paneas (Caesarea Philippi) southward to the Banias waterfall, the most powerful in Israel, and beyond. The perennial stream is sourced from the rain and snowmelt that fosters springs at the foot of the Paneas cave, and in turn supplies the Jordan River with most of its water.

2. **Snir (Hatzbani)** – The longest tributary of the Jordan River, the perennial Snir Stream flows through a forest of plane trees and yellowish travertine rock walls, and is subject to annual flooding. Descending from the western slope of Mount Hermon, Snir (another biblical name for Mount Hermon) runs for over 37 miles (mostly in Lebanon, where it passes by the Druze town of Hatzbaya, hence its Arabic name Hatzbani), and for over 3 miles through an Israeli nature reserve in the Galilee Panhandle ("The Finger of Galilee"). Denizens of the stream include otters, porcupines, wild boars, mongooses, badgers, river crabs, dragonflies, and damselflies.

3. **Dan** – The largest tributary of the Jordan River, rising from a plentiful karstic spring in the ancient Israelite city of Dan (Tel Dan), formerly known as La'yish/Leshem. Rainwater and snowmelt trickling down from Mount Hermon feed the stream, which courses for about 12 miles

through a shady wetland forest of laurel and ash trees and plants such as buckthorn and marsh fern. The vicinity, within the Galilee Panhandle ("The Finger of Galilee"), is also home to Near Eastern fire salamanders, otters, wild boars, river crabs, dragonflies, and damselflies. The cool stream features several rivulets that combine with Hermon Stream and Snir Stream, and is spanned by several wooden bridges. Kibbutz Dan and Kibbutz Dafna are nearby.

4. **Iyyon (Ayun)** – A stream originating in Lebanon and flowing through a gorge in the Galilee Panhandle ("The Finger of Galilee") from the Iyyon (Ayun) Valley to the Hula Valley, passing by en route the ancient ruins of Avel Beit Ma'akhah and the modern town of Metulah, the northernmost town in the State of Israel. In his war against King Basha of Israel, King Asa of Judah bribed King Ben-Hadad of Aram with silver and gold to make war on Basha in the north; Ben-Hadad obliged and attacked the northern sites of Iyyon, Dan, Avel Beit Ma'akhah, etc. During the reign of King Pekah of Israel, Emperor Tiglat-Pileser III of Assyria conquered Iyyon, Avel Beit Ma'akhah, Hatzor, and other northern towns in the Naphtali tribal territory, and exiled their inhabitants to Assyria. The scenic stream includes four waterfalls: Tanur, Tahana, Iyyon, and Eshed. In classical rabbinical literature, the stream and its gorge are referred to in Aramaic as "Nekuvta D'Iyyon"/"Nukvata D'Iyyon" (e.g., Sif. *Deuteronomy* 51; Tos. *Shvi'it* 4:5; JT *Shvi'it* 16a).

5. **Meshushim** – A perennial stream almost 22 miles in length (the longest in the Golan), coursing through a deep basalt canyon within the Yehudiyah Forest amid the central Golan. The Meshushim originates at Mount Avital and terminates in Lake Kinneret (the Sea of Galilee), where it forms an estuary lagoon. The stream leads to the sizable Meshushim pool surrounded by a cliff of hexagonal basalt pillars. The area is replete with oak, eucalyptus, mastic, styrax, jujube, and almond trees, and is also noted for its population of wild boars, eagles, vultures, kestrels, buzzards, mountain gazelles, and hyraxes, among other fauna. The Meshushim, one of four streams in the Yehudiyah Forest (the others being Zavitan, Yehudiyah, and Daliyot) flows near the ancient Jewish town of Gamla, a prominent mountain site famous for its dramatic battle and mass suicide during the Great Revolt (66–73 CE) against the Romans, and the ancient Jewish village of Yehudiyah, whose ruined synagogues remain in evidence.

6. **Kziv** – A perennial stream flowing for over 12 miles through Upper Galilee from Mount Meron to Akhziv, and the longest watercourse in

Galilee. The ruined crusader fortress of Montfort, erstwhile stronghold of Teutonic knights, perches on a spur overlooking the Kziv. The stream features several springs along its course.

7. **Kishon** – A river originating south of the Gilboa mountain range and flowing northwestward through the Jezreel Valley and north of the Kharmel mountain range, reaching its outlet, the Mediterranean Sea, just north of Haifa. The river extends for over 43 miles. In *Joshua*, it is referred to as "the river before Yokne'am" (19:11); in *Judges*, for its role in the triumph of the Israelite Judge and prophetess Dvorah and her general Barak against King Yavin of Hatzor and his general Sisera, it is celebrated thusly: "Kings came; they fought. Yes, the kings of Canaan fought at Ta'anakh, by the waters of Megiddo; but they took no spoil of silver. They fought from heaven, the stars in their courses; yes, they fought against Sisera. The Kishon River swept them away, that ancient river, the Kishon River. O my soul, march on with strength!" (5:19-21). The river is also cited in *Psalms*. The prophet Elijah subsequently had the 450 defeated prophets of Ba'al seized and taken down from the Kharmel mountain range to the Kishon, where they were slain with the sword. In winter the Kishon is often flooded, rendering its fords impassable. In the modern era, the mouth of the river was deepened and developed to establish an auxiliary port near Haifa Bay. In recent decades the river was chemically polluted by industrial effluents and municipal wastewater, but a major cleanup was lately undertaken.

8. **Taninim** – A sparkling coastal stream running for almost 16 miles between the Menasheh Heights of the Kharmel mountain range and the Mediterranean Sea, and named after the former reptile residents (in Hebrew, *taninim* denotes "crocodiles") of the proximate Kebara swamp. The stream is ornamented with yellow water lilies on its surface and contains fish such as tilapia, catfish, and gray mullet, as well as Caspian turtles, below its surface. An extant dam from late in the Roman era (63 BCE–313 CE) or from early in the Byzantine era (324–638 CE) was built to raise the stream's water level so that it could be channeled southward to Caesarea (Caesarea Maritima), which was built by King Herod the Great of Judea and which served as the Roman administrative capital in the Land of Israel. A by-product of the dam was a small lake. Taninim is regarded as the cleanest coastal watercourse in Israel, and it delimits the southern extent of the Hof HaKharmel (Kharmel Coastal Plain). The ancient remnants of a city dating either to the Persian era (539–332 BCE) or to the Hellenistic

era (332–167 BCE) and once known as Crocodilopolis (Tel Taninim) rest along the confluence of the stream and the sea.

9. **Amud** – A stream in eastern Galilee that flows southward for over 15 miles and descends into Lake Kinneret (the Sea of Galilee) at the Ginnosar Valley. The watercourse is named after an isolated limestone pillar (in Hebrew, *amud* denotes "pillar") about 22 yards tall that stands upright along the streambed, beside which rises the seasonal spring Ein Amud. Amud is especially known for its adjacent caves (Dovecote, Amud, Skull/Zutiyeh, Amira), all of which have been excavated, and which were found to contain the remains of Neanderthals and other prehistoric humans, as well as for its cliff-dwelling vultures, eagles, kestrels, falcons, and buzzards. In the stream swim Levantine scraper fish, and its springs feature river crabs, dragonflies, and damselflies. Along the stream can be found lush riparian vegetation and a diverse array of trees: oak, terebinth, carob, styrax, mastic, almond, walnut, jujube, plane, willow, and eastern strawberry. Nearby are the remnants of a pagan temple on Mount Mitzpeh HaYamim dating to the Hellenistic era (332–167 BCE), and of the Jewish village Kfar Hananiah dating to the Hasmonean era (167–63 BCE), as are the eastern slopes of Mount Meron, whereon the Mishnaic sages Shimon bar Yohai and his son Elazar ben Shimon are entombed. Alongside the stream are the ruins of more than two dozen flour and fulling mills dating to the 1500s, attesting to early modern Tzfat's wool industry, introduced by Sephardic exiles post-Spanish expulsion (1492). The National Water Carrier traverses the Amud Stream in a camouflaged siphon pipe.

10. **Alexander** – A coastal flood stream in the Sharon Plain, flowing for almost 20 miles from the western slopes of Samaria westward then northwestward through the Hepher Plain until reaching the Mediterranean Sea, with its estuary between Beit Yannai beach and Mikhmoret. The stream channels through eucalyptus trees, reeds, bulrushes, and brambles, and is home to an abundance of giant soft-shelled turtles, as well as specimens of tilapia, catfish, mullet, and river eel. Its riverbanks feature rich riparian wildlife, including green sea turtles, loggerhead sea turtles, coypus, and mongooses. The terrain near the mouth of the stream consists of calcareous sandstone (*kurkar*) ridges and sand dunes. Close by lie the remnants of a structure dating to the late 1800s, Horvat Samara. In June 1948, the Irgun Tzvai L'Umi (Etzel/the Irgun) vessel *Altalena* anchored at a nearby port before sailing onward to Tel Aviv.

11. **Kanah (Qana)** – A seasonal stream and the Yarkon River's northernmost tributary, rising from the vicinity of Mount Gerizim in Samaria and flowing southwestward into the Sharon Plain. The Kanah has its own tributary, Nahal Hadar, which courses east and south of the mound of Tel Qana, where ancient wine presses have been excavated. The Kanah served as the boundary between the tribal territories of western Menasheh to the north and Ephraim to the south. Today the stream passes by numerous communities including Karnei Shomron, Kfar Saba, and Hod HaSharon.

12. **Yarkon** – A perennial river rising from springs proximate to Aphek (Pegae/Arethusa/Antipatris) and Rosh HaAyin and winding for 17 miles westward till it spills into the Mediterranean Sea in northern Tel Aviv. Its name is derived from its greenish hue (in Hebrew, *yarok* denotes "green"); the name Aphek, incidentally, derives from the Akkadian word Aphek/Aphekum, meaning springs, whence the Hebrew word for riverbed/streambed (*apheek*). The river's source is by the narrow Aphek Passage, through which the ancient Derekh HaYam (The Way of the Sea/Coastal Highway) international trade route connecting Egypt and Syria passed so as to circumvent the quondam marshes. The Yarkon marks the boundary between the northern section of the Coastal Plain (i.e., the Sharon Plain) and the Coastal Plain's lowlands to the south. It receives a number of tributaries from north and south. The stream's water sometimes runs red due to its sandy loam soil (*hamra*), and according to the Mishnah, where it is referred to as *mei pugah*, its water was deemed unfit for ritual service in the Temple because it was marshy. The modern Yarkon Park, through which the stream courses, is replete with oak, carob, and eucalyptus trees. Yellow water lilies grow in the pond near the stream's source, and silver Yarkon bream swim in the stream and in a discrete pool near its spring. Other denizens of the stream include Nile soft-shelled turtles, tilapias, catfish, mosquito fish, coypus, terrapins, mallards, moorhens, swamp cats, and porcupines. Vestiges of Canaanite palaces and of a Roman odeon (music theater) are found at Tel Aphek, and a 16th century Turkish fortress, Pinar Basha, crowns Tel Aphek near the stream. In the modern era, cities that have cropped up in the vicinity include Petah Tikvah, Bnei Brak, Ramat Gan, and Tel Aviv. General Edmund Allenby crossed the stream with his British army during his campaign against the Ottoman Turks in 1917. From the 1950s, the stream became increasingly polluted, but hydrological rehabilitation efforts have

meliorated the water quality in recent years. Since 1955, much of the Yarkon's headwaters has been diverted via the National Water Carrier to the Negev Desert for irrigation purposes.

13. **Sorek** – A stream flowing through the Sorek Valley in the tribal territory of Judah, where the Israelite Judge and strongman Samson encountered the duplicitous Philistiness, Delilah. Several of its tributaries feature waterfalls. The Sorek served as the boundary between the original (southwestern) tribal territory of Dan and Philistia, and the Philistine city of Ekron and the Israelite city of Beit Shemesh were located proximate to the stream. Today the old Jerusalem-Tel Aviv railway parallels the watercourse.

14. **Kisalon** – A Judean river flowing for over 12 miles through the Jerusalem Hills from Mount Adar to the outskirts of Beit Shemesh in the Sorek Valley. The Kisalon features the picturesque spring of Ein Hemed (Aqua Bella), where a crusader farmhouse dating to the 1100s and probably belonging to the Knights Hospitaler is preserved. Today the Kisalon passes by Martyrs' Forest, whose 6 million trees commemorate Jewish victims of the Holocaust.

15. **Gerar** – A brook that rises from the southwest foothills of the Judean Hills and courses westward through rich pastoral country in the northwestern Negev Desert and past several ancient Egyptian archaeological sites dating to the Bronze Age (3300–1200 BCE). During the subsequent Iron Age (1200–550 BCE), the Gerar Brook and the royal city of the same name were under Philistine control. The Philistine ruler, King Avimelekh of Gerar, took the matriarch Sarah captive when Abraham had to sojourn in Gerar due to famine; later, the patriarch Isaac likewise sojourned in Gerar for identical reasons, and soon dwelt in the river valley and unstopped the wells of his father Abraham that the Philistines had since filled up with earth. Here Isaac's servants dug two new wells of living water, called Esek and Sitnah, of which the Philistines contested ownership, then a third well called Rehovot that went uncontested. The brook also flowed near the Philistine fortress of Tziklag, where David and his followers sojourned while hunted by an unstable King Saul. Thereafter King Asa of Judah battled against Zerah the Ethiopian and his vast army and hundreds of chariots, pursuing the fleeing Ethiopians from Mareshah to Gerar, routing them and despoiling the local towns. In the Hasmonean era (167–63 BCE), in a hasty treaty between Emperor Antiochus V Eupator of Syria (and his regent Lysias) and the Hasmonean hero Judah Maccabee, Gerar served as the southern border of the coastal region

under Seleucid (Syrian-Greek) control. The city of Gerar has been identified with several ruins, perhaps most convincingly with the large mound known as Tel Haror/Tel Abu Hurayra. Today the Gerar Brook passes by the Bedouin town of Rahat, as well as the town of Netivot and the village of Re'im.

16. **Bsor** – The largest stream in the northern Negev Desert, extending for almost 50 miles from Mount Boker across the Agur-Halutzah sand dunes and the Gaza Strip to the Mediterranean Sea. In his pursuit of the Amalekites, who had attacked and burnt his haven of Tziklag, David left behind at the brook 200 of his 600 men, who safeguarded their possessions while the other 400 ventured off to war. The Bsor has numerous tributaries and floods yearly after heavy rains.

17. **Jordan (Yarden)** – The primary watercourse in the Land of Israel, formed by the confluence of a quartet of headwaters (Iyyon/Ayun, Snir/Hatzbani, Dan, Hermon) at the base of Mount Hermon. The Jordan (in Hebrew, *yarden* denotes "the descender"/"descending from Dan") extends for about 225 miles southward through (the former) Lake Hula and Lake Kinneret (the Sea of Galilee) and continues descending southward along a significant gradient until as a delta it empties into the north shore of the Salt Sea (Dead Sea). Declining some 3,000 feet from its northern source to its southern mouth, the Jordan is shallow in summertime and profound in wintertime. Its usually swift current ferries considerable silt, and the salinity of its water increases as it nears the Salt Sea. Coursing through luxuriant vegetation, the river features some 31 fords, and possesses the lowest elevation of any river in the world. During the period of the Israelite repatriation to the Land of Israel (c. 1273–1245 BCE), the Israelites followed Joshua across the Jordan near Jericho. When the men of Reuven, Gad, and eastern Menasheh departed from the rest of the Israelite tribes, they paused while still on the western riverbank of the Jordan and erected a large altar to serve as a symbolic "witness" attesting to the fact that they, too, had a share in the God of Israel. The Jordan was the tribal border between eastern Menasheh, Gad, and Reuven to the east (in Transjordan and atop the Mishor) and Naphtali, Issachar, western Menasheh, Ephraim, and Benjamin to the west (in Cisjordan). In the era of the Judges (c. 1228–1020 BCE), Gidon adjured the Ephraimites to capture the lower fords to prevent the Midianites and their chieftains Orev and Ze'ev from fording the Jordan, and later Yiftah and the Giladites secured the lower fords and slew 42,000 Ephraimites in battle after the Ammonites had been defeated. In time King Solomon

established his brass-foundries in the clay ground of the Jordan Plain between Sukkot and Tzartan. The river's water was deemed unfit for ritual use in the Temple due to its impurity. The prophets Elijah and Elisha both forded the Jordan dry-shod after striking it with Elijah's rolled-up cloak, thereby dividing it. Elisha performed further riverine miracles when he directed the disease-ridden Aramean general Na'aman to immerse himself seven times in the Jordan's waters, which healed Na'aman's skin, and when he caused an iron axe blade to surface from the Jordan's depths after one of his prophetic disciples had inadvertently dropped it into the river. In the Hasmonean era (167–63 BCE), Judah Maccabee and Jonathan Maccabee crossed the Jordan prior to their rescue campaign in Gilad; later, after Judah's decease, Jonathan Maccabee, Shimon Maccabee, and their force of Maccabean freedom fighters bivouacked by the marshes and thickets of the Jordan during their campaign against the formidable Seleucid (Syrian-Greek) general Bacchides, at one point swimming across the river after routing the enemy. Jewish reformer Jesus of Nazareth was baptized in the river by his relative John, who was perhaps a member of the Essene sect. In the modern era, half a dozen bridges were erected to span the river, including: Arik Bridge, between Galilee and the Golan; Jordan River Crossing/Sheikh Hussein Bridge, a border crossing, between Galilee and Jordan; Gesher Adam/Damiya Bridge, between Samaria and Jordan; and Allenby/King Hussein Bridge, another border crossing, between Judea and Jordan. The malign attempt by Syria, Lebanon, and Jordan to divert the river's headwaters in 1965 was a contributing factor to the ensuing Six-Day War of 1967. Immortalized in the Tanakh (Hebrew Bible), the Jordan has been celebrated further in many spiritual hymns and folk songs. Today the river is used for irrigation in order to grow fruits and vegetables and for recreational rafting, and remains revered by Christians as a baptismal site.

18. **Yarmuk** – The largest tributary of the Jordan River, with its sources amid a lava plateau in the Golan. The narrow and shallow Yarmuk flows with many convolutions southwestward, widening and deepening as it joins the Jordan several miles south of Lake Kinneret (the Sea of Galilee). The river has its own tributaries, which feature numerous waterfalls. The Yarmuk served as the northern boundary of the southern Transjordanian region of Gilad. According to the Mishnah, its water was deemed unfit for ritual use because it was "mixed", which the medieval sage (Estori) Isaac HaParhi explained meant blended with the waters of Hammat Gader (Gadara), whose hot

springs the Yarmuk skirts. In the Talmud, the sage Yohanan bar Nappaha asserts that the Yarmuk is second only to the Jordan (in volume) among Israel's rivers. In 636 CE, the Battle of Yarmuk River proved to be a decisive victory for the Muslim Arabs under Khalid ibn al-Walid against Theodorus Trithurius and the Byzantine Christians, whose Armenian and Christian Arab allies had deserted them. In 1946, during Operation Markolet ("The Night of the Bridges"), the Haganah bombed the Hejaz Railway bridge spanning the Yarmuk. For most of its length (approx. 50 miles) it serves as Israel's northeastern border with Jordan.

19. **Kireet (Cherith)** – An eastern tributary of the Jordan River where Elijah the prophet was divinely directed to hide and dwell, there to be sustained by the brook's water and fed by its ravens who brought him bread and meat morning and evening. When the brook dried up during the drought which he had foretold, Elijah was directed to move on to be sustained by the widow of Tzarphat.

20. **Yabok (Jabbok)** – The second-largest tributary of the Jordan River, joining the latter between Lake Kinneret (the Sea of Galilee) and the Salt Sea (Dead Sea). Stretching some 62 miles, the Yabok emanates from a spring proximate to Rabbat-Ammon and divides mountainous Gilad into two. After departing Haran, the patriarch Jacob forded the Yabok en route to his long-awaited yet dreaded reunion with his brother Esau. He conveyed his household and their possessions across the Yabok, and that night at the site known thereafter as Penu'el (Peni'el), a future capital of the Kingdom of Israel, he wrestled with a mysterious figure until daybreak. The Yabok served as the Ammonite-Amorite frontier – the dominion of King Sihon of the Amorites extended between the Yabok and Arnon rivers – until the Amorites were defeated by Moses and the Israelites in the preliminary stages (c. 1273 BCE) of the period of the Israelite repatriation to the Land of Israel (c. 1273–1245 BCE). It subsequently served as the boundary between the Israelite tribes of Gad and Reuven (to the west and southwest) and Ammon (to the east and northeast), and coursed by the Israelite capitals of Penu'el and Mahanayim, as well as the town of Sukkot. In the Hellenistic era (332–167 BCE), the Yabok also functioned as the border of the domain of a prominent Jewish clan, the Tobiads, based in Perea (southern Gilad and the Mishor). Thereafter the Romans erected a bridge spanning the Yabok. In Arabic the Yabok is known as the Zarqa.

21. **Heshbon** – An intermittent stream in Transjordan descending westward from the vicinity of the town of Heshbon in the heights of

Moab through a verdant ribbon toward the longer watercourse Wadi al-Kafrein, which it joins in the Jordan River Valley north of the Salt Sea (Dead Sea). The stream served as the boundary between the tribal territories of Gad to the north and Reuven to the south, and as the southern boundary of the southern Transjordanian region of Gilad. The oft-contested town of Heshbon first belonged to Moab, then served as the capital of King Sihon of the Amorites, then was allotted by Moses to the tribal territory of Reuven, then became a Levitical city in the tribal territory of Gad, then was reclaimed by King Mesha of Moab, then was reconquered by the Hasmonean monarch King Yannai Alexander of Judea, then became a military veterans' colony in Perea (southern Gilad and the Mishor) under King Herod the Great of Judea. In *Song of Songs*, the male persona romanticizes his beloved with the description, "your eyes [are] like the pools in Heshbon" (7:5). Ruins of a reservoir are extant at the town.

22. **Arnon** – The meandering Arnon flows northward then westward through limestone hills and a steep gorge into the eastern shore of the Salt Sea (Dead Sea), opposite Ein Gedi. It extends for approximately 50 miles, is alternately broad and narrow, and deepens considerably (down to about 10 feet) during winter. It served as the boundary between the Amorites in the north and the Moabites in the south; following the period of the Israelite repatriation to the Land of Israel (c. 1273–1245 BCE), it similarly divided the tribe of Reuven to the north and Moab to the south. King Mesha of Moab mentions the Arnon, and the roads (or fords) across it that he constructed, in his famous stela. The Arnon's fords were indeed a critical link along the King's Highway (Road to Bashan) international trade route connecting Egypt and Mesopotamia, which traversed the tableland east of the Jordan Rift Valley from Etzion-Gever (near Eilat) to Damascus. The river figures in the Tanakh (Hebrew Bible) when it cites "the masters of Arnon's high places" (*Numbers* 21:28); when the prophet Isaiah avers that the "daughters of Moab at the fords of the Arnon are like fluttering birds pushed from the nest" (16:2); and when the prophet Jeremiah relates the divine prophecy declaring: "Proclaim it by the Arnon that Moab has been laid waste" (48:20). The largest settlement in the vicinity in ancient times was the city of Aro'er. In the Hasmonean era (167–63 BCE), the region was claimed by Yohanan Hyrcanus and his son King Yannai Alexander of Judea, with the Arnon again serving as the boundary between the Judean kingdom to the north and Nabatea to the south. In the Roman era (63 BCE–313 CE), a legion was stationed

by the Arnon to secure the Eilat-Bozrah road crossing it. Upon beholding the Arnon, and in commemoration of a legendary miracle that occurred when the Ark of the Testimony (Ark of the Covenant) caused the ambuscading Amorites to be crushed in their cavernous hideouts, allowing the Israelites to proceed unmolested northward across the mountains of Gilad, the Sages instituted a special blessing: "Blessed be He who performed miracles for our forefathers at this place" (BT *Brakhot* 54a-b). The Arnon also became renowned for its plentiful fish and diverse wildlife. In Arabic the Arnon is known as Wadi Mujib.

23. **Zered** – A verdant stream in northeastern Moab whose name denotes "lush", the Zered was a camping site of the Israelites in their roundabout approach to the Promised Land. The stream was long identified with Wadi al-Hasa – which served as the Moab-Edom border – but is likely either Wadi es-Sawaqa (the Arnon's eastern tributary), Wadi Nukheile/an-Nukhayla (which discharges into the Arnon), or Wadi Tarfawiyye/e-Tarfawiya (which discharges into Wadi Nukheile).

24. **Tze'elim** – Named after its shady lotus trees, the Tze'elim Stream courses from the Hebron Hills through the Judean Desert toward the Salt Sea (Dead Sea) between Ein Gedi and Masada. The stream passes by a trio of caves and four pools of water.

25. **Tzin** – The largest seasonal stream in the Negev Desert, rising in the northwest of the erosion cirque Makhtesh Ramon and flowing northward then eastward for almost 75 miles through an arid limestone landscape. The watercourse meanders south of Kibbutz Sdei Boker through the narrow Ein Avdat canyon, which features springs, waterfalls, and pools, as well as poplar trees and saltbush shrubs. Ibexes forage for provender in the area, and birds of prey (eagles, hawks, vultures) and bulbul songbirds hunt and swoop overhead. The wilderness of Tzin was where the Israelite spies began their reconnaissance mission in Canaan; where the Israelites encamped after Etzion-Gever (near Eilat); where Miriam died and was buried; where at Kadesh (Meribat-Kadesh/Rekem/Petra) Moses twice struck the rock he was divinely instructed to speak to, which gushed forth the water of Meribah; and whence the southern border of the Promised Land traversed westward to Kadesh-Barnea. Today the stream is known for its surging flash floods after heavy rainfall in winter, and the area is popular among hikers.

26. **Paran** – Coursing for over 93 miles through the Negev Desert and the Sinai Peninsula, the Paran Stream is the widest and the third longest watercourse in Israel. The Paran wilderness is traversed by Wadi el-

Arish's eastern affluents. This beige desert landscape, southwest of the Tzin River Valley and north of the Gulf of Eilat and the Red Sea, was where King Khedarlaomer of Elam and his royal alliance assailed the Horites. The patriarch Abraham's concubine Hagar was dispatched from Be'ersheva to Paran with their son Ishmael, who in this locus became an archer and married an Egyptian wife. During their wilderness wanderings, the Israelites traveled from the Sinai Desert and via Hatzeirot encamped at Paran. Moses dispatched the 12 Israelite spies into Canaan from Paran, to which they returned after reconnoitering for 40 days, and later he addressed the people "between Paran and Tophel and Lavan and Hatzeirot and Di Zahav" (*Deuteronomy* 1:1). Later the fugitive David, having effected a temporary truce with King Saul, retreated to Paran after the decease of the prophet Samuel. Thereafter the young prince of Edom, Hadad, fled King David and Yo'av his general, escaping to Midian then crossing Paran and collecting local men there to join him in his flight to Egypt. In the Roman era (63 BCE–313 CE), a road traversed the area. Today the stream is known for its flash floods in wintertime, and the surrounding desert for its recently introduced population of Arabian oryxes.

Hebrew contains numerous words denoting rivers, including: *nahar* (river); *ziroa nahar* (tributary); *nahal* (stream/brook/watercourse); *peleg* (rivulet/ stream/streamlet/brook/runnel); *peleg kattan* (rill); *meephratzon* (creek); *arutz* (creek/channel); *ti'alla* (canal/channel); *apheek* (trough/streambed/ riverbed/watercourse); *niteev mayyim* (waterway); *zerem* (stream/flow/ flux/gush); *sheteph* (flow/flood/stream); and *shephekh* (estuary).

Without the life-sustaining watercourses of the Land of Israel, the history of the Jewish people would have been certainly different and almost certainly abbreviated.

The State of Israel's sophisticated water usage allows for the irrigation of farmlands and arid desert, but such diversions of water must be delicately balanced with the ecological needs of riverine wildlife and riparian plants dependent upon the sustained flow of watercourses along their original channels. Toward this end, the Israel Nature and Parks Authority has designated many important rivers, riverbanks, springs, waterfalls, and pools protected nature reserves, and has facilitated the continuous or seasonal efflux, and when necessary the rehabilitation, of Israel's cherished rivers.

Hermon Stream

6
Lakes of Israel

Lakes of Israel

Hebrew's lacustrine vocabulary includes *agam* (lake) and *agamon* (lakelet). The Land of Israel historically featured two larger lakes referred to as seas (Kinneret, Salt), as well as two smaller lakes (Hula, Ram). The Kinneret, Hula, and Ram are freshwater bodies; the Salt is, unsurprisingly, a saltwater body. The Hula underwent significant transformation in modern times, from a single sizable lake to a pair of discrete lakelets.

Israel's lakes vary substantially in water volume and quality. However, they share their general geographical alignment within or proximate to the Jordan Rift Valley, formerly the boundary between the Cisjordanian and the Transjordanian tribes of Israel and presently the boundary between Israel to the west and Jordan to the east. Moreover, all lakes have changed, and continue to change, in terms of their length, width, depth, circumference, and altitude due to several major factors: natural inflow reduction; inflow diversion; precipitation; evaporation; drainage; and seismic events.

For the Jewish people, these waters have possessed great value as ecosystems, natural resources, income sources, political boundaries, strategic assets in wartime, and leisure and recreation sites.

1. **Breikhat Ram (Lake Phiale)** – A natural reservoir situated in the crater of an extinct volcano in the northeastern Golan, near Mount Hermon. Ram rises almost 3,100 feet above sea level, and formerly measured approximately 3,280 feet long, 2,000 feet wide, and 33 feet deep, though in recent years its size has diminished due to evaporation and pumping for irrigation purposes. Known as Breikhat Ram ("Ram Pool") in Hebrew, the lake is a maar whose sources are an underground spring, precipitation, and snowmelt. Peach, pear, and apple trees contour the lake. The amora Yohanan bar Nappaha is quoted in the Babylonian Talmud as stating that the Ram ("Beiram"), Hammat Gader (Gadara), and Hammat Tiveryah (Tiberias' hot springs) were the three underground springs breached during the primordial Flood that continued to spout boiling water. In 1973, Ram featured on an Israeli postage stamp. In 1981, a volcanic pebble that apparently portrays a female figure was discovered between layers of ash and named the "Venus of Berekhat Ram"; it dates to 233,000 years ago during the Lower Palaeolithic, indicating it was incised either by *Homo erectus* or by Neanderthals and rendering it the oldest work of art ever found. Today the Druze villages of Mas'ade, Buq'ata, and Majdal Shams are located close by, as is the tourist-oriented Bambook Village and Park.

2. **Lake Hula (Lake Semechonitis)** – A marsh-like lake lying in the Hula Valley of Upper Galilee, a major stopover for birds migrating via the Great Rift Valley/Syrian-African Rift between Europe, Africa, and Asia.

As many as 500 million birds and 400 bird species, including cranes, storks, coots, pelicans, herons, raptors, cormorants, and egrets, pass through the valley annually during the migration seasons (spring and autumn). Sourced primarily from the Jordan River and enclosed by the Naphtali Mountains to the west and the Golan to the east, the lake has been home to various fish species such as catfish, tilapia, and carp, as well as the Hula painted frog, and to rare aquatic plants including the yellow-flag, paper reed, and white water-lily. Grazing water buffaloes and preying wildcats also form part of the local wildlife. Historically, Lake Hula and its surrounding marshes occupied a third of the Hula Valley. During the period of the Israelite repatriation to the Land of Israel (c. 1273–1245 BCE), Joshua triumphed in battle over a Canaanite coalition under King Yavin of Hatzor at the waters of Merom, springs lying on the western side of the Hula Valley. Thereafter the Israelites established the city of Dan (formerly La'yish/Leshem) at the northern end and developed the city of Hatzor at the southern end of the valley. From 1951–1958, the Keren Kayemet L'Yisrael-Jewish National Fund (KKL-JNF) drained malarial swamps surrounding the lake. In 1953, the Society for the Protection of Nature in Israel (SPNI), a nonprofit environmental conservation organization, was founded in response to concerns about the Hula's drainage. In 1963, a small area of recreated papyrus marshland was preserved and designated Israel's original nature reserve, which was officially inaugurated in 1964. The Hula Valley was also reflooded by heavy rainfall in the 1990s, and the deluged area was left intact and developed into a second wetland habitat, Agamon HaHula ("Lakelet Hula"); the lakelet is much smaller and shallower than the historical Lake Hula was prior to its drainage. The Hula region and its wildlife featured on Israeli stamps in 2007 and 2014. Today Lakelet Hula is a distinct park managed by the KKL-JNF while just to the south the Israel National Parks Authority operates the official Hula Nature Reserve; both wetland paradises are highly popular with flocks of birds and birdwatchers alike.

3.   **Lake Kinneret (Lake Gennesaret/Sea of Galilee/Lake Tiberias)** – A pear-shaped lake in eastern Galilee, about 33 miles in circumference, 13 miles in length, and eight miles in width, on the site of an extinct volcanic crater. On average, the lake reaches approximately 696 feet below sea level and a maximum depth of 144 feet. It is the lowest freshwater lake on Earth, and the second-lowest lake after the Salt Sea (Dead Sea). As a result of cool air from the uplands rushing down the gorges, the Kinneret is regularly subjected to abrupt storms that imperil small craft. The Jordan River flows in and out of the Kinneret from

north to south and is the main source of the lake, which is also plenished by underground springs. The biblical name "Kinneret" is believed to be an inflection of the Hebrew word for harp or lyre (*kinor*), a reference to the lake's salient shape; the later appellation "Gennesaret", applied to both the lakeside town of Kinneret and to the eponymous lake, is perhaps a Grecized form of "Ginnosar", itself a derivation of Kinneret (alternatively, a midrashic etymology in *Genesis Rabbah* 98:17 explicates the name as a derivation of the Hebrew *Gannei Sarim*, "Gardens of Princes"). Dating to the Bronze Age (3300–1200 BCE), the ancient Derekh HaYam (The Way of the Sea/Coastal Highway) international trade route connecting Egypt and Syria skirted the lake's western and northern borders, passing through Tiberias, Migdal (Magdala-Tarichaeae), Kfar Nahum (Capernaum/Capharnaum), and Hatzor. The Kinneret features along the eastern boundary in one set of borders of the Land of Israel and served as part of the western border of the Transjordanian tribe of eastern Menasheh. Its western shore formed part of the tribal territory of Naphtali, its eastern shore part of eastern Menasheh, and its southern shore was possessed by the Transjordanian tribe of Gad. Riparian cities of the tribe of Naphtali included Hammat, Rakkat, and Kinneret. During the Davidic era (1010–970 BCE), part of the northeastern coastline was possessed by the independent kingdom of Geshur. The Arameans later vied for control of the eastern shore with the royal Omride dynasty. The area was entirely Jewish during the Hasmonean era (167–63 BCE). Fisheries occupied a prominent place in the Judean economy, and the lakeside city of Migdal (Magdala-Tarichaeae) became renowned for its preserved fish (in Greek, Tarichaeae denotes "place of processing fish"). In 30 BCE, King Herod the Great of Judea received Hippos (Sussita), a Seleucid (Syrian-Greek) colony turned Greek polis of the Decapolis, from Octavian (Augustus Caesar). In the Roman era (63 BCE–313 CE), the city of Tiberias was built on the lakeshore by the ruins of Rakkat, and was completed in 18 CE by Herod Antipas, tetrarch of Galilee and Perea, who named the site, his new capital, after the then reigning Emperor Tiberius of Rome. Much of the ministry of Jewish reformer Jesus of Nazareth took place in and around Lake Kinneret, particularly at Kfar Nahum, Tabgha (Heptapegon/Ein Sheva), and the Mount of Beatitudes on the southern slope of the plateau Ramat Khorazim. In the aftermath of Jerusalem's destruction, Tiberias became a Jewish holy city and a locus of learning; the Great Sanhedrin convened there and the Jerusalem Talmud was largely indited and edited there. Many leading Jewish sages, such as

Akiva ben Joseph, Meir Ba'al HaNeis, Moses ben Maimon (Rambam/Maimonides), and Isaiah Horowitz (Shlah HaKadosh) were interred in the vicinity. In the 600s, the Masoretes developed their scriptural vocalization system in Tiberias. Numerous lacustrine fish – including carp, perch, sardines, mullet, tilapia, catfish, damselfish, scaleless blennies, mouthbreeders, barbels, cichlids, and Kinneret bream – flourish in the lake, which has provided a reliable livelihood for fishermen since ancient times. Bananas, mangoes, grapes, olives, and dates now grow in the fertile perimeter environing the water. Modern communities built on the lakeshore include Ginnosar, Migdal, Kinneret, Deganiah Aleph, Deganiah Bet, Ein Gev, Ma'agan, HaOn, Tel Katzir, and Almagor. In 1964, the lake became the National Water Carrier's principal reservoir, which from a pumping station in the northwest corner siphons water away to irrigate disparate parts of the country. From 1964–1967, Syrian aggression near the lake's eastern shore was a factor in the outbreak of the Six-Day War of 1967. In 1986, during a drought when water levels receded, an ancient fishing boat made of cedar was discovered on the lake's northwestern shore. Today the Kinneret separates the provinces of Galilee in the west and the Golan in the east, and is a major tourist area for Jews and Christians alike. In 2018, the Israeli government approved a plan to pump desalinated water into Lake Kinneret as part of a drought recovery program.

4. **Salt Sea (Dead Sea/Lake Asphaltitis)** – An inland saltwater lake whose source is the Jordan River, which flows in from the north. Located in the Jordan Rift Valley, the Salt Sea has the lowest surface elevation and is the lowest body of water on Earth; its surface lies approximately 1,412 feet below sea level. The hypersaline lake is terminal (without an outlet). It formerly measured 50 miles in length and 11 miles wide, though its size is inconstant and has decreased dramatically since the 1960s. Its extremely saline water, which contains hydrogen sulfide, magnesium, potassium, chlorine, bromine, and sodium chloride, has a high density that buoys bathers. Bacteria are the only life forms in the lake, which possesses an oily consistency and on which blocks of asphalt float due to sulfur on its shores. Parts of the dark blue saltwater have occasionally turned red due to blooms of the alga *Dunaliella salina*, a microbial organism that possesses reddish halobacteria. Steep mountain ridges enclose the lake to the west and to the east, amid which dwell ibexes, jackals, foxes, hares, and leopards. The Salt Sea was also known biblically as the "Sea of the Aravah" or the "Eastern Sea" (as opposed to the Mediterranean), and was later

known in Latin as "Lacus Asphaltites" (an appellation used by classical writers Pliny the Elder and Flavius Josephus) and in the Talmud as the "Sea of Sodom". The lake's western shore formerly resided in Canaan while its eastern shore was eventually occupied by Moabites and Edomites; following the period of the Israelite repatriation to the Land of Israel (c. 1273–1245 BCE), the tribal territory of Judah included the western shore while that of Reuven included the eastern shore's northern half from the Heshbon Stream to the Arnon River (Moab retained the eastern shore's southern half from the Arnon River to Wadi al-Hasa). The infamous biblical towns of Sodom and Gomorrah, destroyed for their wickedness, were situated nearby, perhaps on the lake's southeastern shore. The young fugitive David sought refuge from the jealous and paranoid King Saul at the Ein Gedi oasis in the desolate wasteland west of the lake. The ascetic Essene sect settled at the Ein Fashkha oasis and composed and compiled the Dead Sea Scrolls at nearby Qumran (where pottery storage jars containing their manuscripts were discovered in caves from 1947–1956). The Hasmonean monarch King Yannai Alexander of Judea battled the Nabateans for control of the lake's lucrative bitumen resources. King Herod the Great of Judea retreated to his refuge at nearby Masada during the Parthian siege of Jerusalem in 40 BCE. The hermetic Jewish preacher John the Baptist was beheaded at the fortress of Mikhvar (Machaerus), which overlooks the lake's northeastern edge. During the Great Revolt (66–73 CE), Jewish refugees fled by boat across the sea and were pursued by Roman antagonists, and the Roman general Vespasian notoriously ordered a prisoner thrown into the lake to see if he would float; toward the revolt's end, Masada was besieged and, after a mass suicide of almost 1,000 Jewish Sicarii rebels and their families, fell to the legionaries in 73 CE. During the Bar Kokhba Revolt (132–135 CE), Ein Gedi served as a key supply port in the latter stages of the conflict. A peninsula – "HaLashon" in Hebrew, "Al-Lisan" in Arabic (i.e., "the tongue") – near the middle of the lake's eastern side juts out to divide it into two basins, the larger northern basin achieving a depth of 1,300 feet and the much shallower southern basin plunging less than 10 feet deep. Since 1977, the marl peninsula has extended completely to the western shore, forming a ribbon of dry land, and the southern basin has been reconfigured into dozens of sizable evaporation pools. Both Israel and Jordan extract potash (a key component of agricultural fertilizer) from the lake's brine. Hundreds of sinkholes have since formed in the vicinity. Today the lake boasts beaches, thermal springs, tourist spas, and hotels, and local salt, minerals, and mud are sold worldwide as therapeutic treatments and cosmetics.

Modern Israel also possesses several small, artificial lakes including in the heart of Modi'in, in Golda Meir Park on the banks of the Revivim River, and Lake Timna in Timna Park, the latter two located in the Negev Desert.

Although relatively modest in size, the lakes of Israel continue to exert much influence on the lives of locals and to attract visitors from near and far. Israeli regulators tasked with monitoring environmental conditions and devising and implementing policies have been sensitized to the necessity for striking a delicate balance between water usage and conservation. Sourcing potable water, supplying daily household and public use needs, and irrigating for agricultural purposes are all crucial for a functioning society, particularly in a country that remains largely desert, yet these legitimate demands must be tempered in a sensible and sustainable manner by the need to preserve thriving ecosystems. Maintaining equilibrium remains an ongoing challenge to which Israel's environmental stewards and technological innovators are increasingly applying creative solutions.

Lake Kinneret (the Sea of Galilee)

7
Seas of Israel

Seas of Israel

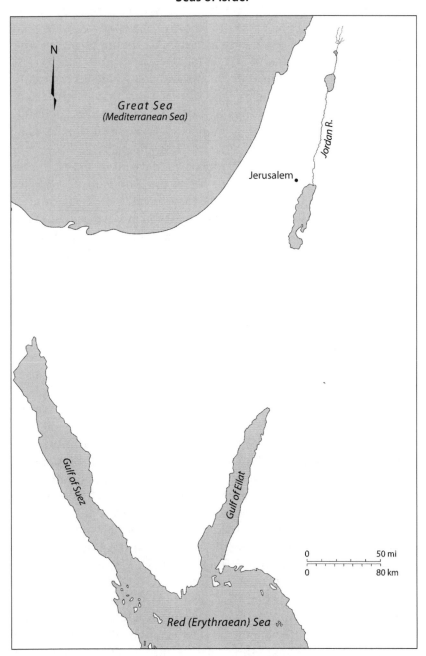

The Land of Israel has two seas on its borders, the Mediterranean along the northwestern boundary and the Red at the southern end. Unlike the Egyptians, Phoenicians, Greeks, and Romans, the Israelites were not a seafaring people, yet both seas served the nation for the important purposes of travel and maritime trade.

The Tanakh (Hebrew Bible) describes various seagoing vessels such as ships made from papyrus bundles, ships with oars, sailing ships with a deck, and bulky merchant ships ("ships of Tarshish"). *I Maccabees* describes carved ships ornamenting the monumental Hasmonean family tomb erected at Modi'in. Hundreds of nautical terms appear in the Babylonian Talmud. In addition, artistic depictions of navigation dating to the Maccabean Rebellion (167–134 BCE) and to the Herodian era (37 BCE–73 CE) were found in Jerusalem at the monumental, rock-cut Tomb of Jason (featuring three ships with unfurled sails) and in Mareshah, and those dating to the Roman era (63 BCE–313 CE) were found at the Beit She'arim catacombs in Galilee. Likewise, nautical imagery appears on the coins of King Yannai Alexander of Judea, King Herod the Great of Judea, and Archelaus (ethnarch of Judea, Samaria, and Idumea).

While Jews did not employ seagoing vessels for discovery or for conquest, sea lore occupied an important place in the Jewish imagination. Famed Mishnaic sages Gamliel II, Eliezer ben Hyrcanus, Joshua ben Hananiah, and Akiva ben Joseph are among the figures who feature in midrashic legends set at sea.

1. **Mediterranean Sea (Great Sea)** – The world's largest inland sea and an intercontinental sea lane environed by Europe, Africa, and Asia. Nearly landlocked, the Mediterranean has since ancient times served as a waterway connecting the civilizations that arose along its circuitous shores, thereby facilitating regional communication and exchange. The sea's southeastern Levantine Basin, which extends from southeastern Turkey to northeastern Sinai, abuts the Land of Israel. The Mediterranean thus formed the western border of the Land of Israel, and the Hebrew word for seaward (*yammah*) became synonymous with westward. In the Tanakh (Hebrew Bible), the Mediterranean is most commonly known as "the Great Sea"; it is also referred to as the "Western Sea", the "Sea of Jaffa", the "Sea of the Philistines", and simply as "the sea". Scripture specifically depicts the Israelite tribes of Zevulun and Dan availing themselves of the Mediterranean, though the tribal territories of Asher, western

Menasheh, and Judah also reached the coastline. Jaffa became the main port of Judea during the Hasmonean era (167–63 BCE), by which time there were capable Jewish seamen based at Jaffa, Ashdod, and Gaza. Hasmonean monarch King Yannai Alexander of Judea also captured Straton's Tower (Stratonos Pyrgos/Migdal Sharshon), a Hellenistic naval station/trading post named after the Phoenician ruler Abdashtart I of Tzidon, which was incorporated into Judea until the Roman general Pompey the Great sundered it therefrom. According to the priestly historian Joseph ben Matityahu (Flavius Josephus), Galilean refugees from the Great Revolt (66–73 CE) sought refuge in Jaffa and became corsairs, building a flotilla to interrupt the grain supply from Alexandria to Rome and to generally disrupt commerce along the coasts of Syria, Phoenicia, and Egypt; their efforts were ultimately thwarted by a violent "black north wind" that dashed the ships against each other and against coastal rocks, leaving some 4,200 Jews dead either from drowning, suicide, being dashed against the rocks, or being slain by awaiting Roman legionaries (*War* 3.9.3). In the Herodian era, King Herod the Great of Judea reconstructed Straton's Tower as Caesarea (Caesarea Maritima), complete with a new fleet. The legendary sea monster Leviathan was believed to dwell in the depths of the Mediterranean, a myth perhaps based in part on the rare appearance of sperm whales or of blue whales off the coast of Israel. Some 400 fish species inhabit the sea, many of which – e.g., sole, flounder, sea bass, sea bream, anchovy, hake, mackerel, and sardine – are kosher and would have featured in the Israelite diet. Key harbors included Akko, Dor (Dora), Caesarea, Jaffa, Ashdod, and Ashkelon, and nowadays include the natural harbor at Haifa Bay. Most of modern Israel's population centers contour the Mediterranean coastline, including such seaside cities as Nahariyah, Akko, Haifa, Haderah, Netanyah, Herzliyah, Tel Aviv-Yafo, Bat Yam, Rishon L'Tzion, Ashdod, and Ashkelon.

2. **Red (Erythraean) Sea** – A seawater inlet of the Indian Ocean and part of the Great Rift Valley/Syrian-African Rift, the Red Sea at its northern end bifurcates into the Gulf of Suez to the northwest (which formerly reached as far north as Pitom in Wadi Tumilat) and the Gulf of Eilat to the northeast. Its name is a direct translation of its Greek counterpart Erythra Thalassa, and may have originally derived from the seasonal blooms of the reddish algae *Trichodesmium erythraeum*, which, upon expiring, tinge the normally blue-green water rubicund.

The Tanakh (Hebrew Bible) employs the appellation *Yam Suph* (perhaps best translated as "Stormy Sea", from the Hebrew word *supha*) to refer to both northern branches of the Red Sea. The Red Sea figures in one set of borders of the Land of Israel and in the seafaring ventures of King Solomon, who had an argosy constructed at Etzion-Gever (near Eilat) on the seashore and whose servants sailed with Phoenician navigators to procure gold from Ophir. Access to this southern outlet was first acquired by King David, and after being lost it was later regained by Judahite kings Yehoshaphat and Uziyahu. Yehoshaphat thought to replicate Solomon's merchant fleet with his royal counterpart, King Ahaziah of Israel, but the enterprise foundered. The Red Sea is also mentioned in the apocryphal books *I Maccabees*, *Judith*, and *The Wisdom of Solomon* (*The Book of Wisdom*). The Jewish kings of Himyar (Yemen) contended with Byzantium for control over the sea, then as now a strategic trade route to the East. Hydrologically, the Red Sea is the hottest and most saline of the world's open seas, and its waters are believed to be completely renewed every 20 years. Today Israel shares the northeastern arm with Egypt and Jordan (which refer to the Gulf of Eilat as the Gulf of Aqaba).

In 1869, the two seas were connected at Egypt via the Suez Canal, which was enlarged in 1975. (For information on Lake Kinneret [the Sea of Galilee] and the Salt Sea [Dead Sea], see "Lakes of Israel".)

The Hebrew word for sea (*yam*) inflected into *yammah* (lit. "seaward"), a term connoting "west" because of the Mediterranean Sea's western situation relative to the Land of Israel. Subsequently, rabbinical sources used the term *okyanos*, derived from the Greek word *okeanos*, to refer to the sea.

Finally, the relationship between Jews and the sea is perhaps captured best in *Psalms*:

> Some go down to the sea in ships, ply their trade in the great waters; they have seen the deeds of the Lord and His wondrous works in the deep. By His word He raised a stormy wind that made the waves surge. Mounting up to heaven, plunging to the depths, disgorging in their misery, they reeled and staggered like a drunkard, and all their skill did not avail. In their adversity they cried to the Lord, and He delivered them from their distress. He reduced the storm to a whisper; the waves were hushed. They rejoiced when all was quiet,

and He brought them to their desired port. Let them praise the Lord for His steadfast love, and His wondrous deeds for mankind! Let them extol Him in the assembly of the people, and acclaim Him in the council of elders. (107:23-32)

Mediterranean Sea

8
Deserts of Israel

Deserts of Israel

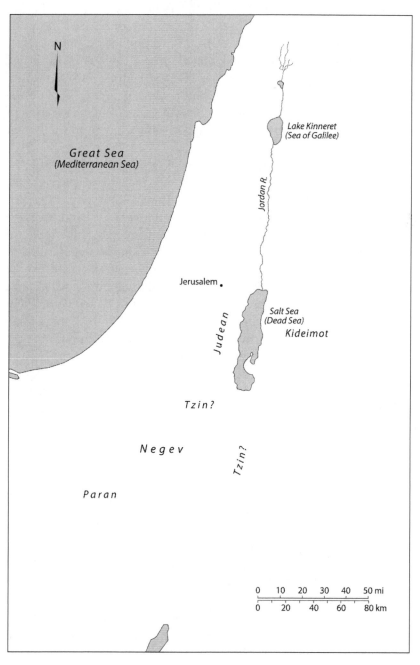

The Land of Israel comprises several desert regions on both sides of the Great Rift Valley/Syrian-African Rift: the Wilderness of Judah (Judean Desert) and the Negev (according to certain sets of borders, only the northern portion, including the Be'ersheva Basin and the northern Aravah Valley) in Cisjordan, as well as semiarid or arid regions in the tribal territories of eastern Menasheh, Gad, and Reuven – also known as Bashan, Gilad, and the Mishor – in the Transjordanian highlands and atop the eastern tableland overlooking the Salt Sea (Dead Sea), i.e., the section of escarpment extending from Mount Hermon in the north to the Arnon River in the south.

At the height of the United Monarchy of Israel (1030–931 BCE), the expansive dominion of kings David and Solomon included arid areas of the Syrian Desert (now in Syria and Jordan), featuring volcanic lava and basalt, and the Ard as-Sawwan Desert (now in Jordan), featuring sandstone and granite outcrops. The Hasmonean kingdom regained all of the semiarid Transjordanian highlands and eastern tableland from Mount Hermon to the Aravah Valley. The Herodian kingdom retained most of the Transjordanian highlands and eastern tableland excepting the Decapolis (which excised part of Gilad in Transjordan and northeastern Samaria in Cisjordan) and Moab (then occupied by Nabatean Arabs), and gained Iturea, which extended northwards beyond Mount Hermon, and the northeastern provinces of Batanea (Bashan), Trachonitis, and Hauran (Auranitis), the latter two stretching eastward into the Syrian Desert.

Despite initial impressions evoked by notions of barren wastelands, Israel's deserts are abundant in history and variegated in topography, as adumbrated in the following précis.

1. **Judean** – The wilderness lying in the eastern half of the tribal territory of Judah (eastern Judea), bordered by the Judean Hills in the west and the Salt Sea (Dead Sea) in the east and extending approximately from Jericho in the north to Masada in the south. In the Tanakh (Hebrew Bible), the name "Yeshimon" ("wasteland") is sometimes applied to the Judean Desert, which comprises seven distinct wilderness sections stacked roughly north to south, each named after an important locus in the Judean Hills: Beit Aven, extending southeast of Beit El; Givon, extending east of its eponymous city; Yiruel, extending east of Jerusalem; Tekoa, extending east of its eponymous town; Ein Gedi, extending northwest of its eponymous town and around Nahal Arugot and Nahal David; Ziph, extending southeast of Hebron; and Maon, extending further southeast of Hebron toward Nahal Tze'elim. The

rugged desert – almost 45 miles in length and 12.5 miles in width –
lies in the rain shadow of the Judean Hills, whose leeward side features
a precipitous drop-off of almost 5,000 feet (from 3,366 feet above sea
level to 1,412 feet below sea level). It features mountains, plateaux,
riverbeds, cliffs, canyons, and salt flats, and its key sites include
Jericho, Cypros, Qumran, Hyrcania, Herodium (Herodion), Beit
Hananiah (Bethany), Ein Gedi, and Masada. Historically, the Judean
Desert has proven a refuge for rebels and a haven for hermits. The
region contains springs and oases at Jericho and at Ein Gedi, where
balsam, dates, and persimmons flourished. Jericho ("City of the
Moon", from the Hebrew word *yarei'ah*), known also as the city of
palm trees, is one of the oldest fortified towns in the ancient Near East
and among the earliest sites of continuous settlement in human
history, dating to 7800 BCE. During the period of the Israelite
repatriation to the Land of Israel (c. 1273–1245 BCE), Joshua besieged
and captured Jericho, whose walls in the biblical account tumbled after
being repeatedly encircled and upon the priests' blaring shofar blasts
and the Israelites' resounding shouts; only the helpful harlot Rahav
and her household were spared. Thereafter the wilderness was
allocated to the tribal territories of Judah and Benjamin. Ein Gedi, an
aquifer-derived perennial spring and an oasis village, was assigned to
Judah and served as a refuge for David in his flight from King Saul.
The prophets Elijah and Elisha sojourned at Jericho before Elijah's
final departure, heavenward in a whirlwind, and afterwards Elisha
cured local waters by casting salt into them. During the reign of King
Pekah of Israel, the Judahite captives of the Israelites were returned to
Jericho following the prophet Oded's injunction. King Zedekiah of
Judah took flight from Jerusalem but was overtaken by the
Babylonians on the plains of Jericho. In the Hasmonean era (167–63
BCE), a royal winter palace was constructed adjacent to Jericho, and
Shimon Maccabee was murdered with most of his family by his
treacherous son-in-law Ptolemy ben Abubus at a banquet in the
nearby desert fortress of Dok (Docus/Dagon) in 134 BCE. The
Hasmonean mountain forts guarding the approaches to Jericho –
Threx and Taurus – were destroyed by the Roman general Pompey
the Great in 63 BCE (one of the forts is identified with the subsequent
Herodian fortress Cypros). Jewish sectarians (the self-styled "Yahad"),
perhaps Essenes, retreated to the Judean Desert in the Hasmonean
era (probably under the rule of Yohanan Hyrcanus or else of his
forerunners Jonathan Maccabee or Shimon Maccabee); they

developed Qumran into a pottery factory and later added waterworks and a scriptorium, in the latter of which numerous biblical works were copied and communal documents were composed on parchment or on papyrus. Southwest of Qumran, halfway to Herodium, lies Hyrcania (Horkania/Hyrcanium), a Hasmonean fortress erected by Yohanan Hyrcanus, used as a treasury by Queen Shlomtzion (Salome Alexandra), refortified by Alexander II of Judea (Alexander Maccabeus) in his short-lived mutinies against the Roman proconsul Gabinius (57–55 BCE), refurbished and used as a prison and as an execution site by King Herod the Great of Judea (his son Antipater, whom he ordered executed, was interred there), and later repurposed by Byzantine hermits as the monastery of Castellion. To commemorate the site of his victory against his foes when he fled Jerusalem for Masada in 40 BCE, Herod built Herodium, a multi-towered fortress resting atop a natural mound near Tekoa, hometown of the prophet Amos; Herodium, which included a lower town at the mountain base, later served as Herod's burial place, wherein he was inhumed with much ceremony, and as a citadel for Judean freedom fighters during both the Great Revolt (66–73 CE) and the Bar Kokhba Revolt (132–135 CE). In addition, Herod built southwest of Jericho the citadel of Cypros, which he named after his Nabatean mother, and which was destroyed during the Great Revolt. He also ordered the drowning of the young Hasmonean high priest Aristobulus III at Jericho in 35 BCE, eliminating a highborn and popular rival. The Jewish reformer Jesus of Nazareth lodged in Beit Hananiah, a desert village with Jewish structures, cisterns, and tombs dating to the Second Temple era (516 BCE–70 CE), and where Christians believe the decedent Lazarus was resurrected. In 68 CE, amid the Great Revolt, Sicarii based at Masada raided and destroyed Qumran and Ein Gedi, their ruins occupied thereafter by Roman garrisons; both sites later served Jewish freedom fighters during the Bar Kokhba Revolt. The rhomboid-shaped citadel of Masada, crowning a mesa rising 1,475 feet above the Salt Sea's western shore, was first constructed by Jonathan Maccabee (or else by King Yannai Alexander of Judea), and Herod later erected there a triple-tiered cliffside palace, a mountaintop palace, a water system, and a turreted casemate wall around the plateau's perimeter to further fortify the site as a refuge from his potentially rebellious Jewish subjects and from Queen Cleopatra VII Philopator of Egypt. The Sicarii, under their leader Menahem ben Judah, seized Masada and slew its Roman garrison at the outset of the

Great Revolt; under Menahem's nephew, Elazar ben Ya'ir, the Sicarii hosted for a time Zealot leader Shimon bar Giora and held the nearly impregnable stronghold until the bitter end of the war in 73 CE, diehard holdouts refusing to submit to the besieging Roman legions under the Roman legate Flavius Silva by committing mass suicide instead. In the Byzantine era (324–638 CE), Christian monks built many remote monasteries among the Judean wilderness' cliffs and crevasses, including those of Masada, Mar Saba, Saint George, Martyrius, and Euthymius. Since 1971, a cable car has transported visitors to and from Masada's summit. Today the Society for the Protection of Nature in Israel operates a field school in the Judean Desert at Ein Gedi.

2. **Kideimot** – A wilderness area atop the Mishor, in the tribal territory of Reuven, opposite the Wilderness of Judah (Judean Desert) with the Salt Sea (Dead Sea) in between. The name in Hebrew indicates both "easternmost" and "beginnings", doubly apropos due to Kideimot's geographical location and chronological position in the Israelites' return to their ancestral homeland. Moses dispatched hence messengers to King Sihon of the Amorites, who reigned from Heshbon, requesting permission for the Israelites to traverse the latter's lands, which was refused. Kideimot Desert, north of the Arnon River, environed its eponymous city located northeast of Divon-Gad and cited along with Yahtzah and Meipha'at as cities of Reuven; Kideimot the city became a Levitical city (of the Merari family) within Reuven.

3. **Negev** – The desert region comprising the inverted triangle that is the southern half of modern Israel. The name in Biblical Hebrew denotes "south" and derives from a linguistic root denoting "dry". An extension of the Sinai Desert and part of the broader Saharo-Arabian desert belt, the Negev is bounded by the Sinai Peninsula in the west and by the Great Rift Valley/Syrian-African Rift in the east. Be'ersheva is the largest city in the Negev and its northern gateway; Eilat is the southern tip of the desert that opens out to the Gulf of Eilat, the northeastern branch of the Red Sea. The arid and rugged wilderness comprises limestone, dolomite, chalk, flint, sandstone, and granite, and possesses metals and minerals including copper, magnesium, gypsum, phosphates, bromine, and potash. A desert primarily of rock, canyons, and caves, the Negev also possesses deposits of glass sand and clay. Its northern Be'ersheva Basin features a surface of loess as well as the Halutzah, Shunrah, and Agur sand dunes. Three erosion cirques or erosional craters (*makhteshim*) environed by high cliffs dot the

landscape: Makhtesh Ramon (23 miles long, 5 miles wide); HaMakhtesh HaGadol/Makhtesh Hatirah (9 miles long, 4 miles wide), and HaMakhtesh HaKattan/Makhtesh Hatzeirah (3 miles long, 4.5 miles wide). Such discrete and rare craters – found primarily along the Syrian Arc System in southern Israel, northeastern Sinai, and northwestern Jordan – are formed through geological processes distinct from those of volcanic craters and meteor-impact craters. Mount Ramon, in the southwest of the largest *makhtesh* (lit. "mortar", to whose shape the natural feature is likened), is the loftiest summit in the Negev at over 3,400 feet. Desert flash floods are common during the rainy winter season. The desert's eastern border is the narrowing Aravah Valley, which extends from the Salt Sea (Dead Sea) southward to the Gulf of Eilat, passing by Hatzeivah, the Timna Valley, and Eilat en route. In biblical times, the Negev was a semiarid pastoral region in which the Patriarchs and Matriarchs settled. Abraham, Sarah, Isaac, and Rivkah dwelt in Be'ersheva, dug wells, and forged local alliances. Following the period of the Israelite repatriation to the Land of Israel (c. 1273–1245 BCE), the tribes of Judah and Shimon possessed the northern Negev, including Be'ersheva. King David established Israelite sovereignty over the region by defeating the Amalekites and Edomites. King Solomon inherited from the ancient Egyptians, and further developed, a metallurgic industry based at the copper mines of Timna, whose wind-sculpted rock formations include Solomon's Pillars, sphinx outcrops, mushroom-shaped hoodoos, and sandstone arches. Solomon and King Uziyahu of Judah each erected fortresses to protect desert routes to Eilat and to Egypt. During the Persian era (539–332 BCE), Be'ersheva was resettled by Judahite repatriates from the Babylonian Captivity. In the Hellenistic era (332–167 BCE), intrepid Nabateans from Arabia settled the region, wherein they developed the northern segments of their overland Incense Route between Oman and Sheba/Himyar (Yemen) in southern Arabia and the Mediterranean ports of Gaza and Rhinokoroura (El-Arish) and fostered desert agriculture by developing terracing and rainfall conservation methods featuring dams, channels, cisterns, and reservoirs; preserved ruins remain of their classical towns Halutzah, Mamshit, Avdat, Shivta, Nitzanah, and Rehovot-in-the-Negev (Ruhaibe), of their caravanserais/khans Ein Yahav, Ein Rahel, Moyat Awad (Moa), Saharonim, and Ein Zik, and of their forts Katzra, Nekarot, Mahmal, Grafon, and Horvat Ma'agorah. In the Hasmonean era (167–63 BCE), King Yannai Alexander of Judea possessed the northern Negev, which served as the southern border of his Judean kingdom. For more than 1,200 years the region remained desolate, populated only by nomadic Bedouin. In 1949, during the War of Independence (1947–1949), the Israel Defense Forces defeated the Egyptian army to regain the Negev. In 1953, Israeli prime minister David Ben-Gurion temporarily retired and removed to Kibbutz Sdei Boker. Desert flora include tamarisks, acacias, pistachios, doum palms (gingerbread trees), saltbushes, white broom bushes, bladder senna shrubs, rhubarb plants, pennyworts, red anemones, yellow asphodels, and orchids; desert fauna include eagles, onagers, ibexes, gazelles, leopards, tortoises, shrews, sand rats, porcupines, hyenas, foxes, and wolves. Modern Negev towns include Eilat, Dimona, Arad, Yeruham, Mitzpeh Ramon, Netivot, and Ofakim. The resort district of Ein Bokek, near the Nivei Zohar village and the Zohar hot springs, is popular with tourists and spa goers. Hatzeirim air base, the first in modern Israeli history, lies just outside Be'ersheva, which today is home to the respected Ben-Gurion University of the Negev. In 2019, Israel opened just north of Eilat the Ilan and Asaf Ramon International Airport, which hosts Israel's domestic airlines Arkia and Israir, as well as several European carriers.

4. **Tzin** – A sere region south of the Salt Sea (Dead Sea) abutting the northern Aravah Valley and Edom, and containing Mount Tzin and the city of Kadesh (Meribat-Kadesh/Rekem/Petra). The Tzin Desert is mentioned nine times in the Tanakh (Hebrew Bible) in connection with the Israelites' wilderness wanderings during the Exodus from Egypt (c. 1313–1273 BCE) and with the borders of Canaan. At Tzin, the momentous incident of the Meribat-Kadesh spring occurred, and the southern border passed through the area. Aaron, who was buried on Mount Hor (Hor HaHar), may have died and been buried on Mount Tzin, sometimes identified with Mount Hor. Following the period of the Israelite repatriation to the Land of Israel (c. 1273–1245 BCE), the Tzin abutted the southeastern frontier of the tribal territory of Judah. Scholars debate whether the Tzin lay in the northeastern Negev Desert or in the highlands on the opposite side of the Aravah Valley. Today the Society for the Protection of Nature in Israel operates a field school in or adjacent to the Tzin Desert, at Hatzeivah, in the northern Aravah Valley.

5. **Paran** – A section of the Negev extending from Kadesh-Barnea southward to the Red Sea. The Paran Plateau inclines from the northeast to the southwest. Israel's largest and longest desert watercourse, Nahal Paran, traverses the plateau. The Paran Desert is

mentioned 11 times in the Tanakh (Hebrew Bible). At Paran, Ishmael lived as an archer and married; the Israelites arrived from the Sinai Desert and encamped during the Exodus from Egypt (c. 1313–1273 BCE); Moses dispatched 12 spies to reconnoiter Canaan for 40 days, after which time they returned to Kadesh-Barnea to deliver their report and samples of the fruit of the land; God "shone forth" from Mount Paran, according to Moses' blessing given to the Israelites; a young David sojourned following the prophet Samuel's decease; the young Edomite prince Hadad and his servants took men to join him en route to his exile in Egypt; and, according to the prophet Habakkuk's poetic prayer concerning errors, God departed, spreading his splendor across heaven and earth. Today the Society for the Protection of Nature in Israel operates field schools in the Paran Desert at Har HaNegev and at Eilat.

Hebrew words denoting desert include: *midbar* (desert), *aravah* (wilderness/plain/steppe), *shimamah* (wilderness/desolation/wasteland), *yeshimon* (wasteland), *horavah* (dry land), *yabashah* (dry land), and *tziyah* (desert/wilderness/wasteland). Throughout Jewish history, the wilderness has been a locus of spirituality and of self-preservation. The Nabateans set precedents for harnessing the harsh environment's untapped resources and capitalizing on the desert for commerce. In the modern era, the deserts of Israel – which constitute approximately 62 percent of the country – are appreciated for their natural bounty and national development potential. Desertification, characterized by soil erosion and a diminishment of variety among flora and fauna, is nowadays being reversed. The Negev, for example, has been undergoing afforestation, and possesses numerous fish farms, olive groves, fruit orchards, vegetable plantations, and wineries. Just as desert agriculture and viticulture thrive, so does desert recreation: Israel's breathtaking wilderness vistas attract visitors from around the globe, especially outdoor enthusiasts including hikers, mountain climbers, sandboarders, and riders of camels, horses, mountain bikes, ATVs, dune buggies, jeeps, and hot air balloons. That said, industrial hazards and Bedouin relations are ongoing concerns for local inhabitants and environmentalists. The future well-being of Israel's deserts depends on responsible development (e.g., planning incorporating environmental impact assessments), addressing and settling outstanding intercommunal issues (e.g., unrecognized Bedouin villages), and sedulous law enforcement.

Negev Desert

9
Forests of Israel

Forests of Israel

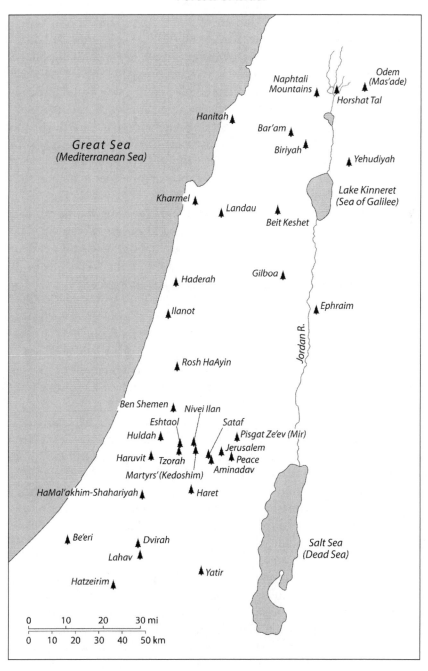

Hebrew possesses several words for forest: *yaʿar, horesh, horshah, pardeis*. Forests serve as the backdrop for a number of episodes in the Tanakh (Hebrew Bible): in the lush Garden of Eden, Adam and Havah sewed together fig tree leaves to conceal their nudity; the important Judahite-Benjaminite border town of Kiryat Ye'arim ("Town of Forests") hosted the Ark of the Testimony (Ark of the Covenant) for 20 years; fighting the Philistines, King Saul's weary soldiery discovered in a forest a honeycomb upon the surface of the ground – cane sugar, according to medieval sage Solomon Yitzhaki (Rashi) – whose flowing honey was readily eaten by the Israelite prince Jonathan, unaware of his father Saul's curse upon any who ate before he was avenged of his foes; David hid from Saul in the copse of the Ziph Desert; King Solomon made "cedars as common as sycamores that are in the lowlands in abundance" (*I Kings* 10:27; *II Chronicles* 1:15, 9:27); at a forest on the road between Jericho and Beit El, jeering youths mocked the prophet Elisha's baldness and for their insolence were soon mauled by a pair of forest bears until 42 youths lay dead; the prophet Amos was an inspector of sycamores; the prophet Isaiah enounced the divine pledge, "I will give in the desert cedars, acacias, myrtles, and pines; I will place in the wilderness box trees, firs, and cypresses together" (41:19); King Yotam of Judah built fortresses and towers in Judean forests; the prophet Ezekiel was divinely adjured to prophesy against "the forest of the field in the south"/"the forest of the south" (21:2-3); and Asaph, guardian of Emperor Artaxerxes II of Persia's orchard and overseer of the imperial forests, was instructed to supply timber for use in the Temple, in Jerusalem's city wall, and in Nehemiah's residence in Judah.

The Land of Israel's forests span its Mediterranean and desert biomes, comprising a variety of coniferous and deciduous tree species. In ancient times, the sylvan uplands abounded in indigenous terebinth, tamarisk, Kermes oak, Mt. Tabor oak, Cyprus oak, and Aleppo pine (Jerusalem pine), while the sycamore fig and olive flourished in the Shephelah foothills west of the country's mountainous central spine. Lebanon oak, European Turkey oak, and apple proliferated upon Mount Hermon. Boars, antelope, and deer made their habitat among the woodlands and scrublands.

Aleppo pine, or *pinus halepensis*, was long preferred in construction and in furniture making due to its straight limbs (today manufacturers use it to make crates and barrels), and its seeds and nuts were consumed as food. Terebinths were used for handles and tools and in ancient medicine, its resin treating facial skin, teeth, and dysentery. Mt. Tabor oak was a choice wood for handicrafts. Tamarisks were utilized in construction as foundations and supports, and for eating utensils. Cypresses were used in the Temple, and in manufacturing furniture, boats, and coffins. Date palms furnished fronds for ritual use as lulavim on the Sukkot festival; in addition, their leaves were braided into baskets, mats, ropes, and brooms, and their trunks were used for beams and pillars. The grapevine, one of the seven species for which the Land of Israel was known, was cultivated for its sweet fruit bunches (consumed fresh or as raisins) and for producing grape juice and wine. The olive tree, another of the seven species, was prized for its oily fruit, consumed as fresh olives or edible oil and used in medicinal balms and in cosmetic creams and lotions, as well as for oil lighting, including for lighting the Temple menorahs. The fig tree, also among the seven species and a symbol of peaceful living, was valued for its dried fruit that served as a salve for boils and that treated digestive ailments. The pomegranate tree, also among the seven species and a symbol of beauty, love, and fertility, offered fruit consumed as food and used in winemaking and in leather tanning and dyeing. Acacias were fit for construction purposes, as when the Israelites used it liberally in constructing the Tabernacle, and for heating, animal fodder, and medicinal use by nomadic Bedouin. Other fruit-bearing species, such as apple and almond, primarily supplied nutriment.

Over the millennia, the country's arboreal landscape gradually attenuated as a result of the increase in local populations and their growing demand for timber. When apportioning the tribal territories in the Land of Israel, Joshua told the tribes of Ephraim and Menasheh, "You are a numerous people, and have great power; you shall not have one lot. But the mountain shall be yours, for it is a forest, and you shall cut it down" (*Joshua* 17:17-18). Later, Isaiah limned some of the uses of timber in peacetime, especially by pagan gentiles: "A carpenter…goes to chop down cedars; he takes a cypress and an oak; he especially tends one tree in the forest, plants a pine for the rain to nourish. In time, when it's ready for use as fuel, he takes some of it to keep himself warm and burns some more to bake bread. Then he makes a god and worships it, carves it into an idol and falls down before it" (44:13-15).

In wartime, forests were felled to eliminate hiding places, prevent construction of defensive fortifications, and simply for the sake of destruction. Once densely forested, the Golan was largely denuded of its trees, including the famous oaks of Bashan, employed in shipbuilding and in fabricating oars. The Jordan River Valley featured a thick jungle of tamarisks and willows running along the terrace above the riverbed, an area once roamed by thirsty lions. In Gilad, evergreen ilexes (holm oaks) were prevalent throughout the region; oak forests abounded between the Yarmuk and the Yabok rivers and, southwards, arbutus, fir, and valonia-oak trees thrived. Parts of the Sharon Plain along the Mediterranean coastline were treed, as at the Turkey oak forest north of Rishpon (Apollonia/Arsuf), a woodland that paralleled the seashore for 12 miles, where King Richard I the Lionheart of England and King Guy of Jerusalem defeated Sultan Saladin of the Ayyubid Sultanate in 1191 CE, during the Third Crusade. The classical fishing outpost of Sycaminum/Sycamine (Tel Shikmonah, which over the millennia expanded into modern Haifa) derived its name from the local sycamore fig groves. Native species such as oak – the dominant species in the Land of Israel – and pine were felled in large numbers and used to lay railways and to fuel trains by the Ottoman imperial authorities in the 19th century and up to WWI. Tree thinning and bald spots amid formerly contiguous forests eventually enlarged until the country's woods were almost entirely extirpated.

The following précis includes forests mentioned in the Tanakh and many of the major forests planted throughout the Land of Israel in the modern era.

1. **Odem (Mas'ade)** – Situated in the northern Golan, this natural woodland features a trio of oaks, as well as pistacias, snowdrop trees, spiny hawthorns, and single-seeded hawthorns. In the vicinity rises lofty Mount Odem, whose summit affords scenic views of verdure. Odem, whose name derives from the Hebrew word for red (*adom*), an allusion to its rust-colored soil, is a relict of the expansive forest that formerly blanketed the northern Golan. In the 1800s, Circassians who settled the region denuded the trees, which were sold as timber. Local flora species include Etruscan honeysuckle, rough bindweed, eastern sowbread, broad-leaved helleborine, violet limodore, and various fungi. Local fauna include deer, antelope, ibexes, and cows. Human remains dating to the Middle Bronze Age (2100–1550 BCE) were discovered in the area. Within the forest lie sundry ruins, comprising a dozen sites such as Horvat Ra'abna, ascribed to the classical Itureans (an Arabic or an Aramaic tribe against whom the Hasmonean monarch King Judah Aristobulus I of Judea waged war in Lebanon, conquering then forcibly circumcising and converting them to Judaism) and for the most part dating to the Byzantine era (324–638 CE); there are also remnants of a French fortress built in 1920 before the formalized French Mandate (1923–1946). The area also features an apple and cherry plantation, a deep quarry where the

multicolored volcanic rock, scoria, was extracted, and some 23 circular volcanic craters known as "jubas", from the Arabic word for pockets (*juyub*). In 1973, Odem was the site of intense warfare during the Yom Kippur War, and a local memorial commemorates fallen soldiers of Reconnaissance Platoon 7 of the Israel Defense Forces' Seventh Brigade. The forest is proximate to the Druze village of Mas'ade, the moshav Odem, and Kibbutz El Rom.

2. **Horshat Tal** – A grove of just over 25 acres in the northern Hula Valley, featuring Mount Tabor oaks and pistachios. Local flora include horse parsley, hop clover, fringed fescue, chamomile, Phoenician rose, spurge, yellow wort, fen-sedge, great horsetail, water germander, jointleaf rush, broad-leaved speedwell, Spanish cane, and centaury, and rare species such as Saint John's wort and Greek silk-vine grow on travertine rocks. Anemones bloom abundantly in winter, and a large variety of orchids thrives in the area. The resident wildlife comprises otters, egrets, lapwings, European bee-eaters, hooded crows, and black kites. Rock-hewn burial caves occupied during the Byzantine era (324–638 CE) are situated on the western side of the nature reserve.

3. **Naphtali Mountains** – Growing in the west of the Galilee Panhandle ("The Finger of Galilee") upon the Ramim Ridge, the forest overlooks the Golan, the Hula Valley, Mount Hermon, and southern Lebanon. The Naphtali Mountains forest was planted beginning in the 1940s, and today encompasses 2,000 acres between Metulah and Keren Naphtali. The woodland comprises oaks, terebinths, cedars, jujubes, mastics, eucalypti, Syrian pear trees, spiny hawthorn bushes, ferns, orchids, anemones, narcissi, snapdragons, and irises. Amid the heights are the notable sites of Tel Hai, in whose defense Zionist hero Joseph Trumpeldor fell, and Kfar Giladi, as well as ruins of the crusader castle Chateauneuf (Hunin Fortress), built in 1107 and restored in 1267 by Sultan Baybars of the Mameluke Sultanate of Egypt. Local wildlife includes hyraxes and birds of prey. Remains of Kedesh-Naphtali (Tel Kedesh), captured circa 1300 BCE by Pharaoh Thutmose III of Egypt and later designated an Israelite city of refuge, lie nearby, as does the Yesha Fortress (Metzudat Ko'ah), a strategic site captured after repeated attempts by Jewish forces in 1948 during the War of Independence (1947–1949).

4. **Bar'am** – A forest covering steep slopes in Upper Galilee and in the Golan up to the Lebanese border, 2,500 acres in total. The Bar'am was planted between 1950 and 1965. The forest comprises Aleppo pines (Jerusalem pines), Calabrian pines, cypresses, cedars, and poplars, as

well as irises, daffodils, mushrooms, and toadstools. It also includes a nature reserve, scenic lookout, and national park featuring impressive ruins of the ancient Bar'am synagogue. Deer, wild boars, and vultures inhabit the forest. The Bar'am borders Nahal Gush Halav, a gully descending from the ancient Jewish town of Gush Halav (Gischala), whose native son Yohanan was a Zealot leader during the Great Revolt (66–73 CE) against the Romans.

5. **Biriyah** – Galilee's largest planted forest features Aleppo pines (Jerusalem pines), Brutia pines (Calabrian or Turkish pines), Canary pines, cypresses, and aromatic cedars of Lebanon (the species imported from Phoenicia by King Solomon to build the First Temple in Jerusalem). The Biriyah contains the tombs of several prominent sages, including Jonathan ben Uziel (a Mishnaic sage and the leading student of Hillel the Elder), Elazar of Modi'in (a priestly aggadist and an uncle of Bar Kokhba), and Honi HaMe'agel (a renowned thaumaturge), as well as ruins of the Naburiyah synagogue, among the oldest Jewish prayer houses in Galilee, which thrived between 564 and 640 CE. In the early modern era, the preeminent sage Joseph Karo dwelt in the eponymous town, where he completed a section of his influential halakhic code *Shulhan Arukh*. Also amid the forest is the Biriyah Fortress, an important Palmah stronghold in the pre-state era, whose lookout tower and scenic observation point offer panoramic views of Upper Galilee.

6. **Yehudiyah** – Among the largest and most important forests in the Golan, Yehudiyah sparsely covers an area of 16,500 acres between Lake Kinneret (the Sea of Galilee) and Katzrin, and possesses Mount Tabor oaks, jujubes, styraxes, and almonds. Local flora include Golan irises, anemones, cyclamens, Jerusalem spurges, Egyptian honestys, jujube bushes, common myrtle bushes, brook willows, oleanders, and giant reeds. The woods are home to songbirds, gazelles, wild boars, porcupines, rodents, foxes, jackals, and wolves, and raptors such as kestrels, eagles, buzzards, and vultures inhabit the cliffs of the canyons. Yehudiyah also features abundant water, including springs, waterfalls (e.g., Ein Nataf and Amit), deep pools, and four streams that flow through the area: Daliyot, Yehudiyah, Zavitan, and Meshushim. The streams are home to fish, water insects, amphibians, and river crabs. Archaeological ruins on-site include the classical Jewish village of Yehudiyah and synagogues from the Byzantine era (324–638 CE), basalt stone buildings with arches, and dolmens (ancient burial stones made of basalt boulders) dating to the third millennium BCE.

7. **Beit Keshet** – Carpeting the eastern slopes around Nazareth, Beit Keshet overlooks the Jezreel Valley and Lower Galilee and includes vestiges of an expansive Mt. Tabor oak forest that formerly blanketed the region. In addition to oaks, there are terebinths, pines, and carobs. The area is also adorned with buckthorns, cyclamens, anemones, orchids, navelworts, and moss. Ruins from the Roman era (63 BCE– 313 CE) linger nearby in the village of Tur'an.

8. **Gilboa** – Lower Galilean woods comprising 5,000 acres on the Gilboa mountain range, where King Saul and his sons Jonathan, Avinadav, and Melkishua died in battle against the Philistines. The forest is ornamented with irises, crocuses, cyclamens, mandrakes, anemones, tulips, poppies, Persian buttercups, and orchids. It is home to fauna such as mountain gazelles, rock hyraxes, bats, rabbits, porcupines, badgers, mongooses, weasels, rodents, tortoises, lizards, snakes, foxes, wildcats, and swamp lynxes. Perched on a rocky spur in the foothills lies ancient Jezreel, military headquarters of King Ahab of Israel and the site where the ruthless rebel Yehu slew King Yehoram of Israel before defenestrating the wicked Queen Jezebel.

9. **Kharmel** – A forest of 20,000 acres clothing the Kharmel mountain range, from Haifa and the Mediterranean Sea to the Jezreel Valley and the hills of the Menasheh Heights. The Kharmel has oaks, terebinths, carobs, mastics, stone pines, Aleppo pines (Jerusalem pines), arbutuses, figs, and Judas trees. There are also various shrub and herb species here, including broom, rockrose, sage, and hyssop (wild marjoram; *eizov* in Hebrew, *za'atar* in Arabic), as well as crocuses, narcissi, orchids, and mushrooms. Atop Mount Kharmel, the prophet Elijah famously contested the heathen priests of Ba'al and of Asherah, a dramatic triumph that resulted in the defeat and demise of his rivals. Several local sites, such as Elijah's Cave, are dedicated to the prophet's memory. In 2010, a conflagration claimed 6,250 acres in the worst forest fire in the State of Israel's history. Orchard and fruit trees were planted in the wake of the great blaze, including olives, carobs, pomegranates, and almonds. The Kharmel also has several hanging bridges with steel cables suspended high above a gully. Local wildlife includes songbirds, mongooses, deer, foxes, and jackals. The forest features Kharmel National Park, Kharmel Hai-Bar Nature Reserve (wherein Persian fallow deer, wild goats, and sheep are bred for release into the wild), Nahal Me'arot Nature Reserve (featuring prehistoric caves), the Kdumim stone quarries, the Ein Hod artists' colony, and the Druze communities Daliyat al-Kharmel and Isfiya.

10. **Hanitah** – Occupying about 575 acres of western Galilee, the pine forest encompasses Lower Hanitah at the base of Mount Hanitah, atop which rests Kibbutz Hanitah (Upper Hanitah), originally established in 1938 as a tower-and-stockade settlement. The forest features a tower-and-stockade reconstruction and recreation area, and the kibbutz displays artifacts, models, and natural samples in Hanitah Museum. The karst subterrane known as the Ladder Cave or as Hanitah Cave lies on the northern slope of the mount.

11. **Landau** – Mount Tabor oaks are joined by Aleppo pines (Jerusalem pines) and carob trees in this forest commemorating the young HaPo'el HaMizrahi leader, rabbi, and newspaper editor Samuel Hayyim Landau (1882–1928). Other species the forest possesses include terebinth, snowdrop bush, Mediterranean buckthorn, spiny hawthorn, hyssop (wild marjoram; *eizov* in Hebrew, *za'atar* in Arabic), white-leaved savory, cyclamen, and anemone. The Landau contains the necropolis of Beit She'arim, once the home of patriarch Judah HaNasi and the seat of the Great Sanhedrin circa 170 CE; many sages, including Judah HaNasi, were buried therein. The monument to Zionist hero Alexander Zaïd, co-founder of Jewish self-defense organizations Bar Giora and HaShomer, rises nearby.

12. **Haderah** – An Australian eucalyptus forest covering over 320 acres in the Sharon Plain, planted in 1896 on a site formerly a malarial marshland frequented by swamp lynxes, wild boars, and water buffaloes. One of Israel's first planted woodlands, Haderah Forest also features Tabor oaks as well as idyllic ponds containing spiny rushes and narrow-leaved water plantains; the wetlands are nowadays frequented by wild boars and waterfowl. Local flora include red anemones, yellow groundsels, and blue-flowered dyer's buglosses. On the western side of the forest, atop a sandstone hill, lies Tel Ibrektas, believed to be the ruins of the ancient Jewish community of Birkta, cited in the Mishnah.

13. **Ephraim** – A Transjordanian forest in the tribal territory of Gad (the Gilad region) opposite the Cisjordanian tribal territory of Ephraim, where Ephraimites used to pasture their flocks and where a major battle occurred during a civil war in the Davidic era (1010–970 BCE). Some 20,000 Israelite men were slain, and it was said, perhaps in relation to the wild beasts inhabiting the forest, that "the forest devoured more of the people than the sword devoured on that day" (*II Samuel* 18:8). Among the slain was King David's rebellious son Avshalom, whose head got caught in the thick boughs of a great

terebinth while he was riding his mule, suspending him "between the heaven and the earth" (ibid. 18:9). After Avshalom was dispatched by the general Yo'av and his 10 armigers, his corpse was tossed into a forest pit and covered with a cairn.

14. **Haret** – A forest in the tribal territory of Judah, perhaps located southeast of Adulam and northeast of K'eelah, to which David was prompted to go by the prophet Gad. Here David sought refuge from King Saul after returning to the Land of Israel from Moab, where he had taken his family for their safety. It is thought to lie in the vicinity of the modern town Kharas, northwest of Hebron.

15. **Ben Shemen** – The largest forest in central Israel, encompassing almost 5,500 acres east of Lod (Lydda/Diospolis). In its early days, land was set aside for an oil factory, giving the forest its name (in Hebrew, *ben shemen* denotes "son of oil", and the related phrase *ben-shamen* is a biblical reference to *Isaiah* 5:1, where it denotes "very fruitful"); the factory was prosperous until it burned down in 1915. The forest comprises olive groves, pines, cypresses, jujubes, Judas trees, prickly pears, carobs, almonds, figs, and pomegranates, and flowers such as cyclamens and anemones. Peckish storks graze in nearby fields. The Hasmonean Tombs, featuring a cave and nine tombs carved into bedrock, lie within the woods and commemorate Matityahu the priest and his five sons who successfully led the Maccabean Rebellion (167–134 BCE) against the Seleucids (Syrian-Greeks) and restored Jewish independence in the second century BCE; they also gave rise to the Hanukah festival, celebrated ever since. The Hasmonean town of Shilat lies in ruins nearby. Ben Shemen abuts Modi'in Forest, which covers about 2,000 acres.

16. **Haruvit** – Carobs, pines, almonds, olives, jujubes, and tamarisks constitute Haruvit Forest, which also contains caves and ancient agricultural terraces, wine presses, and cisterns. To the south the woods abut the Elah Valley and Tel Tzafit, the ancient Philistine town of Gath, hometown of the giant Goliath and capital of King Akhish, a Philistine ruler who had granted asylum to the fugitive warrior David. King Rehoboam of Judah later fortified Gath.

17. **Huldah** – What began in 1909 as an olive tree farm dedicated to the memory of Theodor Herzl developed into a full-fledged forest featuring almonds, pines, acacias, cypresses, and carobs, and later became a national park covering some 50 acres. The Huldah features the beautiful edifice Herzl House; a round pool; a grove planted in 1931 to commemorate the poetess Rahel; a memorial to Zionist siblings

Ephraim and Sarah Chisik, dating to 1937; and a stone quarry. Zionist pioneers of the Gordonia youth movement replanted the incinerated forest in 1931 before establishing on a nearby hilltop Kibbutz Huldah, the organization and embarkation point for Jewish stalwarts who penetrated the blockade of the road to Jerusalem during the War of Independence (1947–1949).

18. **Ilanot** – A unique arboretum in the center of the Sharon Plain. Established in the 1950s, Ilanot features 750 tree species across more than 32 acres. The forest served as a living laboratory wherein researchers studied local planting suitability, seed collection, and tree pests, among other forestry subjects. The vast array includes specimens of eucalyptus, bay laurel, cluster fig, rose she-oak, turpentine pine, mottlecah, tecate cypress, sulphur bark, Chilean mesquite, and cork oak. In 1986 the arboretum was abandoned and left derelict until its restoration in 2013.

19. **Rosh HaAyin** – Encompassing 260 acres on the southeastern edge of the Sharon Plain, in the foothills of the Samarian Hills, Rosh HaAyin Forest contains several archaeological sites such as the Bronze Age (3300–1200 BCE) locus Even HaEzer (Isbet Sartah), wherein buildings, houses, and granary pits were discovered and excavated, yielding important artifacts such as an ostracon with Hebrew writing believed to have formed part of an abecedary. A pair of significant battles between the Israelites and the Philistines occurred nearby, including one that involved the loss of the Ark of the Testimony (Ark of the Covenant) to the Philistines. The forest also features remnants of a Byzantine era (324–638 CE) settlement and a rock-hewn cistern. Local tree species include carob, almond, mastic, olive, jujube, Judas, stone pine, eucalyptus, cypress, and styrax, supplemented by clematis vines and rough bindweed. Cyclamens, white and red anemones, bee orchids, tulips, asphodels, sea squills, and pancratia bloom locally. The Raba tributary of the Yarkon River courses through the woods. The forest lies directly below a seminal bird migration route, and hundreds of thousands of migratory birds soar overhead annually in spring and in autumn.

20. **Tzorah** – A forest dedicated to the memory of Chaim Weizmann, first president of the State of Israel. The Israelite Judge and strongman Samson, and his father Manoah, were born in the eponymous town, now at the center of Tzorah Forest; the site's ancient remains include burial caves, cisterns, and wine presses. Autumn crocuses, narcissi, cyclamens, anemones, Persian buttercups, giant fennels, and *ferulae* mushrooms adorn the woods.

21. **Eshtaol** – Covering almost 3,000 acres on low chalk hills, Eshtaol Forest comprises tree species such as olive, carob, and stone pine, and includes the Eshtaol Nursery, where saplings are cultivated and nurtured for future afforestation projects. The Eshtaol features ruins of an ancient olive press and a lime pit. The Israel National Trail (Shvil Yisrael) and the Jerusalem-Tel-Aviv Bicycle Trail both traverse the woods. Nearby lie the Burma Road, a vital bypass forged to reach Jerusalem, and Latrun Monastery, two key sites in Israel's War of Independence (1947–1949), as well as the Jewish-Arab village Nivei Shalom (to the north) and the city of Beit Shemesh (to the south).

22. **Nivei Ilan** – Planted in 1952 west of Jerusalem and southeast of Modi'in, the forest commemorates UN mediator Count Folke Bernadotte, assassinated in Jerusalem in 1948. The woods possess evergreens, almond trees, red anemones, streamside trails, and wild boars. There are also ruins dating to the Hasmonean era (167–63 BCE) and built along the classical Jerusalem-Emmaus road in the northern section of the forest at Horvat Metzad, as well as more intact ruins of houses, wine presses, wells, and rock-hewn cisterns from the Byzantine era (324–638 CE) in the center of the forest at Horvat Aleket. The road skirting the woods to the south offers lovely views of Sha'ar HaGai.

23. **Aminadav** – Part of the lush greenbelt on the outskirts of Jerusalem. Aminadav Forest possesses oaks, carobs, almonds, natural springs, agricultural terraces, caves, memorials, and remnants of ancient orchards, wine presses, olive presses, and limekilns, as well as the Horvat Saadim nature reserve. There are also impressive views of the Jerusalem Hills and of the Sorek and Rephaim gullies.

24. **Peace** – A hillside forest in southern Jerusalem, sloping downward (northward) from the Armon HaNatziv/East Talpiot ridge and up again toward the Old City. Established in the immediate aftermath of the Six-Day War of 1967, the woods comprise 100 acres replete with pines, cypresses, cedars, and olive groves. Peace Forest is today a gathering place for nature-loving Jerusalemites and visitors. Several graves dating to the Second Temple era (516 BCE–70 CE) were discovered herein, including that of the infamous high priest Joseph Caiaphas (Yosef Kayafa), as was an aqueduct dating to the Hasmonean era (167–63 BCE). Breathtaking panoramas of Temple Mount and of the Ben Hinnom and the Kidron Valleys are available from Trottner Park and from the adjacent Sherover, Haas, and Goldman Promenades – collectively known as "The Promenade" (*tayelet*) – that skirt the southern edge of the forest. Nahal Atzal runs through the basin and

the area also features a large menorah sculpture and an open-air amphitheater.

25. **Jerusalem** – A green lung for residents of Israel's capital, Jerusalem Forest comprises pines, cypresses, cedars, oaks, terebinths, olives, figs, carobs, and pomegranates. Spring flowers include orchids, daffodils, anemones, and cyclamens. Local plants include thyme and rockrose. The area features ancient agricultural terraces, burial caves, wine presses, and cisterns. The forest is also home to songbirds, sparrow hawks, gazelles, and jackals. The Holocaust museum Yad Vashem is adjacent to the woods, on the western slope of Mount Herzl.

26. **Martyrs' (Kedoshim)** – Planted along the banks of the Kisalon Stream in 1951, Martyrs' Forest contains 6 million trees symbolically commemorating the 6 million Jews murdered in the Holocaust (1933–1945). The forest covers 10,000 acres of the Judean Hills west of Jerusalem. Tree species include terebinth, Kermes oak, styrax, pine, cypress, carob, and eucalyptus. Local flora such as white rockrose, three-lobed sage, and rough bindweed ornament the woods. The bronze Scroll of Fire monument by sculptor Nathan Rapoport looms large over the middle of the forest, which also features Martyrs' Cave and the Anne Frank memorial by Holocaust survivor and sculptor Piet Cohen.

27. **Pisgat Ze'ev (Mir)** – A forest northeast of Jerusalem that abuts the Judean Desert. Pisgat Ze'ev features Aleppo pines (Jerusalem pines), Calabrian pines, stone pines, Mediterranean cypresses, Arizona cypresses, mastics, and seven discrete types of eucalyptus. Flora such as autumn crocuses, autumn squills, asphodels, tulips, anemones, cyclamens, and eastern groundsels abound. Denizens of the forest include hyraxes, gazelles, foxes, wild boars, songbirds, jays, crows, partridges, wagtails, bulbuls, and Syrian woodpeckers. Amid the woods can be found a memorial to the Jews of Mir (Belarus); a memorial to 37 Palmah paratroopers (including Hannah Szenes) dispatched to Europe in WWII; ancient vestiges of wine presses, four limekilns, and two cisterns; and several burial caves.

28. **Sataf** – Situated just east of Mount Eitan, on the western fringes of Jerusalem, and sloping toward Nahal Sorek, Sataf contains two local springs (Ein Sataf and Ein Bikura), vegetable gardens, vineyards, olive groves, and almond orchards. Prehistoric remnants have been discovered in situ.

29. **Be'eri** – Named after the prominent socialist Zionist Berl Katznelson (whose pen name was Be'eri Ya'akov), the forest rises in the Bsor region

of the northwestern Negev Desert. Within the forest lie the Be'eri Badlands (Crater Nature Reserve), comprising almost 1,250 acres and featuring an agave grove and vegetation including Spur flax, brushwood, rockrose, thorny saltwort, Pink Sun-rose, Deverra tortuosa, and Egyptian sage. Local flora such as irises, anemones, scarlet crowfoots, bee orchids, asphodels, grape hyacinths, and squills flourish in springtime. In terms of fauna, the reserve is home to gazelles, Indian porcupines, turtles, and Monitor lizards. The area possesses the impressive ruins of Maon, a Jewish town dating to the Byzantine era (324–638 CE), whose ancient synagogue and mosaic floor were discovered in 1957 (and built on the Hellenistic site Menois); a memorial to the ANZAC soldiers of WWI; abandoned sulphur mines encompassing half an acre and dating to the period 1933–1946; a British military installation including ammunition storehouses, from WWII; and a monument to Baghdad Jewry (members of which were founders of Kibbutz Be'eri).

30. **Dvirah** – Planted in the 1990s, Dvirah forms the northern part of Lahav Forest and functions as a green corridor between the Judean Hills and the Mediterranean Sea. Dvirah comprises deciduous terebinths, carobs, acacias, jujubes, and eucalypti; coniferous pines; and orchard trees such as olives and figs. Sycamores and date palms appear along the streambed of the seasonal watercourse Nahal Shikmah. At Dvirah, desert floodwaters are harvested by means of terraces, furrows, and ridges; this process of savannization prevents runoff by capturing rainwater that is absorbed into the earth for use by the trees and vegetation. The forest hosts rodents, hares, foxes, jackals, wolves, gazelles, porcupines, lizards, and butterflies (lured by the acacias). Anemones and bee orchids bloom in winter. Dvirah also features the ruins of Migdalit, including cave dwellings, building foundations, and a cistern, and of Za'ak, whose Bronze Age (3300–1200 BCE) vestiges include a secret tunnel and a cave with a wine press inside.

31. **Lahav** – An expansive forest encompassing over 7,400 acres. Planted from 1952 onward, Lahav rises from a backdrop of desert shrubs. It includes conifers, terebinths, mastics, eucalypti, carobs, and olive groves. Its glades bloom with Jerusalem sage, yellow Sternbergia, and wildflowers. Attracted by the abundance of oil-rich mastic fruits, migrating songbirds – e.g., the Eurasian blackcap, the black-eared wheatear, the western Orphean warbler, the common redstart, and the lesser whitethroat – sojourn for a fortnight in the woods en route to their overwintering destination. In autumn, Lahav functions as an

overnight roost for raptors such as the European honey buzzard, the Levant sparrowhawk, and the lesser spotted eagle. Spanish sparrows are compelled to the area by saltbushes beside the Ein Rimon Well; warblers by fig trees; and greenfinches by thymelaea bushes. Remnants of Ein Rimon, a village in the tribal territory of Shimon, lie nearby, including an ancient synagogue with an ornamental floor dating to the Second Temple era (516 BCE–70 CE). The Halif ruins, also in the vicinity, feature Jewish burial caves from the second and third centuries CE.

32. **HaMal'akhim-Shahariyah** – A forest east of Kiryat Gat and of the eponymous Shahariyah transit camp established in 1956 (in Hebrew, *HaMal'akhim* denotes "The Angels", a reference to the donors of Los Angeles). Surrounded by desert brush (e.g., buckthorn, Thorny burnet, Coolatai grass), the forest rises from the southwestern Shephelah foothills and features carobs, olives, and figs. Local flora include hyssop (wild marjoram; *eizov* in Hebrew, *za'atar* in Arabic), anemones, cyclamens, buttercups, as well as fungi such as pine mushrooms. The woods contain the Karua ruins (featuring a three-level public building, possibly serving as a synagogue, with an adjoining rectangular cistern that doubled as a mikvah), ancient wine presses, an ancient olive press, a limekiln, as well as herb gardens growing thyme, sage, lavender, rosemary, white-leaved savory, and vetiver (an aromatic root yielding oil used in perfumery).

33. **Hatzeirim** – A sparsely treed oasis in the tribal territory of Shimon, now the northwestern Negev Desert, just southwest of Be'ersheva near Kibbutz Hatzeirim. The landscape resembles a savannah and possesses groves of tamarisks, acacias, and eucalypti, in addition to jujubes, carobs, South American mesquites, and fruit trees. Adjacent to the forest is a plain of loess soil, a natural habitat for rare fauna such as the leopard fringe-fingered lizard, houbara bustard, cream-colored courser, long-eared hedgehog, and greater Egyptian jerboa. Kibbutz Hatzeirim served as a crucial command post during the War of Independence (1947–1949), and its entrepreneurial members founded Netafim, the prosperous drip irrigation manufacturing company, in 1966. A local Sculpture Trail showcases the works of scores of Israeli artists. The Israeli Air Force Museum is also located nearby.

34. **Yatir** – The largest desert forest in Israel, and the country's largest planted forest, named after a Levitical city whose ruins reside within it. Planted beginning in 1966, the Yatir was meant to help make the desert bloom. In 1967, the Foresters' Fortress was erected to

accommodate foresters. Located northeast of Be'ersheva on the lower slopes of the Hebron Hills, the forest now comprises almost 10,000 acres and some 5 million trees, including conifers such as Aleppo pines (Jerusalem pines) and cypresses; broadleaf trees such as tamarisks, terebinths, pistachios, carobs, and jujubes; orchard trees such as olives and figs; as well as eucalypti, acacias, and assorted shrubs such as desert brooms and vitexes. The Yatir also features agricultural plots wherein vineyards and orchards thrive, as well as cherry trees and peonies. Stone terraces harvest runoff rainwater that soaks into the soil. The ruins of Anim, including a Judahite fortress from the First Temple era (960–586 BCE), cave dwellings and secret tunnels, and a Byzantine era (324–638 CE) synagogue, are on-site, as are cisterns and caves.

The State of Israel, today about 10 percent treed, is famously one of few nations in the world that commenced the 21st century with more trees than it possessed a century earlier. About a third of the nation's forests are natural (unplanted), mostly located in the uplands of central and northern Israel. The diversity of trees in Israel today owes much to the various climatic regions. Species range from Kermes oak and Syrian juniper on Mount Hermon; terebinth, black mulberry, and olive in Galilee; sycamore and eucalyptus in coastal cities; poplar, cypress, and pine in Judea; acacia in the Judean Desert; pine, acacia, and tamarisk in the Negev Desert; and acacia, tamarisk, date palm, and doum palm (gingerbread tree) in the Aravah Valley.

As Israel's forestry service, Keren Kayemet L'Yisrael-Jewish National Fund (KKL-JNF) has taken the lead in greening the country and to date has planted upwards of 240 million trees, created 280 forests across some 300,000 acres, developed over 1,000 forest recreation areas, and built more than 4,350 forest access roads. The organization's heuristic silviculture has prompted adjustments in forestry practices over the decades: it has adopted salutary forest management protocols such as prescribed burnings and controlled grazing by livestock (cattle, sheep, and goats foraging in rural forests doubling as pastures), and has pioneered the innovative savannization (sparse planting) process wherein single trees or tree clusters are planted wherever climatic conditions prevent woods or shrubs from growing absent significant human intervention; by employing advanced water harvesting techniques to capture runoff rainwater, these trees are able to grow while simultaneously retarding soil erosion.

Most of Israel's forestlands are designated multiple-use, and there are also recreational forests for the general public, community forests for use primarily by proximate residents, and research forests for projects designed to improve forest management activities. Fuel breaks are incorporated to deter the advance of forest fires across the landscape. Forests increasingly incorporate fruit groves (*bustanim*) for tree diversity, with their fruit free to consume. Some 12 million people visit Israel's forests annually, taking advantage of scenic roads, observation points, picnic spots, hiking and cycling trails, playgrounds, parks, and historic sites free to the public. Regions still awaiting substantial afforestation or reforestation include the Jezreel Valley, the Coastal Plain, Samaria, the Jordan River Valley, eastern Judea, the Aravah Valley, and the Paran Desert. Israel's forests remain vulnerable to forest fires (e.g., the Kharmel forest fire of 2010, the Eshtaol/Tzorah forest fire of 2015) and to incendiarism – arson or pyroterrorism – (e.g., in Haifa, the Sharon Plain, and the Judean Hills in 2016; in the Bsor/Eshkol region of the northwestern Negev Desert in 2018), making vigilance and resolute law enforcement key to preserving natural resources.

Jews today look forward to the reification of the prophet Mikhah's vision, when "everyone shall sit under his vine and under his fig tree, and none shall make them afraid; for the mouth of the Lord of hosts has spoken" (4:4).

Forested Judean Hills

10

Heartland of the Homeland: What Judea and Samaria Mean to Jewry

Heartland of the Homeland: What Judea & Samaria Mean to Jewry

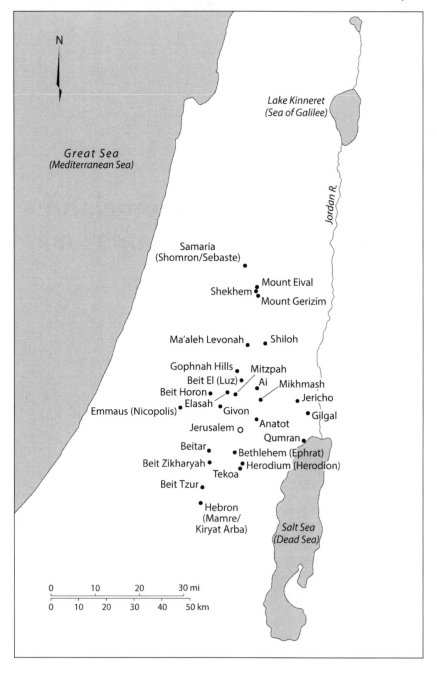

For the Jewish people, the ancient tribal territories of eastern Judah, Benjamin, Ephraim, and western Menasheh – also known as "Judea & Samaria" – form the very heartland of the homeland. In the contemporary political climate, ceding these foundational areas remains an ongoing possibility, and many individual Jews disconnected from their heritage and their history remain unacquainted with what these crucial regions of the Land of Israel mean to Judaic civilization and to Jewry as a whole.

Here, then, is a précis outlining the provinces' most important geographical sites, personages, and historical contexts, thereby highlighting their momentous significance to Jewish identity.

1. **Samaria (Shomron/Sebaste)** – Capital of the Omride kings of Israel (Omri, Ahab, Yehoram, etc.), and the ancient center of thriving wine and oil industries. Mentioned in *I & II Kings* and *II Chronicles*, as well as by the prophets Amos, Isaiah, Mikhah, Jeremiah, Ezekiel, and Ovadiah, Samaria also appears in the writings of the priestly historian Joseph ben Matityahu (Flavius Josephus) and its orchards are praised in the Mishnah. The ruined city was later possessed by the Hasmonean monarch King Yannai Alexander of Judea, rebuilt and renamed Sebaste (Sebastia) by King Herod the Great of Judea, and controlled by King Agrippa I of Judea until the advent of the Roman procurators (44–70 CE). The prophet Elisha is said to be buried here, as is the hermetic Jewish preacher John the Baptist.

2. **Shekhem** – Situated in the narrow valley between Mounts Eival and Gerizim, and along the regional Derekh HaAvot (The Way of the Patriarchs/Ridge Route) connecting Upper Galilee and the Negev Desert, Shekhem is where Abraham built an altar under the oak of Moreh; where Jacob encamped, bought a field, and buried idols and earrings; where Dinah was raped and brutally avenged; and where Joseph is buried. Here Joshua drew up the Mosaic statutes, erected a stone monument under the oak tree, and convened the elders and judges of Israel before his decease, adjuring them to pledge allegiance to God. Gidon's sons fought over the city after that great Judge's decease. King David twice versified the city in *Psalms*. King Rehoboam of Judah was crowned here and King Jeroboam I of Israel was elected here and made the city his initial capital. Shekhem, deemed the midpoint of the Land of Israel – exactly 71.5 miles from both Dan in the north and Be'ersheva in the south – is also a Levitical city and one of the biblical cities of refuge. Emperor Vespasian of Rome built Neapolis (Nablus) near the ruins of the city, which is also mentioned

by the prophets Hosea and Jeremiah, by the priestly historian Joseph ben Matityahu (Flavius Josephus), and in *Midrash Rabbah*. Shekhem is the Jerusalem of Samaritans.

3. **Mount Eival** – Here Joshua built an altar of unhewn stones and made a peace sacrifice to God following the fall of Ai, and inscribed and read the Torah before the Israelites and in the presence of the Ark of the Testimony (Ark of the Covenant). Eival is the taller counterpart of Gerizim, toward which the Levites pronounced the Mosaic curses.

4. **Mount Gerizim** – Gerizim is where the other half of Israel stood listening to Joshua, and toward which the Levites pronounced blessings. The smaller counterpart of Eival is known foremost as the holy mountain for Samaritans, who celebrate their version of the Passover festival atop its peak. It is also where the Hasmonean ruler and high priest Yohanan Hyrcanus destroyed the Samaritan temple in 111/110 (the date of this victory, 21 Kislev, was thenceforth celebrated as "the Day of Mount Gerizim"), and where the Samaritan leader Baba Rabbah built a synagogue in the 300s CE.

5. **Shiloh** – At Shiloh Joshua made plans with the assembled Israelites to finish apportioning the Promised Land to the tribes. As the first religious center of the repatriated Israelites, Shiloh was for more than two centuries home to the Tabernacle and the Ark of the Testimony (Ark of the Covenant), and where the high priest Eli and his sons officiated. Elkanah made an annual pilgrimage to Shiloh, which is also where his barren wife Hannah vowed to consecrate a son to God if she could conceive a child. After giving birth to the future Judge and prophet Samuel, Hannah recited her song of praise here. Mentioned repeatedly in *Jeremiah*, Shiloh was also home to the prophet Ahiyah of Shiloh.

6. **Ma'aleh Levonah** – The site of the first major Maccabean battle and victory, in which the Hasmonean hero Judah Maccabee defeated the Seleucids (Syrian-Greeks) and slew the Samarian mysarch Apollonius, taking his sword for himself.

7. **Gilgal** – The first campsite and base of Joshua and the Israelites upon entering Canaan, where Joshua erected 12 stones gathered from the Jordan River, and where the people celebrated the Passover festival and circumcised those born in the desert. The prophet Samuel sojourned here to judge the people, and King Saul was crowned at this sacred site. The prophets Elijah and Elisha passed through the site prior to Elijah's whirlwind ascent. Gilgal was a Levitical city in the time of Nehemiah, and the site is mentioned by the prophets Amos and Hosea and in the Talmud.

8. **Gophnah Hills** – In the hill country of Ephraim, just northwest of Beit El, the Maccabees trained in guerilla warfare to prepare for battle against Emperor Antiochus IV of Syria and his Seleucid (Syrian-Greek) forces. In the secluded heights and caverns of Gophnah, east of their hometown of Modi'in, the glorious brothers Yohanan, Shimon, Judah, Elazar, and Jonathan established a command center and drilled their followers into a formidable Maccabean army, which went on to liberate Judea and to regain Jewish independence and sovereignty in the Land of Israel in the second century BCE.

9. **Beit El (Luz)** – A key locus along the regional Derekh HaAvot (The Way of the Patriarchs/Ridge Route) connecting Upper Galilee and the Negev Desert. Abraham erected a sacred altar to the Lord between Beit El and Ai. Here Jacob spent a night dreaming he saw a ladder rising heavenward, with angels ascending and descending it. A heavenly voice then assured him of divine protection, confirming the promise that the land upon which he rested would be for him and his descendants. When morning came, Jacob built a sacred pillar over which he poured oil as a thanksgiving offering. For a time the Tabernacle and the Ark of the Testimony (Ark of the Covenant) were stationed in Beit El, and in the conflict with the tribe of Benjamin the Israelites prayed, fasted, and offered sacrifices here. The Israelite Judge and prophetess Dvorah lived nearby, and later the Judge and prophet Samuel sojourned here to judge the people. During the United Monarchy of Israel (1030–931 BCE), King Saul mustered his forces here against the Philistines. Frequented by King Jeroboam I of Israel as a central shrine, Beit El hosted a community of prophets during the prophethood of Elisha (who was mocked by the children of Beit El), and witnessed the prophet Amos' righteous indignation against illegitimate worship and the impious priest Amaziah. Later, the pious King Josiah of Judah cleansed the city of its cultic practices. Beit El hosted the formidable Seleucid (Syrian-Greek) general Bacchides' garrisons during the Maccabean Rebellion (167–134 BCE), and is mentioned often in *Joshua, Judges, I & II Kings, Hosea, Jeremiah*, and *Ezra*. Beit El is most likely modern Beitin/Baytin, just northeast of Al-Bireh.

10. **Mitzpah** – Here the Israelites gathered to punish the tribe of Benjamin after the outrage committed by the men of Givah. Home of the reluctant Israelite Judge Yiftah who repeated his conditions for leadership in Mitzpah. This is also where the Judge and prophet Samuel assembled the people to fight and defeat the advancing Philistines, and where he annually judged Israel. King Asa of Judah fortified the place,

and the Babylonian-appointed governor Gidalyah established Judah's capital here after the fall of Jerusalem (586 BCE) and was later assassinated in Mitzpah (giving rise to the fast day in his memory near the Jewish New Year). The city was also a district capital in Nehemiah's time under Persian rule, and was later where the Maccabees prayed, tore their clothing, wore sackcloth and ashes, fasted, and read the Torah before the Battle of Emmaus (166 BCE). There are several loci named Mitzpah in the Land of Israel; Mitzpah of Benjamin is most likely Tel en-Nasbeh, just southeast of modern Ramallah.

11. **Mikhmash** – At Mikhmash King Saul gathered his army before the Philistines encamped there, until their defeat and flight. Mikhmash is mentioned in *Isaiah, Ezra, Nehemiah, I Maccabees*, and by the priestly historian Joseph ben Matityahu (Flavius Josephus), and praised in the Mishnah for its excellent wheat. The Hasmonean leader Jonathan Maccabee resided here prior to assuming the high priesthood. Mikhmash is the modern village Mukhmas.

12. **Emmaus (Nicopolis)** – Emmaus is where the Hasmonean hero Judah Maccabee defeated the general Nicanor and frightened off another general, Gorgias, in a stunning and strategic double victory over the Seleucids (Syrian-Greeks). The town was known for its hot springs and is mentioned often in the Talmud. Tannaim held discussions here, including local scholar Nehunya ben HaKanah, and Yohanan ben Zakkai's prized disciple Elazar ben Arakh took up residence in Emmaus, where his erudition diminished in the absence of his rabbinical colleagues. Emmaus, whose name likely derived from the (construct form of the) Hebrew word for hot springs (*hammat*), received its Greek name Nicopolis ("City of Victory") once rebuilt at the request of Christian traveler and historian Sextus Julius Africanus in 220/221.

13. **Beit Horon** – Both a steep pass where the Canaanites fled from Joshua, and a two-tiered town fortified by King Solomon; where the Hasmonean hero Judah Maccabee defeated Seleucid (Syrian-Greek) general Seron and his phalanx of hoplites; and where Zealot leader Shimon bar Giora and other stalwarts similarly defeated the Roman general Cestius Gallus during the Great Revolt (66–73 CE). Lower Beit Horon is the modern village of Beit Ur al-Tahta; Upper Beit Horon is the modern village of Beit Ur al-Fauqa.

14. **Givon** – Givon is the city whose men negotiated in bad faith with Joshua, and where according to Scripture the sun stood still for Joshua in battle. King David's nephew and general Yo'av fought his military

counterpart Avner by the Givon pool, and later slew his own cousin and rival Amasa here. David conquered the Philistines nearby, and Givon is also the site at which King Solomon sacrificed a thousand burnt offerings to God, who reportedly appeared to Solomon in a dream eliciting then granting the king's request for wisdom. Givon is mentioned in *I Kings, I & II Chronicles, Jeremiah, Nehemiah,* and the Talmud. Givon's ruins lie at the southern edge of the modern village of al-Jib.

15. **Elasah** – A town near Beit Horon apparently named after a scion of Benjamin, and the site of the tragic battle wherein, woefully outnumbered, the Hasmonean hero Judah Maccabee fell. Elasah is identified with Khirbat al-Ishshi, southwest of Al-Bireh, but also equated by others to Mount Ba'al-Hatzor (near Ramallah), mentioned in the Dead Sea Scrolls.

16. **Anatot** – The Levitical hometown of Evyatar the high priest and of the prophet Jeremiah, in which the hopeful prophet redeemed property from his cousin Hanamel in defiance of Judah's dire situation under the conquering Babylonians, giving the lie to his reputation as a preacher of doom and gloom. The site is also mentioned in *I Chronicles*. Anatot is most likely the modern village of Anata.

17. **Ai** – Abraham encamped on the hill between Beit El and Ai, where he erected an altar and called upon the Lord. After Jericho, Ai was the second royal fortress to fall to Joshua and the Israelites, following the initial failed assault hindered by the misdeeds of Akhan ben Kharmi, who had absconded with forbidden spoils of war. Joshua's army pitched camp on Ai's north side, with other troops left to ambush and capture the city. Ai is also mentioned in *I Chronicles, Isaiah, Ezra,* and *Nehemiah*. Ai's ruins likely lie beneath the modern village of Deir Dibwan.

18. **Jericho** – The "City of the Moon", one of the most famous cities in the Tanakh (Hebrew Bible) and in the Talmud, Jericho was a walled palm and balsam oasis encountered by the likes of Joshua, Rahav, King David's ambassadors to Ammon, the prophets Elijah and Elisha (two onetime residents), the doomed fugitive King Zedekiah of Judah, the Hasmonean rulers, King Herod the Great of Judea, etc. Centuries later the Arabian Jewish tribe of Banu Nadir sought refuge here from Muhammad.

19. **Qumran** – The former desert monastery of the sectarian "Yahad" community (probably Essenes) on the shores of the Salt Sea (Dead Sea), whose scriptorium hosted the creation of the Dead Sea Scrolls ultimately found in the surrounding, cave-pocked Judean Hills.

20. **Beitar** – The only man ever anointed as the Jewish Messiah, Shimon bar Kosiba (Bar Kokhba), finally fell in his hilltop headquarters in 135 CE after the city had endured a prolonged Roman siege. The sage and priest Elazar of Modi'in, Bar Kokhba's uncle, also died here. The bastion was known for its natural spring and its defensible location as a steep neck of land bounded by valleys on three sides. Often mentioned in the Mishnah, Tosefta, Talmud, and *Midrash Rabbah*. Beitar is known today as Khirbet al-Yahud ("Ruin of the Jews") and lies at the western edge of the modern village of Battir.

21. **Bethlehem (Ephrat)** – A key locus along the regional Derekh HaAvot (The Way of the Patriarchs/Ridge Route) connecting Upper Galilee and the Negev Desert. Bethlehem is the storied locus just outside of which the matriarch Rahel is buried, and where the Moabite convert Ruth married the wealthy Israelite landowner Bo'az. Bethlehem was the home of the shepherd youth and slinger (a descendant of Ruth) who would become the warrior and psalmist King David, and the recorded birthplace of the Jewish reformer Jesus of Nazareth, who inspired a new world religion.

22. **Tekoa** – The village of Tekoa was home to the wise woman who convinced King David to pardon his rebellious son Avshalom, and was thereafter fortified by King Rehoboam of Judah. Most of all, it was home to the herdsman and prophet Amos who gathered its sycamore fruit and who is buried there. Tekoa was also home to Calev's descendants and the site where King Yehoshaphat of Judah withstood the attack from neighboring nations. Tekoa was renowned for its oil and honey.

23. **Herodium (Herodion)** – Herodium is a partially manmade mountain where King Herod the Great of Judea commemorated an early military victory and later had himself inhumed. The mound was fortified during the Great Revolt (66–73 CE) and fell only after the destruction of Jerusalem. A synagogue from the Great Revolt era remains in situ. It was thereafter refortified as a district headquarters during the Bar Kokhba Revolt (132–135 CE).

24. **Beit Zikharyah** – Elazar Maccabee fell in battle here in his bold attempt to kill an elephant by stabbing its underbelly. The falling beast crushed him, and thus died the first of the five glorious Maccabee brothers.

25. **Beit Tzur** – A strategic site mentioned in *Joshua* that was later fortified by King Rehoboam of Judah and that eventually became a key Maccabean fortress along the border between Judah and Edom. It was also the

locus of a major Maccabean victory that paved the way for the Maccabees' recapture of Jerusalem and for the advent of the Hanukah festival.

26. **Hebron (Mamre/Kiryat Arba)** – Hebron is one of the four holiest cities in Judaism and the locus of the Cave of the Patriarchs (and most Matriarchs), where Abraham and Sarah, Isaac and Rivkah, and Jacob and Leah are interred. Jewish tradition also locates the graves of Adam and Havah here. Abraham was a local resident after arriving in Canaan, and Hebron served as a key locus along the regional Derekh HaAvot (The Way of the Patriarchs/Ridge Route) connecting Upper Galilee and the Negev Desert. Hebron was also where King David was anointed and established his capital for seven and a half years before the conquest of the Jebusite citadel of Jerusalem. The first Israelite Judge, Otniel ben Kenaz, is also entombed in Hebron. The Hasmonean hero Judah Maccabee and later the Zealot leader Shimon bar Giora reconquered the city from its Idumean and Roman occupiers, respectively. Renowned for its terebinths, Hebron is also one of the six cities of refuge in the Torah, and is mentioned therein 87 times. Numerous rabbinical authors have lived here, such as: Elijah de Vidas (1525), author of *Reishit Hokhmah*; Israel Tzvi (1731), author of *Urim Gedolim*; Aaron Alfandari (1772), author of *Yad Aharon* and *Merkevet HaMishneh*; Hayyim Abraham Israel Tzvi (1776), author of *Be'er Mayyim Hayyim*; Mordekhai Ruvio (1785), author of *Shemen HaMor*; Elijah Sliman Mani (d. 1878), author of *Kisei Eliyahu*; Rahamim Joseph Franco (d. 1901), author of *Sha'arei Rahamim*; and many more. For Jews, Hebron is second in stature only to Jerusalem.

The exempla above are only some of the seminal places, events, and key figures associated with the heartland of the homeland, wherein lie the modern communities and inhabitants of Ariel, Elon Moreh, Hashmonaim, Ma'aleh Adumim, Mevasseret Tzion, Ephrat, Alon Shevut, Kfar Etzion, Migdal Oz, and many, many others. In sum, the length and breadth of eastern Judah, Benjamin, Ephraim, and western Menasheh are steeped in 4,000 years of Jewish history, religion, culture, and civilization – ongoing in the present day and into the future.

Herodium (Herodion)

11

18 Must-See Sites in Israel

18 Must-See Sites in Israel

Great Sea
(Mediterranean Sea)

Litani R.

N

Lake Kinneret
(Sea of Galilee)

Beit She'arim

Mount Tavor

Megiddo

Kokhav HaYarden (Belvoir)

Ma'ayan Harod (Ein Harod)

Beit She'an

Jordan R.

Rishpon (Apollonia/Arsuf)

Emmaus (Nicopolis)

Castel

Aqua Bella (Ein Hemed)

Jerusalem

Sorek Cave

Tel Ashkelon

Herodium (Herodion)

Mareshah (Marisa)/
Beit Guvrin (Eleutheropolis)

Salt Sea
(Dead Sea)

Tel Be'ersheva

0   10   20   30 mi

0   10   20   30   40   50 km

Nitzanah

Shivta (Sobeita/Sobota)

Hatzeivah (Tamar/Ovot)

In the Land of Israel, the road less traveled was almost certainly once a busy thoroughfare for residents, nomads, pilgrims, merchants, travelers, or wildlife.

If only these rocks could speak – and not only the rocks.

In a land where every tree, blade of grass, and wilderness stone has a scroll-length tale to tell, there is no shortage of historical or natural treasures to discover in every province and corner, including: the Golan (eastern Menasheh); Upper Galilee (Naphtali, Asher); Lower Galilee (Zevulun, Issachar); the Jezreel Valley; Samaria (western Menasheh); the Sharon Plain (western Menasheh); Judea (Judah, Shimon, Benjamin, Dan, Ephraim); the Jordan River Valley; the Shephelah foothills (western Judah, Dan, western Ephraim); the Aravah Valley (Edom); and the Negev Desert (southern Judah, Shimon, Edom).

If, like the famed rabbi, physician, and Beit She'an resident (Estori) Isaac HaParhi (c. 1280–1357 CE), one spends seven years exploring the length and breadth of the Land of Israel, one will doubtless encounter a fair share of what the country has to offer in terms of archaeology, antiquities, flora, and fauna. Tourists with more limited itineraries will have to make difficult choices.

Ultimately, what *must* be seen depends on individual tastes; what *should* be seen is invariably a much longer list. What follows is a sample of sites numbering among the most worthwhile loci.

1. **Megiddo** – Predating recorded history, Megiddo became historically important as a strategic commercial and military locus along the ancient Derekh HaYam (The Way of the Sea/Coastal Highway) international trade route connecting Egypt and Syria, and also along the regional Derekh HaAvot (The Way of the Patriarchs/Ridge Route) connecting Upper Galilee and the Negev Desert, and was often fought over by Egyptians and Canaanites in ancient times. Pharaoh Thutmose III of Egypt conquered the site in the 15th century BCE. In the 10th century, King Solomon made it one of his three regional administrative cities, along with Gezer and Hatzor; whoever controlled these three strategic fortresses was master of the Land of Israel. Here fell noble King Josiah of Judah in battle (609) against the Assyrian ally Pharaoh Neco II of Egypt. In WWI, British and Arab troops defeated the Ottoman imperial army here as well. Today Har (Mount) Megiddo (also known as Armageddon) is an Israeli national park. Kibbutz Megiddo is nearby.

2. **Kokhav HaYarden (Belvoir)** – A crusader fortress built by the Knights Hospitaler, Belvoir is perhaps the best preserved crusader castle in

Israel. In the 12th and 13th centuries, the fortress repeatedly changed hands between the Franks and the Saracens, and its concentric walls, glacis, and surrounding moat today give visitors a sense of its erstwhile fortitude.

3. **Mount Tavor** – Unlike the Kharmel and Gilboa mountain ranges, Tavor is a single mount where the tribal territories of Naphtali, Issachar, and Zevulun converged. It is famous as the site of the battle between the Israelite Judge and prophetess Dvorah and her general Barak against King Yavin of Hatzor and his general Sisera, who fled the muddy battlefield only to meet his fate in the tent of Yael. The site was later fortified in the Hasmonean era (167–63 BCE), and during the Great Revolt (66–73 CE) by the Galilean governor Joseph ben Matityahu (Flavius Josephus). Today the Church of the Transfiguration, a monastery, and a hostel run by the Franciscans sit atop the storied peak, while the Israeli Arab village of Daburiyah (named after the Israelite prophetess) hangs off the mountainside.

4. **Beit She'arim** – An important Jewish town during the Roman era (63 BCE–313 CE), Beit She'arim became a necropolis where famous sages were buried, including the patriarch Judah HaNasi, redactor of the Mishnah. In addition to numerous cavernous tombs, including some featuring Greek or Aramaic inscriptions and salient menorah carvings, there are also ruins of an ancient synagogue, basilica, and olive press.

5. **Beit She'an** – One of the most well-preserved ancient and classical sites in Israel. Once controlled by the Egyptians, Canaanites, and even the otherwise coastal Philistines, Beit She'an sits at the junction of the Jordan River and the Beit She'an Valley (the eastern extension of the Jezreel Valley and the Harod Valley). In the 11th century BCE, after defeating King Saul in battle nearby, the Philistines hung his body from the city walls until it was retrieved by his loyalists. In 732, Emperor Tiglat-Pileser III of Assyria destroyed the city in his military campaign against King Pekah of Israel. In 63 BCE, following a period of Hasmonean rule, the Romans conquered the site and it soon became one of the Greco-Roman cities of the Decapolis. Today the site features a layered tel, columned avenues paved with basalt stone slabs, a Roman temple and a 7,000-seat Roman theater dating to the second century CE (and once again hosting performances), and a Byzantine basilica and bathhouse.

6. **Ma'ayan Harod (Ein Harod)** – Flowing from the foot of the Gilboa mountain range, the spring emerges from Gidon's Cave and forms the centerpiece of a beautiful landscape of lawns and pools. Around the 12th century BCE, the Israelite Judge Gidon selected his 300 most alert

fighters here to do battle against the Midianites encamped nearby. The Battle of Ayn Jalut also occurred here in 1260 CE, when the triumphant Sultan Saif ad-Din Qutuz of the Mameluke Sultanate of Egypt halted the Mongolian conquest of Asia in one of history's most fateful victories. The 20th century home and adjacent tomb of Zionist land procurer Yehoshua Hankin (the "Redeemer of the Valley") and his wife Olga are also in the immediate vicinity. The national park is today tucked away inside the moshav Gidonah, which also features an international hostel on-site.

7. **Rishpon (Apollonia/Arsuf)** – A calcareous sandstone (*kurkar*) promontory along the Sharon Plain first settled by seafaring Phoenicians during the Persian era (539–332 BCE). Named Rishpon after the eponymous Phoenician/Canaanite deity Reshef (god of war and storms), the natural cove anchored ships and became a busy commercial port specializing in the purple dye trade. In the Hellenistic era (332–167 BCE), Greek-speaking residents identified Reshef with the god Apollo and thus renamed the city Apollonia. Hasmonean monarch King Yannai Alexander of Judea later incorporated the site into his kingdom. During the Byzantine era (324–638 CE), the site was renamed Suzussa and was again a key port town engaged in the trade of wine, oil, and glass. Samaritans who dwelt locally in this period and beyond referred to their home as Rashpan, a version of its original name. In the wake of the Arab conquest of the Levant (634–638 CE), the site was renamed Arsuf, the Arabic form of Reshef. After failing to conquer the city in 1099, the crusaders tried again under King Baldwin I of Jerusalem and, aided by the Genoan fleet, succeeded in 1101; they renamed the place Arsour (a corruption of Arsuf) and eventually constructed a fortress and a moat on-site. Typically, control of the site shifted between the crusaders and the Muslims over the next two centuries, until Sultan Baybars of the Mameluke Sultanate of Egypt conquered Arsuf in 1265. Today Rishpon survives as Apollonia (Tel Arsuf) National Park in the northwest corner of urban Herzliyah.

8. **Castel** – Nestled among the Judean Hills inside modern Mevasseret Tzion, Castel was once a crusader bastion overlooking the road leading to Jerusalem. The site gained its greatest fame, however, only much later during the fateful 1948 battles here (including the one wherein the Arab commander Abd al-Qadir al-Husseini died) between Jewish and Arab forces during the War of Independence (1947–1949). Castel today is a national heritage site exhibiting documentary films about its 20th century history. The site also features an ancient well with

remnants of an olive press, as well as walkable trenches leading to the summit where the Mukhtar's House is situated. Kibbutz Tzovah/Tzubah (medieval Belmont, a crusader fortress), with an upscale hotel, is nearby.

9. **Aqua Bella (Ein Hemed)** – This lovely valley features several springs emerging from dolomite and marl, whose waters form the Kisalon Stream that channels through the area's verdant lawns. Amid the olive, oak, and buckthorn trees is a well-preserved and fortified crusader farmhouse, probably formerly managed by the Knights Hospitaler and dating to the mid-12th century CE, which still dominates the picturesque site. Aqua Bella is a hidden delight near Kibbutz Kiryat Anavim and the Israeli Arab town Abu Ghosh.

10. **Sorek Cave** – Discovered accidentally by quarriers, the prehistoric cavern features remarkable stalactites and stalagmites with various natural designs and colors. Located in the Sorek Valley next to Beit Shemesh, the cave is today a nature reserve that exhibits a documentary film about its origins. Guided tours are conducted in which individual rocky formations, often given names, are pointed out, including the "Romeo and Juliet" spikes that almost touch and a cave coral that uncannily resembles the decapitated head of the felled Philistine giant, Goliath of Gath.

11. **Emmaus (Nicopolis)** – Named Emmaus after the (construct form of the) Hebrew word for hot springs (*hammat*), the town was the site of a key military victory of the Hasmonean hero Judah Maccabee against the Seleucid (Syrian-Greek) generals Nicanor and Gorgias in the Battle of Emmaus (166 BCE). In the Roman era (63 BCE–313 CE), Emmaus was the home of famous sages including Nehunya ben HaKanah and Elazar ben Arakh and was a popular spa resort. Christians believe that here, circa 30 CE, the resurrected Jewish reformer Jesus of Nazareth met his disciples, who recognized him by the way he blessed and broke bread with them. Emmaus received its Greek name Nicopolis ("City of Victory") once rebuilt at the request of Christian traveler and historian Sextus Julius Africanus in 220/221. Today the site, operated as a convent by Kharmelite monks charging a nominal admission fee, features ancient Jewish tombs, remains of mosaics, a Byzantine basilica and quarry, and a crusader chapel.

12. **Herodium (Herodion)** – The locus of a battle between the last Hasmonean king, Mattathias Antigonus, and the future King Herod the Great of Judea. After defeating his rival for the throne, Herod in 28 BCE built a partially manmade mountain and fortified estate,

named after himself, at the site. Lower Herodium, at the foot of the mount, was an additional palace complex with pools, gardens, and a bathhouse. Herod was buried here, and his mausoleum was finally discovered in 2007. During the Great Revolt (66–73 CE), the Zealots seized the mountain fortress until the Romans recaptured it following the destruction of the Second Temple in Jerusalem in 70. In the Bar Kokhba Revolt (132–135 CE), Herodium was again used as a rebel base by Jewish stalwarts who carved secret tunnels and caves on-site. The biblical town of Tekoa and the modern village of the same name are nearby.

13. **Mareshah (Marisa)/Beit Guvrin (Eleutheropolis)** – Biblical Mareshah (known in Greek as Marisa) was an early Israelite site that endured until 40 BCE when it was destroyed by the Parthians during the war between the Hasmoneans and the future King Herod the Great of Judea. The adjacent settlement of Beit Guvrin (originally Beit Gabra in Aramaic and subsequently renamed Eleutheropolis by the Romans), with its natural bell caves, flourished in the Roman era (63 BCE–313 CE) and in the Byzantine era (324–638 CE). Besides the numerous and vast caves, there are Phoenician tombs with colorful wall paintings, cisterns, a well-preserved Roman amphitheater and bathhouse, a wine press, an olive press, and remains of a crusader fortress with a church and underground vaults.

14. **Tel Ashkelon** – Ancient Ashkelon, located along the ancient Derekh HaYam (The Way of the Sea/Coastal Highway) international trade route connecting Egypt and Syria, was an important coastal station for maritime trade and overland commerce. Ashkelon, whose name derives from the Hebrew word for a unit of weight (*shekel*), developed into a key fortified city of the Canaanites, Egyptians, and Philistines. Here the Israelite Judge and strongman Samson slew 30 Philistines after his wedding feast. Ashkelon was later attacked by Emperor Sennacherib of Assyria in 701 BCE, and Emperor Nebuchadrezzar II of Babylonia destroyed the city in 604. Seafaring Phoenicians then populated the city during the Persian era (539–332 BCE), and their cemetery filled with a thousand dogs (connected to Phoenician healing rites) is on-site. Ashkelon also features the Canaanite Gate, the world's oldest portal. During the Roman era (63 BCE–313 CE), Ashkelon thrived once again as a commercial and agricultural center, and a special onion grown here (the scallion) takes its name from the eponymous city. Today the site is situated in the southwest corner of modern Ashkelon.

15. **Tel Be'ersheva** – An important biblical city, Tel Be'ersheva lies just east of modern Be'ersheva, Israel's fourth-largest city. The site features the Negev Desert's deepest well (226 feet), perhaps the one used by Abraham and Isaac and where Abraham swore an oath to the Philistine ruler King Avimelekh of Gerar and gave him seven ewes, concluding an eponymous pact (in Hebrew, *sheva* denotes both "seven" and "oath"). There is also an elaborate ancient water system, remains of streets, squares, gates, and pools, and an observation tower. In ancient times, Be'ersheva served as a key locus along the regional Derekh HaAvot (The Way of the Patriarchs/Ridge Route) connecting Upper Galilee and the Negev Desert. In WWI, the Ottoman imperial army used the site as a staging ground for attacking the Suez Canal, but it was overcome by ANZAC forces that conquered the site in 1917. The Bedouin town of Tel Sheva is nearby.

16. **Shivta (Sobeita/Sobota)** – Nabateans first settled here around the first century BCE, and developed the site as an important stopover along their overland Incense Route between Oman and Sheba/Himyar (Yemen) in southern Arabia and the Mediterranean ports of Gaza and Rhinokoroura (El-Arish). Named after a common Nabatean first name, Shubitu, Shivta was inherited by Byzantine Christians (some of whom were pagan Nabatean converts) who built impressive churches, houses, gates, wine presses, and other structures atop the lofty summit. Today Shivta also features the remains of a mosque and the Colt Expedition building (now managed as an inn). Below the peak are terraced orchards with various fruit trees.

17. **Nitzanah** – One of the most beautiful sites in Israel, Nitzanah sits near the border of Israel and Egypt (Sinai). Founded in the third century BCE by the Nabateans as a caravan trading post along their overland Incense Route between Oman and Sheba/Himyar (Yemen) in southern Arabia and the Mediterranean ports of Gaza and Rhinokoroura (El-Arish), the ancient tel features Nabatean ruins from the second and/or first centuries BCE, including an impressive monumental staircase leading down from the summit to the remains of churches in the plain below, as well as ruins from the Byzantine era (324–638 CE). A uniquely shaped water tower – a remnant of an Ottoman railroad station built in WWI – lies in the plain, as does a lovely orchard and a monument commemorating the Israel Defense Forces victory against the Egyptian army during Operation Volcano (1955). The modern village of Nitzanah and Nitzanah Forest are nearby.

18. **Hatzeivah (Tamar/Ovot)** – Known as the "Jewel of the Aravah" and situated at an important crossroads, the ancient desert oasis and fortress site features the oldest Israelite four-room house in the country, remains of a Solomonic gate, and what is perhaps the oldest tree in Israel. It also boasts Roman baths, aqueducts, and fortress walls. Hatzeivah later became an outpost serving Ottoman Turks then British expeditionary forces, whose members built an office and a jail on-site. Today Kibbutz Ir Ovot is adjacent to the site and the modern towns of Ein Hatzeivah and Hatzeivah are nearby.

Israel is the ancestral and modern homeland of the Jewish people, and it is also a palimpsest upon which are inscribed the goings and comings and doings of many other peoples who inhabited or traversed the land. Every river, streambed, cave, forest, hill, mountain, valley, and plain holds untold secrets and stories awaiting discovery.

Nitzanah

12
Peripheral Israel

Peripheral Israel

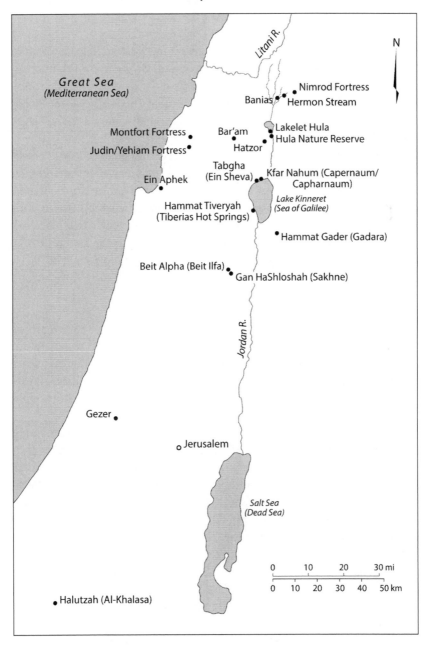

Most modern travelers and tourists who visit the State of Israel keep to the center of the country or to its largest cities (Jerusalem, Tel Aviv, Haifa, Be'ersheva). In so doing, many of the Land of Israel's greatest sites – historical, archaeological, and natural – are overlooked.

In addition, perhaps the worst kept secret in Israel is that the warmest welcome often comes from natives living outside of the main urban areas, inhabiting instead the kibbutzim, moshavim, and villages scattered around every peripheral region such as the Golan, Galilee, the Jordan River Valley, the Sharon Plain, the Shephelah foothills, the Aravah Valley, and the Negev Desert.

Visitors to Israel who cleave to the luxuries of the great indoors (hotels, museums, art galleries, fine dining restaurants) would do well to expand their comfort zones. Those for whom Israel evokes images and memories of the Kotel, the Church of the Holy Sepulcher, the Knesset, the Israel Museum, the beaches of Tel Aviv, the Mamilla or Azrieli shopping malls, the Mahaneh Yehudah and Kharmel markets, and the Baha'i Gardens will doubtless be surprised to learn how much of the country remains to be discovered.

Here is a sample of what awaits the intrepid who dare to venture beyond the beaten track.

1. **Ein Aphek** – There are several historical sites named Aphek in the Land of Israel; this one lies in Galilee between Haifa and Akko, not far from the town of Kiryat Motzkin, and features both a beautiful nature reserve with a police station from the British Mandatory period (1920–1948 CE) and an adjacent tel dating to the Canaanite era (second millennium BCE).

2. **Judin/Yehiam Fortress** – Judin is a ruined crusader bastion built atop the remnants of a Roman fort and a Byzantine structure. It is conveniently attached to Kibbutz Yehiam, and is a national park called Yehiam Fortress in honor of the fallen Palmah soldier Yehiam Weitz, killed in action nearby around the Akhziv bridge during the British Mandatory period (1920–1948 CE).

3. **Montfort Fortress** – One of the trickiest sites in the country to locate unless you happen to hike the Kziv Stream in Upper Galilee. Situated northeast of Nahariyah and just south of the expansive Goren Park (the easiest way to reach it is from the moshav Goren, heading south and downward to the stream then up the ruined hilltop), Montfort is a stunning and haunting crusader site that leaves an indelible impression. It is also accessible to trekkers of a red hiking trail (not for the faint of heart).

4. **Bar'am** – Bar'am was a Jewish town during the Roman era (63 BCE–313 CE), and today is a national park that features an ancient synagogue and a modern Maronite church, both of which remain in use for special events. The tombs of the prophet Ovadiah and of the Babylonian amora Mar Zutra (former head of the Pumbedita academy) are nearby.

5. **Hermon Stream** – Trickling down from Mount Hermon into a spring and forming part of the headwaters of the Jordan River, Hermon Stream is a stunning nature reserve that also features archaeological ruins of the pagan city of Paneas (Caesarea Philippi/Neronias/Banias) and of the Herodian ruler King Agrippa II's luxurious palace, as well as crusader ruins. Hiking the trail alongside the streambed is a peaceful pleasure suitable for all.

6. **Banias** – The nearby city of Paneas was pronounced "Banias" by the Arabs, and the name was applied to the proximate 10-foot waterfall that cascades into a large pool. Banias is part of a nature reserve and also features a suspended trail through a narrow basalt canyon above rushing waters. Kibbutz Snir and an SPNI field school are located in the vicinity.

7. **Nimrod Fortress** – Northeast of Hermon Stream lie impressive ruins on the slopes of Mount Hermon, vestiges of the Ayyubid fortress named Nimrod after the biblical hunter who also features in Muslim lore. Built in 1227 CE, it resisted the crusaders, fell to the Mongols, and was reconstructed by Sultan Baybars of the Mameluke Sultanate of Egypt, whose regal leonine emblem is depicted at the site in a stone sculpture.

8. **Lakelet Hula** – An *agamon* in Hebrew, the picturesque lakelet is situated in the Hula Valley, which divides northern Galilee's Naphtali Mountains to the west from the Golan to the east. Visitors can rent bicycles or golf carts to tour the area and behold some of the migratory birds, numbering in the hundreds of millions, which use the area as an ideal pit-stop en route to and from Africa every year. The site is currently managed by Keren Kayemet L'Yisrael-Jewish National Fund (KKL-JNF) and includes a Bird Sanctuary and Education Center named after Stephen Harper, former prime minister of Canada.

9. **Hula Nature Reserve** – A short distance south of Lakelet Hula is the Hula Valley's official nature reserve, where visitors can climb a wooden observation tower and walk along a furtive hideaway overlooking lush swampland and a serene pond. Mallards, swamp turtles, African

catfish, water buffaloes, squacco herons, great cormorants, and pelicans all call the area home.

10. **Hatzor** – A key locus along the ancient Derekh HaYam (The Way of the Sea/Coastal Highway) international trade route connecting Egypt and Syria, and also along the regional Derekh HaAvot (The Way of the Patriarchs/Ridge Route) connecting Upper Galilee and the Negev Desert. Once commanded by King Yavin of Hatzor and subsequently conquered by Joshua, Hatzor became one of King Solomon's three regional administrative cities, along with Gezer and Megiddo; whoever controlled these three strategic fortresses was master of the Land of Israel. In the plain of Hatzor the Hasmonean leader Jonathan Maccabee won a victory against Emperor Demetrius II Nicator of Syria. Hatzor today is a national park whose tel includes a temple, a tower, and an underground water system dating to the Canaanite era (second millennium BCE) and to King Ahab of Israel (r. 874–853 BCE). The site features an upper and a lower city and is located near Kibbutz Ayelet HaShahar, among the largest kibbutzim in Israel.

11. **Kfar Nahum (Capernaum/Capharnaum)** – Once a station along the ancient Derekh HaYam (The Way of the Sea/Coastal Highway) international trade route connecting Egypt and Syria, Nahum's village experienced renewed importance with the advent of Christianity, whose Jewish founder Jesus of Nazareth moved here from Nazareth to preach to his disciples on the shore of Lake Kinneret (the Sea of Galilee). The Jewish village had several synagogues, and the remains of the ornate White Synagogue can be seen today alongside churches ancient and modern associated with the apostle Peter. Archaeological ruins are displayed outdoors, giving a sense of the ancient site's grandeur. Today the site is managed by Franciscans who charge a nominal fee.

12. **Tabgha (Ein Sheva)** – Close to Kfar Nahum (Capernaum/Capharnaum) is Tabgha (a corruption of the Greek name Heptapegon), also known as Ein Sheva in Hebrew for its seven springs. Important to Christians as the site of the multiplication of bread loaves and fish, and for the Sermon on the Mount that took place on the nearby Mount of Beatitudes, Tabgha today features Franciscan churches and monasteries including the Church of the Primacy. By the shoreline lies the lovely Ein Iyov mini waterfall, a perfect place to relax and enjoy views of Lake Kinneret (the Sea of Galilee).

13. **Hammat Tiveryah (Tiberias Hot Springs)** – Located at the southern end of the city of Tiberias, the hot springs of the ancient town of

Hammat – which merged with Tiberias during the Roman era (63 BCE–313 CE) – were frequented by the sages of the Mishnah and the Talmud and the site, today a national park, sits immediately below the tomb of the revered sage Meir Ba'al HaNeis. The ancient Derekh HaYam (The Way of the Sea/Coastal Highway) international trade route connecting Egypt and Syria ran nearby. The site features remnants of several synagogues, including one whose magnificent mosaic floor is the earliest ever found in Israel, as well as a wading pool and a channel, steam chimneys, remains of a Roman bathhouse, and the Muslim spa Hammam Suleiman.

14. **Hammat Gader (Gadara)** – Located in the southern end of the Golan, southeast of Lake Kinneret (the Sea of Galilee), Gadara's natural hot springs were frequented by Talmudic sages and today attract Israelis from all walks of life. Unfortunately, the site is currently commercialized to a large extent, and instead of being an official nature reserve with a standard and nominal conservation fee, it has been developed as an attraction with a steep admission fee. Towels are not provided as part of the admission fee either, so be sure to bring your own.

15. **Gan HaShloshah (Sakhne)** – Widely considered the most beautiful natural site in Israel, Gan HaShloshah (named after three Jewish pioneers who died in 1938) lies just north of the Gilboa mountain range, near Kibbutz Nir David and the Beit She'an Valley. The water park features underground springs, waterfalls, a tower-and-stockade, an ancient flour mill, an archaeology museum, and picnic areas. Beware the tiny fish that nibble your skin as soon as you enter the warm water.

16. **Beit Alpha (Beit Ilfa)** – Situated on Kibbutz Hephtzibah at the foot of the Gilboa mountain range, this national park features an ancient synagogue with a genizah archive and a marvelous mosaic floor, dating to the second half of the Byzantine era (324–638 CE). A short film exhibited inside the site portrays the synagogue and village in their heyday and a model of the synagogue is displayed just outside.

17. **Halutzah (Al-Khalasa)** – One of the Negev's Nabatean towns, Halutzah later became a Byzantine settlement. There are many well-preserved structures and a deep well, and in every direction are more ruins, attesting to the impressive extent of the ancient site. Unfortunately, Israel has not yet fully prepared the site for visitors; it merits national park status, but there has been relatively limited excavation and trail demarcation and the notable absence of signage

both at the site and on the road thereto makes visiting challenging. There is great hiking to be had along the nearby Nahal Bsor. Halutzah is fairly close to the artful Kibbutz Mashabei Sadeh.

18. **Gezer** – About 5 miles southwest of Modi'in, Gezer is a national park featuring a tel dating to the Canaanite era (second millennium BCE). Gezer was one of King Solomon's regional administrative cities, along with Hatzor and Megiddo; whoever controlled these three strategic fortresses was master of the Land of Israel. The site features a three-stage Solomonic gate, an underground water system, a series of 10 megaliths (*matzeivot*), and three distinct observation points with panoramic views of Modi'in, Tel Aviv, Rosh Pinah, Ashdod, and Ashkelon. Gezer is close to the village Karmei Yosef, the moshav Kfar Bin Nun, and Kibbutz Sha'alvim.

The aforementioned loci constitute only a sample of the many fascinating and breathtaking places Israel has to offer, all of which are seemingly but not actually far away from frequented hubs. With the affordability of car rentals, the many routes offered by the several bus companies, and the burgeoning train network of Israel Railways – not to mention the various hiking trails for committed trekkers and campers – there is little excuse for not getting around and expanding one's sightseeing horizons. To be sure, certain of the less frequented sites require alertness and caution due to their present lack of amenities or demanding terrain, but those adventurous and well prepared will be duly rewarded for their willingness to explore.

Nimrod Fortress

Appendix 1

Davidic Israel

Davidic Israel

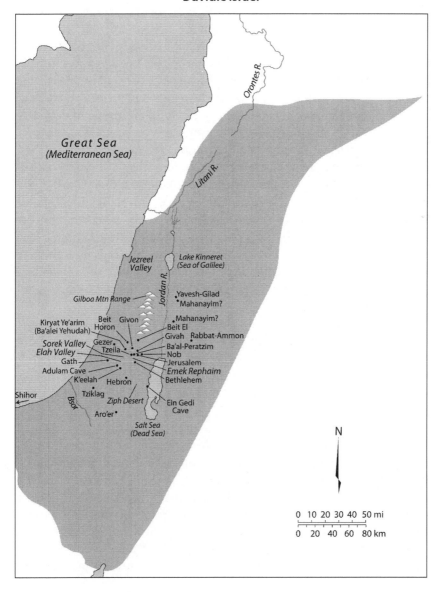

Great Sea
(Mediterranean Sea)

Orontes R.

Litani R.

Jezreel
Valley

*Lake Kinneret
(Sea of Galilee)*

Jordan R.

Gilboa Mtn Range

•Yavesh-Gilad
•Mahanayim?

Kiryat Ye'arim
(Ba'alei Yehudah)

Beit   Givon
Horon

•Mahanayim?

•Beit El

Givah   Rabbat-Ammon

Sorek Valley Gezer•
Elah Valley   Tzeila•

•Ba'al-Peratzim
•Nob

Gath

•Jerusalem

Adulam Cave

Emek Rephaim
•Bethlehem

K'eelah   Hebron•

Shihor

Tziklag•   *Ziph Desert*

•Ein Gedi
Cave

Bsor

Aro'er•

*Salt Sea
(Dead Sea)*

N

0 10 20 30 40 50 mi

0   20   40   60   80 km

Glorified and vilified has been his name, his admirers lauding his historic achievements and messianic legacy, his detractors portraying him as an ambitious warlord or denying his existence.

Perhaps it could not be otherwise, for the pedestaled are so often the vandalized.

To the traditional Jew, King David of Israel (r. 1010–970 BCE) remains exemplary if imperfect, a lionized hero who ushered in the halcyon days of the Jewish people and consolidated a Judaic state under divine law (theonomocracy). He consulted divine prophets – Samuel, Gad, Nathan – as well as the people. He solidified the tenuous reunion of Israelite tribes. He conquered and built up his new capital of Jerusalem as Israel's political and religious center. He brought up the Ark of the Testimony (Ark of the Covenant) to Jerusalem and housed it in a special tent. He acquired Mount Moriah and erected an altar of sacrifice thereon. He drew up plans for the Temple and helped organize the priestly courses for service therein. He is the progenitor of the King Messiah, a worldly scion who is to eventually bring unprecedented peace and prosperity to Jewry and to the world entire. By any measure, such momentous accomplishments bespeak a successful and distinguished sovereign.

So why do others view David so differently?

The short answer is that the Tanakh (Hebrew Bible) limns David not as an immaculate monarch but as a flawed mortal of flesh and blood. It does not expurgate the historical record or bowdlerize the scriptural tale, the reason being to impart important morals from both the good and the bad.

In recent memory, tendentious academics and authors have bandied about the fanciful notion that the entire Torah was but a prelude to his rule; actually, David's silver era was a stepping stone to Solomon's golden age. By overstating David's significance, which needs no embellishment whatever, and by concurrently traducing his personality and deeds, modern detractors thereby discredit the virtue and value of the Tanakh and ultimately seek to disgrace the deity that somehow found a despicable David, scripture's culminating figure, lovable.

Such disparate views and agendas invite a fresh look at what lessons David has to offer us today.

Sweet Singer, Smooth Slinger

We first encounter David ben Yishai (1040–970 BCE) as the runt of the litter, a ruddy shepherd from Bethlehem dripping beneath the oil horn.[1]

He soon turns musical therapist, strumming to soothe the gloom of moody King Saul. He is also made the royal armiger.[2]

His talent as a harper is disremembered by the king, however, when in the Elah Valley David volunteers to oppose the vulgar braggart Goliath of Gath, a Philistine giant taunting the Israelites.[3] David's youth and genteel manner belie his martial skills: already as a herder he has killed lions and bears menacing his lambs. He loads his scrip with five smooth stones from the stream, with his staff his feint, his sling ready at hand, his foe little more than a large target to be felled by a precise projectile.

David steps up; Goliath goes down.

Promoted to captain of a thousand, David leads his soldiers in and out of battle. He leads from the front and earns widespread fame for slaying myriads. His invidious exploits irk the king; Saul seeks to have the Philistines eliminate David (as David would later seek to have the Ammonites eliminate Uriyah the Hittite), but with divine aid David bests the Philistines every time. After repeatedly failing to impale David in the royal palace, Saul dispatches assassins to murder him in his bed.[4]

The narrative at this juncture includes a detail often overlooked: once David defenestrates himself and flees, his wife (and Saul's daughter) Mikhal places a teraphim, a household idol, in bed and bedecks it with a goatskin and garments.[5] David is gone by the time she replaces his figure with an idol that would have had to have been life-size in order for it to have been plausible as an adult male. Is it possible that David was unaware of his wife's idolatry? Yes, though highly improbable. These were not little trinkets tucked away in a pouch or a drawer; this would have been a sizable statue. The ineluctable implication is that David, the hero blessed with divine favor, has been condoning idolatry within the very confines of his own home. He will have to, and will have the chance to, make amends for this going forward.

Fugitive and Outlaw

Expert with instruments, David proves equally adept at playing other people, including Ahimelekh ben Ahituv, the high priest at Nob, from whom he wheedles showbread and Goliath's sword, and King Akhish of Gath, a gulled rube who falls for David's feigned madness and from whom David wangles the town of Tziklag.[6]

But first he flees to the Adulam Cave, which he transforms into a stronghold and where he accumulates about him 400 malcontents, as well as the prophet Gad. He rescues the town of K'eelah from the Philistines before escaping with an enlarged force of 600 fighters. He roams as a vagabond and as an occasional brigand from desert to forest to cave, a relentless Saul ever at his heels.[7]

Saul falls into David's grasp while relieving himself in the Ein Gedi Cave; David spares his life, and merely severs the hem of Saul's coat (which he soon regrets).[8] He does likewise when he creeps into Saul's soporific encampment in the Ziph Desert but restrains his men from slaying the king and only takes Saul's spear and water cruse.[9] No matter how convenient or expedient, he staunchly refuses to stretch forth his hand against the Lord's anointed. As another of the Lord's anointed, David abhors regicide and astutely avoids setting an imprudent precedent.

Forced to return to Philistia, he bases himself in Tziklag and raids Amalekites and other small groups, misleading Akhish into believing he has been assailing his own tribe of Judah.[10] Notably, many archers and slingers from Saul's own tribe of Benjamin defect to David, specialists Saul sorely lacks in battle at the Gilboa mountain range.[11]

When soon it comes time to square off against the Israelites in the Jezreel Valley, the other Philistine lords and officers disdain the presence of Israelites among their camp, understandably fearing betrayal and an ambuscade by the young Judahite champion who had so often routed them in the past.[12] As he pled his innocence variously before his brother Eliav, then King Saul, then Jonathan, David likewise protests before his patron Akhish to no avail, returning to Tziklag only to find it burned by opportunistic Amalekites, who carried off its women and children in David's absence.[13]

This marks a perilous low point for David: his men speak openly about stoning him, but he avoids lapidation and takes strength in his faith. He pulls himself together and pursues. He leaves 200 fighters by Nahal Bsor to guard the baggage, and with the remaining 400 locates and routs the Amalekite bandits, recovering all and sundry. He rules equitably that soldiers on the front lines and those guarding the baggage share the spoils of victory.[14]

Now David the budding politician also spreads the spoils to his tribe of Judah, from Hebron to Beit El to Aro'er, all the haunts his roving band has frequented.[15] The spoils presented serve doubly as emoluments for the past, blandishments for the future.

With Saul slain at Gilboa – beheaded like Goliath, impaled as he meant to impale David – the path to monarchy lies open to David, who moves from Tziklag to Hebron to meet the moment.[16]

King of Judah

For the second time in his life, David is anointed, this time as king of Judah by his fellow Judahites. But his ascension is mirrored by that of Ish-Boshet, instated as king of Israel in Mahanayim – near the border of Gad and eastern Menasheh, and the Transjordanian counter-capital for Hebrew monarchs – by his kinsman and strongman Avner ben Ner.[17]

The initial clash at the Givon pool results in a rout: David loses 20 men, Ish-Boshet 360.[18] The House of Saul is in free fall, yet the statesman David seeks a negotiated solution to the rivalry. He knows the tribes of Israel require unification, and that this vital undertaking would be best done diplomatically and peacefully. And when his refractory nephew and general Yo'av nixes his tactful efforts by murdering Avner, David publicly abjures the bloody deed and humbles Yo'av.[19]

King of Israel

For the third and final time in his life, David is anointed, this time as king of Israel in Hebron, by all the elders of Israel; he has reigned seven and a half years in Hebron (1010–1003 BCE), and will go on to reign another 33 years in Jerusalem (1003–970 BCE).[20] His primary concern is to establish a new capital in the center of the country, in tribally neutral territory: he conquers Jerusalem, a central locus along the regional Derekh HaAvot (The Way of the Patriarchs/Ridge Route) connecting Upper Galilee and the Negev Desert, and at the time a Jebusite site, whose citadel of Zion he renames the City of David. He has a royal palace constructed of cedar, marries more women who bear him more children, and firmly establishes the House of David.[21]

Hitherto the Philistines regarded David as a loyal vassal, but his ambitious and bold moves to establish his kingship and kingdom disabuse the Philistines of their delusion. Additionally, the Jebusite enclave of Jerusalem at this time was perhaps under Philistine protection, in which case David's conquest of Jerusalem decisively signals his overthrow of Philistine suzerainty, which in turn triggers the Philistines' invasion of Israel at the outset of David's reign. Likely ascending from the south along the Sorek Valley, the Philistines advance into Emek Rephaim on the outskirts of Jerusalem and David meets them at Ba'al-Peratzim, where he roundly defeats them and puts them to flight. In their hasty escape, the Philistines abandon their sacred images, affording David the chance to rectify a mistake of the past. He makes sure to burn the images, evincing an intolerance for pagan idolatry that he previously lacked with respect to Mikhal's teraphim. Likely descending from the north by way of Beit Horon, the Philistines again attempt to dethrone David, who repels them anew at Emek Rephaim and strikes down the enemy from Givah (or Givon) to Gezer,[22] indicating that the Philistines' tactical intention had been to divide the tribal territories of Benjamin and Ephraim from Judah in the hope of preventing David from ruling all of Israel.

Repatriating the Ark of the Testimony

Having finally abrogated the longstanding Philistine peril, David refocuses on statecraft and strategically decides to concentrate the national symbols in Jerusalem. Before doing so, he confers with officers from all Israelite tribes and proposes to gather the priests, Levites, and all Israel to collectively retrieve the Ark of the Testimony from Kiryat Ye'arim (Ba'alei Yehudah). He makes a cogent case, and his prerogative is ratified: "And all the congregation said to do so, because the matter was deemed proper by the whole nation."[23] Accompanied by melodious song and the music of harps, psalteries, sistra, cymbals, timbrels, trumpets, and shofars, David and the entire assembly convey the Ark (first by ox-drawn cart, a grave misstep David emends by having the Ark shouldered with staves by the priests) to Jerusalem, where David pitches a tent to shelter it. It is a scene of unity and triumph.[24]

Hell Hath No Fury

The elation is marred by an embittered Mikhal, who mocks David's exhibitionism and is sharply rebuked and spurned by him.[25] He is right to reprove her, but wrong to be so severe to the woman who once saved his life. He has become insensitive and forgotten his lifelong debt of gratitude.

David's character recovers when he soon becomes alive to the incongruity of his living arrangements compared to the Ark's accommodations, and yearns to build a solid structure for God just as he himself dwells in a permanent abode. Appreciating the king's good intentions, Nathan the prophet speaks out of turn: "All that is in your heart, go do; for the Lord is with you."[26] That very night Nathan is divinely enlightened, however, and forced to relate to David that not he but his scion will erect the sacred edifice.[27]

David reduces, one after another, the Philistines, Moabites, Arameans, Ammonites, Amalekites, and Edomites. He amasses booty from his conquests and tribute from his allies, dedicating all of it to God and reserving it for sacred purposes.[28] Most important, "David reigned over all Israel; and David administered justice and charity for all his people."[29]

Now David initiates another opportunity to make amends for erstwhile errors: he shows kindness to Mephiboshet, the lame son of the late Jonathan, in gratitude for Jonathan's friendship and fidelity.[30] Though he shuns Mikhal, he still recalls the goodness he received from the House of Saul. In gratitude mode, he even extends his goodwill to his Ammonite neighbors as repayment for the support shown him by the recently deceased King Nahash of Ammon.[31]

Here is David at his apex: regal but responsible, triumphant yet munificent. He has succeeded and can afford to dispense the victor's largesse.

Moral Nadir

As if to underscore the contrast, nadir follows zenith: David plummets to his moral depths in his ill-conceived affair with Bat-sheva. It was the season wherein kings ventured forth into battle,[32] yet he inexplicably tarried in Jerusalem, roaming his palace, surveying the views. Was this not an abdication of leadership and royal duty? In a similar vein, Saul previously went out to battle in the Elah Valley yet noticeably refrained from challenging Goliath, leaving that daunting responsibility to a stripling shepherd who went on to usurp Saul's kingship while the latter was still on the payroll.

In Israelite society, kingship (as opposed to priesthood or prophethood) was the political-military leadership role. David in particular was famed as a valorous warrior. But now, in the Battle of Rabbat-Ammon, the captain who had always led his soldiers in and out of war was AWOL. Public failure set the stage for private failure, and things spiraled downward thence until the cuckolded Uriyah was consigned to the clutches of the Ammonites.

Exegetical attempts to mitigate David's sins never avail, for they would legitimate the illegitimate. It matters not that Uriyah may well have granted Bat-sheva a conditional divorce writ (*get*), since this was a routine formality for Israelite soldiers heading into battle and not meant to make wives a prey to prowling rivals. Nor is it ultimately germane that Bat-sheva might have intentionally exposed David to her charms for her own purposes. Nor that Uriyah incurred a measure of guilt by disobeying the royal command to go home to his wife. Unlike Joseph in Potiphar's house, David apparently never inquired, "Now how can I commit this great evil, and sin against God?"[33]

Instead, he took possession then murdered, as later King Ahab of Israel would murder then take possession.[34]

David's wrongdoing was unmistakable and inexcusable. It was an egregious abuse of power, the calculated manipulation of an autocrat. It was a betrayal of divine law, of David's unswervingly loyal warrior Uriyah, of David's better self. Israel's monarch was not yet sovereign over his animal impulses…and he well knew it.

The parable, Nathan's approach to reproach, educes David's candor: "I have sinned against the Lord."[35]

He is repaid for his pitilessness with the decease of his illicit child with Bat-sheva.[36] Yet David also wronged the nation, especially its soldiery, by not leading Israel's campaign against Ammon. He now remedies this negligence by joining Yo'av and the army in the field at Rabbat-Ammon, where he assumes command of the siege and promptly completes the conquest.[37]

The Princely Pretender (#1)

Guilty himself of carnal misconduct, David cannot have been surprised, or at least cannot have felt blameless, when his firstborn Amnon rapes his half-sister Tamar, nor when her full brother Avshalom then slays Amnon in revenge and flees Jerusalem.[38] In time David and Avshalom reconcile, but Avshalom has not yet avenged David's tolerance of Amnon's perfidies. In Avshalom's eyes, David is a failure as a father and as a king, and has thereby forfeited his right to rule. Rebellion ensues.

Resorting to self-imposed exile, David vacates Jerusalem and heads for the counter-capital, Mahanayim. On his way out, he is accompanied by the high priest Tzadok and by Levites bearing the Ark of the Testimony. David confirms that he has learned to place the national interest before his own interests by refusing to abscond with the preeminent Israelite symbol and insisting it remain where it belongs, in the national capital. He entrusts his destiny to God, submitting to Providence.[39]

Once again David is a man on the run, the kingdom of Israel hanging in the balance until Avshalom hangs suspended between heaven and earth, his head (not necessarily his hair) stuck in the thick boughs of a great terebinth, dangling precariously when his cousin Yo'av and his armigers deliver the quietus,[40] flouting David's explicit injunction to deal gently with the youthful prince.[41]

David prefers to resume his kingship in Jerusalem at the invitation of the tribes, especially of his own tribe, Judah, which hosted Avshalom in

Hebron and which was heavily implicated in the revolt. This tactic proves savvy when Judah and the other tribes squabble over who has the greater investment in the House of David and the right to escort the king home. The Judahites make up for their disloyalty to David with a restitution of their own by staunchly backing him in the short-lived, follow-up revolt of Sheva ben Bikhri.[42]

Political Reparations

Next, a three-year famine afflicts the kingdom. When the Givonites, an Amorite clan formerly targeted by an overzealous Saul, tell David that they would exact retribution against seven descendants of the House of Saul, David agrees to expiate Saul's wrongdoing and delivers up the descendants. The men are hanged until dead, but David spares the lame Mephiboshet on account of his covenant with Jonathan.[43]

This fidelity is mirrored by that of the grieving Ritzpah, originally Saul's concubine and most recently Avner's lover, which impels a moved David to right another wrong long overlooked: he has the remains of Saul and Jonathan exhumed from Yavesh-Gilad in Gad (in central Transjordan) and reinterred in the Benjaminite town of Tzeila, even inside the sepulcher of Kish, Saul's father.[44] Once again David demonstrates that he is the settler of accounts par excellence.

The Enumeration Violation

In ancient Israel, counting the people was taboo due to the divine promise to Abram: "And I will make your seed like the dust of the earth, so that if a man will be able to count the dust of the earth, so will your seed be counted."[45]

Prompted either by an angered God[46] or by Satan,[47] David orders a reluctant Yo'av to conduct a census to register all arms-bearing men in Israel. Nearly 10 months later, Yo'av returns with the lofty figure of 1,100,000 fighters, 470,000 of them Judahites, the total excepting the Levites and the Benjaminites whom Yo'av declined to count.[48]

David soon regrets his census: "I have sinned greatly in what I have done; and now, Lord, please set aside the iniquity of your servant, for I was very foolish!"[49] Gad the seer presents him with a selection of punishments, of which a three-day pestilence seems most mild. But the heavy toll the plague takes stirs the shepherd in David, who entreats God for mercy on his flock's behalf: "Behold I have sinned, and have acted iniquitously; but these sheep, what have they done? I beg that Your hand be against me, and against my father's house."[50] He purchases King Aravnah the Jebusite's threshing floor atop Mount Zion, erects an altar, and sacrifices to God, stopping the plague.[51]

Leaving a Legacy

As a visionary, David perceives the grand labor that lies ahead for his heir and determines to lay the groundwork for his successor: "And David prepared in abundance before his decease."[52] He sedulously procures gold, silver, stone, iron, brass, and cedar for use in the future Temple. He enlists workmen for the construction: hewers, stonemasons, carpenters, smiths, and artisans.[53] He numbers the mature Levites and divides them into courses rotating to perform the elaborate Temple service.[54]

But exactly who among the many princes is to reign in his stead?

On this crucial point, God, via His spokesman Nathan the prophet, elided the detail: "I will raise up your seed that shall proceed from your body after you, and I will establish his kingdom. He shall build a house for My name, and I will establish the throne of his kingdom forever."[55]

The Princely Pretender (#2)

David had not disciplined his son Adoniyah any more than he had his sons Avshalom or Amnon, thus Adoniyah as the eldest living prince believes himself the heir apparent. Adoniyah enlists Yo'av and Evyatar the high priest to his cause. But David has learned his lesson. Once apprised by Bat-sheva and Nathan of the embryonic rebellion, David moves quickly to nip it in the bud: he orders the other high priest Tzadok, Nathan, and Benaiah the captain of the royal guard to appear before him, to have his true scion Solomon ride his own mule, and to anoint Solomon at the Gihon spring.[56] David thereby secures the succession while yet alive. He pronounces the little-known but remarkably gracious and magnanimous Outgoing Ruler's Benison:

"Blessed be the Lord, God of Israel, who has today enthroned another in my stead before my own eyes."[57]

Solomon Set Up for Success

With Solomon confirmed as heir, David repeatedly exhorts him to "be strong and of good courage";[58] "arise and do, and may the Lord be with you";[59] "be strong and do it";[60] and "be strong and of good courage and do; do not fear and be not dismayed".[61] He adjures his ministers to assist Solomon in his endeavors. He provides Solomon with divinely devised blueprints for the Temple structures, chambers, treasuries, courts, and vessels.[62] And he leads by example in donating from his personal fortune to the future Temple before soliciting contributions from all the assembled leaders of Israel, who heed his precedent and generously follow suit.[63]

Here David shrewdly rehearses the communal construction of the Tabernacle during the Exodus from Egypt (c. 1313–1273 BCE),[64] which united the Israelite tribes then just as popular participation does now: "And the people rejoiced over their donation, for they wholeheartedly donated to the Lord, and King David also rejoiced a great rejoicing."[65]

David is doing what the finest of historic achievers do: he not only sets up for success his successor, but encourages his replacement to surpass him. Just as David once outdid Saul, slaying myriads compared to thousands, now it is David's turn to be exceeded. Whereas David has perforce been a warrior, Solomon is to be a man of rest and peace. Whereas David recovered the Ark and housed it in a tent, he charges Solomon to "arise and build the Sanctuary of the Lord God to bring the Ark of the Covenant of the Lord and the holy vessels of God to the House that is to be built in the name of the Lord."[66] Like Moses, David can take things only so far; it falls to another to go the distance.

The Great and the Humble

In blessing God before Solomon and the assembled leaders of Israel, David exemplifies the modesty and clarity essential for the high and mighty, lest they lose perspective and arrogate the credit for their prosperity: "Yours is the kingdom and [You are He] who is exalted over everything as the leader."[67] He downplays their own virtue as benevolent donors by highlighting the simple truth of the matter: "for all is from You, and from Your hand we have given it to You. [...] ...all this store that we have prepared to build for You a House for Your holy Name – it is from You, and all is Yours."[68] On the morrow, Solomon is anointed and crowned a second time by the leaders, who, along with the champions and princes of Israel, subordinate themselves to his authority.[69]

David wants Solomon, young and tender, to have an easier reign, unencumbered by insurrections. Captious critics aver that David on his deathbed bequeathed to Solomon a hit list, attesting to the bloody warlord version of David. This is a shallow misreading obscuring what David is in fact doing, namely, ensuring the peace and security of Solomon's rule, which otherwise would be seriously jeopardized by the chronically bloodthirsty and disobedient Yo'av and by the contemptuous traitor Shimei ben Geira. David counsels Solomon to dispense with these lingering dangers not due to any vendetta, but for the sake of the stability of the United Monarchy of Israel (1030–931 BCE).

It transpires that David, far from turning Solomon into a vengeful tyrant, is validated after his decease. Solomon initially pardons not only his elder brother Adoniyah but the seditious Shimei as well, until both overstep their bounds and prove unworthy of clemency. Solomon also pardons but deposes the high priest Evyatar for imprudently siding with Adoniyah; in sharp contrast to Saul, who without scruples slew Evyatar's father Ahimelekh ben Ahituv and all the priestly inhabitants of Nob, King Solomon proves unwilling to put to death a holy priest, even one implicated in treason.

A Unitary Perspective

The eminent Talmudic sage Abbahu taught: "Where penitents stand, even the wholly righteous do not stand."[70]

In his 70 eventful years, David made a series of serious mistakes. They cost him and his family dearly. They cost the nation of Israel dearly. The height of his virtue consisted of his abilities to reckon forthrightly with his actions and their consequences and to recommit himself to righteous living. He never altered his values, even when he fell short of adhering to them.

David was an accomplished sinner, but the consummate penitent. In this he took after his tribal forebear Judah, the Tanakh's original atoner.

David was never in love with sinning, never abnegated God, never denied his failings or shifted blame onto others. He was willing to be accountable for his conduct and to edify his character.

Although not a pristine paragon of rectitude, David was nonetheless a great man: his martial feats were great, his moral defeats were great. He was chastened by conscience and motivated by equity. His military prowess facilitated Solomon's irenic reign; his foresight laid the foundation for the Temple.

His subservience to divine sovereignty was total. Unlike his aggrandized neighbors in Egypt and in Mesopotamia, he never deified himself or gloried in his achievements. He knew full well to whom his unlikely rise from sheepcote to royal palace was due, and whom he must always exalt and extol. He gave credit where credit was due.

Tendentious detractors intent on eisegesis will find it facile to depict David in a negative light using the biblical material, which presents a much-blemished personage. But sound exegesis – not to mention accuracy and fairness – demands that David be considered holistically, in the entirety of his character and acts. He is a figure not defined by his flaws, but by his continuous commitment to overcome them. Those who study David's model are unlikely either to attain his heights or to plunge to his depths, but nonetheless have much to glean from his dappled paradigm.

Notes

1. *I Samuel* 16:12-13
2. ibid. 16:12-23. David's narrative is related in the biblical books of *Samuel*, *I Kings*, and *I Chronicles*.
3. ibid. 17
4. ibid. 19:11
5. ibid. 19:13-16
6. ibid. 21
7. ibid. 22-23
8. ibid. 24:4-8
9. ibid. 26:6-12
10. ibid. 27:5-12
11. *I Chronicles* 12:1-2, 16, 29; Cf. *I Samuel* 31:3
12. *I Samuel* 29
13. ibid. 30:1-5
14. ibid. 30:6-25
15. ibid. 30:26-31
16. ibid. 31:4-7; *II Samuel* 2:1-3
17. *II Samuel* 2:4-11
18. ibid. 2:30-31
19. ibid. 3:27-39
20. ibid. 5:3-5
21. ibid. 5:6-16
22. ibid. 5:17-25; almost verbatim in *I Chronicles* 14:8-16, where David strikes down the Philistines from Givon, not Givah, to Gezer.
23. *I Chronicles* 13:4
24. *II Samuel* 6:2-19; *I Chronicles* 13, 15
25. *II Samuel* 6:16, 20-23; *I Chronicles* 15:29
26. *II Samuel* 7:3; almost verbatim in *I Chronicles* 17:2
27. *II Samuel* 7:4-17; *I Chronicles* 17:3-15
28. *II Samuel* 8:1-14; *I Chronicles* 18:1-13

29. *II Samuel* 8:15; almost verbatim in *I Chronicles* 18:14
30. *II Samuel* 9
31. ibid. 10:1-2; *I Chronicles* 19:1-2
32. *II Samuel* 11:1; *I Chronicles* 20:1
33. *Genesis* 39:9
34. *I Kings* 21
35. *II Samuel* 12:13
36. ibid. 12:14-19
37. ibid. 12:29-30
38. ibid. 13
39. ibid. 15:24-29
40. ibid. 18:14-15
41. ibid. 18:5
42. ibid. 19:12-16, 41-44; 20:1-22
43. ibid. 21:1-7
44. ibid. 21:8-14
45. *Genesis* 13:16
46. *II Samuel* 24:1
47. *I Chronicles* 21:1
48. ibid. 21:5-6. *II Samuel* 24:2-9 gives the figures 800,000 fighters, 500,000 Judahites.
49. *II Samuel* 24:10; almost verbatim in *I Chronicles* 21:8
50. *II Samuel* 24:17; almost verbatim in *I Chronicles* 21:17
51. *II Samuel* 24:18-25, citing 50 silver shekels as the price paid; Cf. *I Chronicles* 21:18-28, citing 600 gold shekels paid.
52. *I Chronicles* 22:5
53. ibid. 22:2-4, 14-16; 29:2
54. ibid. 23-26, 28:13
55. *II Samuel* 7:12-13; almost verbatim in *I Chronicles* 17:11-12
56. *I Kings* 1:32-40
57. ibid. 1:48
58. *I Chronicles* 22:13
59. ibid. 22:16
60. ibid. 28:10
61. ibid. 28:20
62. ibid. 28:11-19
63. ibid. 29:3-9
64. *Exodus* 25-31, 35-39
65. *I Chronicles* 29:9
66. ibid. 22:19
67. ibid. 29:11
68. ibid. 29:14-16
69. ibid. 29:22-24
70. BT *Brakhot* 34b

Gezer

Appendix 2

Solomonic Israel

Solomonic Israel

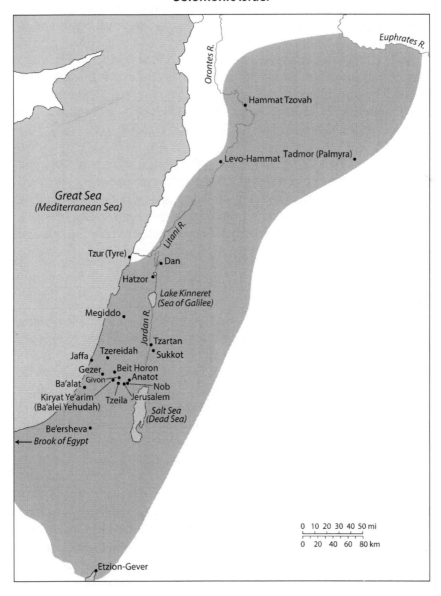

Set up for success by his father King David, King Solomon of Israel (r. 970–931 BCE), also known as Yedidyah and as Kohelet, came into possession of a prosperous realm at a very early age, 12 or 13 according to rabbinical tradition. He married, perhaps for the first time, also at a tender age, while David was yet alive,[1] and would go on to marry 700 royal wives and to maintain 300 concubines.[2]

Jewish tradition ascribes to Solomon the biblical works *Shir HaShirim* (*Song of Songs*), *Mishlei* (*Proverbs*), and *Kohelet* (*Ecclesiastes*). The Tanakh (Hebrew Bible) specifically records that Solomon uttered 3,000 proverbs and composed lyrics for 1,005 songs;[3] not only was he "wise, he also taught the people what he knew; also he listened and researched, correcting many proverbs."[4]

Indeed, numbers prove ubiquitous in the biblical account of Solomon, even if specific figures occasionally differ in the primary sources (viz. *I Kings* and *II Chronicles*). Ostensibly, such details were intended to impress readers by precisely and accurately reifying the glory of Israel's golden age.

But how did the young leader preside over such a splendid epoch, and how was it squandered?

Cleaning the Slate

Despite his adolescence, Solomon commenced his reign by implementing his father's final injunctions, albeit in the manner and timing of his own choosing.

For certain understandable reasons, David had countenanced several disturbing elements within his dominion, yet he knew well that Solomon would prosper only once these had been expunged. After initially sparing his life, Solomon puts to death his presumptuous half-brother Adoniyah after the latter requested their late father's bedroom companion, Avishag the Shunamitess, as a wife.[5] Evyatar the high priest is pardoned for his misplaced support of Adoniyah's royal succession but deposed and banished to the priestly town of Anatot.[6] Yo'av, David's recalcitrant nephew and general (and Solomon's first cousin), is slain even as he desperately grips the horns of the altar.[7] The Benjaminite rebel Shimei ben Geira is kept under surveillance then put to death after he foolishly flouts the terms of his agreement with Solomon.[8] In this way Solomon ensures that the United Monarchy of Israel (1030–931 BCE), the great gift bestowed upon him at considerable expense by David, is purged of internal threats and secured at the outset of his reign: "Thus the kingdom was established in Solomon's hands."[9]

The Givon Vision

The Benjaminite city of Givon, where Scripture states the sun once stood still for Joshua in battle,[10] was the site wherein the Tabernacle remained. David had pitched a tent to house the Ark of the Testimony (Ark of the Covenant) in Jerusalem, where the Ark had been brought with much ceremony, but the Tabernacle itself lingered in Givon, where priestly offerings continued to be made upon the altar of sacrifice.

Solomon convenes all the leaders of Israel at Givon, where he offers 1,000 burnt offerings on the altar.[11] That night, God appears to Solomon in a dream, willing to fulfill any request.[12]

Evincing his innate prudence and pragmatism, Solomon requests "an understanding heart to judge Your people, that I may discern between good and evil."[13] God grants Solomon "a wise and understanding heart", as well as riches and honor.[14] Scripture concatenates wisdom and justice, indicating the utility of wisdom and implying that the royal wisdom would not be for the king's own benefit but for that of all Israel, whose lives and affairs would be subject to his judgment: "the wisdom of God was in him, to do justice."[15] In other words, rulers must preoccupy themselves with fostering an equitable society wherein justice prevails.

The Royal Administration

On his accession, Solomon inherits a religious and a political regime that eases statecraft. Tzadok no longer shares the high priesthood with Evyatar, but officiates alone; Benaiah replaces Yo'av as military commander. The prophets Gad and Nathan are no longer alive; two of Nathan's sons serve Solomon in another capacity, as supervisors overseeing royal officers.[16] Notably, no prophet is mentioned in connection with Solomon between Nathan's intervention in securing Solomon's accession and Ahiyah of Shiloh's anointing of Jeroboam ben Nevat; thus, for nearly 40 years, the phenomenon of prophethood was apparently in abeyance (or else much has been elided in the biblical account). Such a lengthy absence in Israel of a moral, ethical, and spiritual leader sheds light on the eventual decline of Solomon's rectitude and probity.

Solomon implements efficiencies he deems beneficial: he arranges the realm into 12 districts, each with an officer responsible for purveying the royal household for one month annually.[17] He thereby evidences that leaders must be efficient organizers, preparing and implementing plans to manage their domains; moreover, leaders must not be timid with regards to adjusting the status quo or altering the prevailing state of affairs (or, in the case of political leaders, the affairs of state).

These Are the Good Times

The situation in the United Monarchy of Israel is portrayed in glowing terms: "Judah and Israel were many, as the sand which is by the sea in multitude, eating and drinking and making merry."[18] The people's proliferation and mirth are a function of the dearth of war during the reign of Solomon, whose father David could have only dreamed of such tranquility: "and he had peace on all sides round about him. And Judah and Israel dwelt safely, every man under his vine and under his fig tree, from Dan to Be'ersheva, all the days of Solomon."[19] The distinction between mere quiet and true peace is underscored: there was "neither adversary nor calamity."[20]

The nation of Israel enjoys an embarrassment of riches during an epoch in which silver and gold become as common as stones in Jerusalem and cedars as sycamores in the Shephelah foothills.[21]

For Solomon, discernment is accompanied by a sense of noblesse oblige: "God gave Solomon wisdom and understanding exceeding much, and largeness of heart, even as the sand by the seashore."[22] In this Solomon rehearses the admirable blend of equity and generosity that previously characterized his father David: "David reigned over all Israel; and David administered justice and charity for all his people."[23] Despite the kingdom's florescence, Solomon understands the importance of alliances and recognizes that he will need the aid of others to elevate Israel to a loftier level of success.

From Tabernacle to Temple

Having paid tribute to the past, Solomon now points toward the future; whereas he offered 1,000 sacrifices at Givon, where the Tabernacle and brazen altar were, after his dream he returns to Jerusalem and offers sacrifices before the Ark of the Testimony and hosts a banquet for his servants.[24]

Solomon renews ties with King Hiram of Tyre, a Phoenician[25] ruler who had been a friend of David and who had sent ambassadors to Israel to engage its new sovereign. Solomon embraces his destiny, telling his neighboring monarch, "I purpose to build a house for the name of the Lord my God, as the Lord spoke to David my father, saying, 'Your son whom I will set upon your throne in your place, he shall build a house for My name."[26] He requests of Hiram cedar wood, cypress wood, and algum-wood/almog-wood (sandalwood or brazilwood) in exchange for much wheat, barley, wine, and olive oil.[27] The timber is floated in rafts tied together and towed by ships southward to Jerusalem's Mediterranean port of Jaffa, whence the individual logs are hauled by Israelite laborers overland and uphill toward the inland capital.[28]

Under the oversight of Adoniram/Adoram, a corvée of 30,000 Israelite men is conscripted and sent to Lebanon in shifts: 10,000 men at a time labor for a month, then return home for two months before setting out again.[29] Moreover, a census is conducted enumerating gentiles residing in the Land of Israel, whose tally reaches 153,600:[30] these are set to work as 70,000 porters and 80,000 hewers of limestone in the mountains, with 3,300 (or 3,600) supervisors monitoring their efforts.[31]

The king lays the foundation for the Temple in the second month of his fourth regnal year (967 BCE); seven and a half years later, in the eighth month of his eleventh regnal year (960 BCE), it is completed.[32] Gilded are the sacred chambers (walls, doors, floor), the inner altar of incense, the tables of showbread, 10 menorahs, tongs, bowls, musical instruments, basins, spoons, censers, inner door hinges, and doors;[33] in addition, cherubim are fashioned and walls are carved with ornate designs (cherubim, palm trees, open flowers).[34] The Temple is overlaid with precious stone and gold from Parva'im (Yemen), hinting at existing commercial ties between Israel and Sheba.[35]

Solomon hires Huram, an Israelite coppersmith from the tribes of Dan (on his mother's side) and Naphtali (on his father's side), who resides in Tyre and specializes in burnished brass, to craft metallic works for the Temple.[36] Huram is the Betzalel or Oholiav of his day, an expert artisan whom Solomon might have also esteemed for his celerity in fulfilling his commissions: "Have you seen a man quick in his work? He will stand before kings; he will not stand before poor men."[37] Huram's masterful contributions include the porch pillars (the right pillar Yakhin and the left pillar Bo'az)[38] and their bowls and capitals, nets of checker-work, wreaths of chain-work, lily-work, 400 ornamental pomegranates, the molten sea and its knops and 12 oxen, 10 copper bases with wheels, 10 brass lavers that sat on the bases, pots, shovels, and basins.[39] The vessels are cast in a foundry in the clay ground of the Jordan Plain between Sukkot and Tzartan.[40]

Now Solomon finishes what his father had started: as the penultimate touch, he brings the provisions (gold, silver, vessels) David had prepared and dedicated into the Temple's treasuries.[41] The ultimate act of consecration is the installation of the Ark of the Testimony (containing Moses' two stone tablets from Mount Sinai) in the Holy of Holies under the wings of the cherubim, a momentous maneuver for which Solomon once again convenes all the elders and tribal leaders of Israel, this time at the season of the Sukkot festival (Booths/Tabernacles).[42] Solomon hosts a fortnight feast, comprising a week of Temple dedication festivities then the week of the Sukkot festival, wherein all Israelites participate, "a great assemblage from Levo-Hammat to the Brook of Egypt".[43] The priests and Levites convey the Ark from the City of David/Zion, as well as the Tabernacle with all the sacred vessels from Givon, to the Temple in Jerusalem.

The Royal Benison

Solomon, having fulfilled his destiny, overflows with gratitude to God for upholding His promises to David. As all the congregation rises, the king blesses God and all of Israel.[44] He proceeds at length with an earnest entreaty to God to continue fulfilling His pledges, as with the Temple, to be responsive to the prayers of Israelites and of gentiles directed toward the Temple, and to pardon penitents.[45] Here is Solomon at his best: humble, noble, appreciative, selfless, forward-thinking. He is not enamored with his own impressive achievements; rather, he revels in Providence. He does not pray relying on his own spiritual merits, but implores God to "not turn back the face of Your anointed one; remember the kind deeds of David Your servant".[46] He arises from his knees and closes by again blessing the congregation and God.[47] The heady hour also occasions a confirmation of Israelite monotheism: "the Lord, He is God; there is none else."[48]

The Temple's inauguration concludes with sacrificial offerings (22,000 oxen, 120,000 sheep),[49] and "the fire descended from heaven and consumed the burnt offerings and the sacrifices, and the glory of the Lord filled the House.... And all the Children of Israel saw the descent of the fire, and the glory of the Lord on the House, and they kneeled on their faces to the ground on the floor, and they prostrated themselves and [said]: 'Give thanks to the Lord, for He is good, for His loving-kindness is eternal.'"[50] A cloud of divine glory pervades the hallowed precincts such that the priests can no longer minister therein.[51] On the eighth day, Shmini Atzeret, following a solemn gathering, Solomon dismisses the elated people to their homes.[52]

The king of Israel has built the long-awaited national sanctuary, honoring the God of Israel while confirming the sanctity and centrality of the capital, Jerusalem. Israel's national center and foremost institution are now established and ratified, their primacy and legitimacy enshrined by the active and collective participation of all the leaders of the people. In this Solomon illustrates for leaders the importance of enlisting the support of others in leadership roles and presenting a united front to the people, as opposed to exercising power by means of autocratic edict.

Construction Fever

As with sacred architecture, so with royal infrastructure. Solomon spends 13 years building his royal palace complex atop Mount Zion, including the royal guardhouse or ceremonial foyer known as "the House of the Forest of Lebanon",[53] and a discrete palace for his wife, pharaoh's daughter.[54]

Additionally, Solomon erects in Jerusalem the city wall and the Millo (a stepped stone structure or series of terraced platforms supporting houses) and develops and fortifies Hatzor, Megiddo, and Gezer[55] (the last being given as a dowry by the contemporary pharaoh to his daughter, Solomon's wife);[56] militarily, whoever controlled this trio of strategic sites would be master of the Land of Israel. In a sustained building spree that would not be iterated in Israel until the days of the Hasmonean rulers and of King Herod the Great of Judea almost a millennium later, Solomon expands Jerusalem and constructs upper and lower Beit Horon, Ba'alat, Tadmor (Palmyra), store-cities, chariot-cities, cavalry-cities, and sites in Lebanon.[57]

To do all this, he uses his bondservants from among the remnants of the gentile peoples (Amorites, Hittites, Perizzites, Hivites, Jebusites).[58] By contrast, Solomon imposes no permanent forced labor on Israelites, who constitute his officers, military commanders, soldiers, and servants.[59] A hierarchy of officials obtains wherein 250 Israelites supervise 300 proselytes who supervise 3,300 gentile officers who supervise the aforementioned myriads of gentile porters and hewers in the mountains.[60]

Oneiric Encore

In response to the royal benison, God reappears to Solomon at night, this time after the Temple's inauguration when the king is in Jerusalem. At first God reassures him that He has hallowed the Temple and will indeed abide in the abode: "I have heard your prayer and your petition, which you have petitioned before Me. I have consecrated this Temple which you have built to place My name there forever, and My eyes and My heart shall be there at all times."[61]

Then come the caveats: adherence to the divine commandments and statutes would ensure the Davidic dynasty and the security of the Land of Israel; idolatry, on the other hand, would result in catastrophe. Divine favor, Solomon is cautioned, is conditional and corresponds to human deeds. Solomon understands this full well in human terms, writing: "The king's goodwill is to an intelligent servant, but his wrath will be upon a shameful one."[62]

And, indeed, the king's piety endures for an extended period. He appoints the priestly courses to their service and the Levites to their watches, per the ordinances of his father, now lionized as "David the man of God".[63] At least thrice annually does he make burnt offerings and peace offerings on the altar of sacrifice and incense offerings on the inner altar;[64] according to another account, far more often, "as the duty of every day required, to offer up according to the commandment of Moses; for the Sabbaths, for the New Moons, and for the appointed seasons three times a year; on the Feast of Unleavened Bread [Pesah], on the Feast of Weeks [Shavuot], and on the Feast of Tabernacles [Sukkot]."[65]

Toward the end of his life, Solomon will review in some detail his concerted efforts during this earlier stage: "I worked on a grand scale – I built myself palaces, planted myself vineyards, and made myself gardens and parks; in them I planted all kinds of fruit trees. I made myself pools from which to water the trees springing up in the forest. I bought male and female slaves, and I had my home-born slaves as well. I also had growing herds of cattle and flocks of sheep, more than anyone before me in Jerusalem. I amassed silver and gold, the wealth of kings and provinces. I acquired male and female singers, things that provide sensual delight, and a good many concubines. So I grew great, surpassing all who preceded me in Jerusalem; my wisdom, too, stayed with me. I denied my eyes nothing they wanted. I withheld no pleasure from myself; for I took pleasure in all my work, and this was my reward for all my work."[66] The memory is telling, for it speaks of a self-serving leader whose focus has shifted away from the well-being of his people.

The Israelite-Phoenician Alliance

As part of their multifaceted cooperation, Solomon trades 20 Galilean cities in Israel to his royal friend and ally Hiram in exchange for various unnamed cities, which Solomon develops and fortifies, settling Israelites therein.[67]

The partners also embark on a maritime enterprise based out of Etzion-Gever (near Eilat) on the Red Sea. To Solomon's nascent fleet manned by servants Hiram adds experienced seafarers conducting a Phoenician fleet, and together they sail to Ophir, obtaining 420 (or 450) talents of gold delivered to Solomon.[68] Also procured and conveyed via ships of Tarshish – large vessels suitable for lengthy voyages across the Mediterranean, and perhaps named after Tartessus (Spain) – were silver, gems, algum-wood/almog-wood, ivory, monkeys, and peacocks.[69] The location of Ophir remains uncertain; it was probably in southern Arabia, or else in eastern Africa or in India.

The Israelite-Sheban Union

The Tanakh relates that Solomon's fame reached Sheba (Yemen), a kingdom ruled by a wealthy queen named Bilqis in Arabic – likely derived from the Hebrew word for concubine (*pilegesh*) – or Makeda in the Ethiopic tradition, after the voyage to Ophir, possibly suggesting that the latter locus was proximate to, if not identical with, the former. The queen travels northward some 1,500 miles to Jerusalem with a large retinue and a camel caravan laden with precious spices, gold, and gems. She challenges Solomon with riddles and difficult questions, and opens her heart to him; in turn, he answers all her queries and gives her the royal tour. She is so affected by his wisdom, his palace and household, and his Temple, that all of it takes her breath away.[70]

When her composure returns, she divulges her impressions in glowing terms: "It was a true report that I heard in my country of your deeds and of your wisdom. However, I did not believe the words until I came and saw with my own eyes, and I have beheld that not even the half of it was related to me. Your wisdom and goodness surpass that which I heard about. Fortunate are your men; fortunate are these your servants who always attend you and listen to your profound wisdom. Blessed be the Lord, your God, who preferred to place you on the throne of Israel; because of the Lord's enduring love for Israel, He appointed you king to do justice and righteousness."[71]

She gives Solomon 120 gold talents, gems, and spices in abundance.[72] He gives her "all her wish that she requested",[73] an ambiguity often construed as an insinuation that Solomon and the queen were sexually intimate and that an offspring issued upon her return to Sheba. The conjecture is compounded by verses in *Song of Songs*: "I am black but comely, O daughters of Jerusalem! Like the tents of Keidar, like the curtains of Solomon. Do not look upon me [disdainfully] because I am swarthy, for the sun has gazed upon me…"[74]

Six Steps to the Throne

Having amassed 666 gold talents in one particularly lucrative year, Solomon has 200 body shields and 300 shields of beaten gold made and stored in the House of the Forest of Lebanon.[75] But what to do with all that ivory?

Solomon devises the ancient world's status symbol par excellence, an immense ivory throne overlaid with glittering gold. Its six stairs, each flanked by lions at opposite ends, ascend to the royal seat, its armrests also flanked by lions (for a total of 14 lions).[76] Lest anyone believe that such ostentation was precedented, perhaps in Babylonia or in Egypt, the Tanakh makes explicit that "no such throne was made for any kingdom."[77]

Gilded Is Not Golden

A syntactical hint resides in the verse, "King Solomon exceeded all the kings of the earth in affluence and wisdom";[78] riches precede sagacity, implying that commerce took precedence over contemplation. Solomon's success, apparently, engendered an emphasis on materialism at the expense of morality. Indeed, the biblical narrative reveals that even wisdom itself became monetized: "And all the kings of the earth sought Solomon's presence to hear the wisdom with which God had endowed him. And each one would bring his gift, vessels of silver and of gold, garments, weapons, spices, horses, and mules, the tribute due annually."[79] This is a far cry from the explicit reason for which Solomon was endued with wisdom – to mete out justice for his subjects.

In addition to monetary and material wealth, Solomon invests heavily in Israel's military strength. His chariotry and cavalry are substantial: he possesses 40,000 (one account states 4,000) horse stalls, 1,400 chariots, and 12,000 cavalrymen.[80] Solomon's agents procure the horses from Egypt, and perhaps also from a locus called Kvei/Quwê (in the lowlands of eastern Cilicia in Asia Minor, a region renowned for its chargers bred from pedigree studhorses), unless the latter term (קְוֵה) is in fact not a toponym but instead denotes an assemblage.[8] Such robust armed forces were doubtless necessary to maintain law and order throughout Solomon's expansive kingdom, which commanded important overland trade routes in the Near East and stretched all the way from Mesopotamia in the northeast to Philistia and to Egypt in the southwest: "And he reigned over all the kings from the [Euphrates] River and until the land of the Philistines and until the border of Egypt."[82]

Israel's ambitious leader has enhanced his kingdom into an empire. But did Solomon's success go to his head? "The Lord will uproot the house of the haughty",[83] he himself had once warned; "The fear of the Lord is the discipline of wisdom, and before honor there is humility."[84] No clear indication of hubris exists in the biblical narrative itself; rather, what is made plain is that Solomon's appetites are indirectly his undoing.

Moral Nadir

Collections often branch out into different areas, and the king of Israel accumulated with abandon.

Besides accruing wealth and military capabilities, Solomon amassed lovers, populating his harem with gentile wives. In a notable instance of litotes, the Tanakh grossly understates the situation when it posits that "King Solomon loved many foreign women besides the pharaoh's daughter; Moabites, Ammonites, Edomites, Tzidonians, and Hittites", only to divulge two verses later that "he had 700 wives, all princesses, and 300 concubines, and his wives turned away his heart."[85] Small wonder that Solomon was swayed, given that he was outnumbered 1,000 to one. Technically, the verse states that his wives, not his concubines, turned away his heart, but even if all the concubines had been on Solomon's side they would still have been outnumbered by a faction more than twice as large.

The king is unable to bridle his love, of which there is evidently an indefinite supply to go around, despite the divine warning to "not mingle among [foreign women], and they shall not come among you, for certainly they will sway your heart after their deities"[86] and his own dictum that "the mouth of strange women is a deep pit; the one abhorred by the Lord will fall therein."[87] And yet, Solomon held his own for a long time, indeed most of his life: "it was at the time of Solomon's old age, that his wives turned away his heart after other gods".[88] Ultimately, however, enfeebled and perhaps addled due to aging, he succumbs to the pressure of hymeneal influences and goes "after Ashtoreth, the goddess of the Tzidonians, and after Milkhom the abomination of the Ammonites."[89]

He had not in this instance, in contradistinction to his actions at the commencement of his reign, dispensed with negative elements amid his realm, thereby disregarding his own counsel: "The wise king scatters the wicked, and turns the wheel over them."[90]

Solomon's dotage educes unfavorable comparisons with his father David, whose reign retrospectively glows as Solomon's dims: "and his heart was not whole with the Lord, his God, like the heart of David his father";[91] "And Solomon did what was displeasing to the Lord, and he was not completely devoted to the Lord as was David his father."[92] Suddenly David's

presence looms large over the narrative, with over half a dozen references
either to "My servant David",[93] "David your father",[94] or "David his father"[95]
in a single chapter. If Solomon in his regal wisdom and glory had emerged
from under his father's shadow and accomplished his father's great aim, he
is now shaded anew by David. This seems rather unfair, given that a young
David himself had apparently condoned the idolatry (the household idol
teraphim) of his wife Mikhal in their own home.[96] Perhaps Solomon is held
to a higher standard because he was seasoned and elderly while David was
relatively youthful at the time of the commission of this grave sin, or
because Solomon possessed more wisdom than David and therefore should
have known better, or, above all, because Solomon is depicted as ultimately
participating in, and not simply permitting, the idolatry.

The Sages debated Solomon's merits and demerits, arguing about
whether in fact Solomon had debased himself with idol worship or merely
overlooked the worship of his foreign wives. As if anticipating this
controversy, Scripture further avers that the king "built a high place for
Khemosh, the abomination of Moab upon the mountain that is before
Jerusalem, and for Molekh, the abomination of the children of Ammon.
Thus he did for all of his alien wives who offered incense and slaughtered
sacrifices to their deities."[97] Much as one might like to absolve Solomon of
direct wrongdoing, the biblical account itself refrains from doing so, and
indeed leaves little doubt that he was more of an accomplice than an
accessory to his wives' idolatry.

Ironically, Solomon was able to go to great lengths in erecting the
Temple on behalf of God, despite not being divinely obliged to do so, yet
was unable to observe the sole imperative – monotheism – God had issued.
As with Adam and Havah in Eden, one commandment proved one too
many.

Covenants and Consequences

Solomon's breach of the covenant with God is met with divine anger, albeit
with a temporal delay: "And the Lord said to Solomon, 'For as this has been
with you, and you have not observed My covenant and My statutes which
I have commanded you, I will surely tear the kingdom from you, and I shall
give it to your servant. However, in your days I will not do this, for the sake
of David your father; from the hands of your son I shall tear it. But I shall
not tear the entire kingdom away from you; one tribe I shall grant to your
son for the sake of David My servant, and for the sake of Jerusalem, the city
which I have chosen.'"[98] God's communication is typically vague: Who is

the servant of Solomon who will receive the kingdom? Which tribe is alluded to?

The biblical narrative later reveals the servant to be an Ephraimite from Tzereidah, the mighty man of valor Jeroboam ben Nevat, Solomon's overseer of laborers of the tribes of Menasheh and Ephraim and subsequently the first monarch of the northern Kingdom of Israel.[99] Ephraim had formerly been the foremost Israelite tribe during the leadership of Joshua (c. 1273–1245 BCE) and subsequently in the era of the Judges (c. 1228–1020 BCE), and its territory had been of central importance since it possessed at its core Shiloh, amphictyonic center of tribal Israel and its de facto capital, the site wherein the Tabernacle and the Ark of the Testimony had resided for more than two centuries. This rebellion, therefore, was something of a restitution for Ephraim, which had been surpassed in importance first by the tribe of Benjamin during the reign of King Saul then by the tribe of Judah during the reigns of David and Solomon. Tribal loyalties die hard.

The one tribe in question may refer to Solomon's own tribe of Judah, or else to Benjamin, which was, in the aftermath of the decline of the House of Saul, soon to be subsumed within the much larger and stronger Judah, as had happened previously to the tribe of Shimon.

The Advent of Adversaries

Hitherto, there has only been one exception to the prevailing peace during Solomon's reign, a brief narrative note that easily eludes readers: a military engagement occurs between Israel and Aram (southwestern Syria), wherein Solomon besieges and triumphs over Hammat Tzovah.[100]

But now Israel's monarch has fallen out of divine favor, and penalties are being applied.

While the division of the United Monarchy of Israel (931 BCE) and the rivalry between Jeroboam's line and the Davidic dynasty are still to come, God sees fit to elevate enemies of Israel even during Solomon's lifetime. Prince Hadad the Edomite and the Aramean ruler King Rezon of Damascus arise as threats; Hadad is perhaps the more troubling foe, for during his sojourn in Egypt he had married the sister-in-law of the pharaoh,[101] thereby considerably enlarging his clout via affinal relations.[102] Indeed, the Nilotic realm soon turns hostile to Israel, which it invades under Pharaoh Shishak (Sheshonk) I of Egypt,[103] who raids the Temple's treasuries and the royal palace during King Rehoboam of Judah's fifth regnal year (927 BCE).[104]

And it is late in Solomon's reign that another Ephraimite, the prophet Ahiyah of Shiloh, dons new apparel and meets Jeroboam in a field outside Jerusalem, where he rends his garment into 12 pieces and instructs his charge to take 10 of them, a symbolic gesture representing 10 of the 12 Israelite tribes over which Jeroboam will rule.[105]

When Solomon gets wind of this, he seeks to eliminate Jeroboam, who, just as the princely youth Hadad had done, flees to Egypt[106] and marries the pharaoh's sister-in-law.[107] Two aspects of Solomon's conduct are noteworthy here: his brazen refusal to accept God's verdict as transmitted through the prophet Ahiyah, and his willingness to act against Jeroboam, whom he doubtless deemed seditious as well as rivalrous, but not against Ahiyah, a divine spokesperson. In this restraint Solomon rehearses his respect for the inviolability of holy persons (previously demonstrated when upon his accession he pardoned Evyatar the high priest) and renews the contrast between his actions and those of King Saul vis-à-vis the high priest Ahimelekh ben Ahituv and the priests of Nob.

In the Light of Hindsight

In the twilight of life, Solomon indites his disillusioned memoir *Kohelet*, with its recurrent disdain for newcomers who profit from their predecessors' labors. The narrator Kohelet's attitude at times appears proto-Epicurean, with its valorizing of food, drink, and pleasure.[108] He regrets his folly – "Better is a poor and wise child than an old and foolish king, who doesn't know how to accept admonition anymore"[109] – from which neither wisdom nor wealth could protect him: "For in much wisdom is much vexation, and he who increases knowledge increases sorrow."[110] He even doubts whether he was ever wise at all: "I said, 'I will get wisdom', but it was far from me."[111]

He abjures the pursuit of wealth because he has come to realize that "he who loves silver will not be satisfied with silver, nor he who loves abundance, with increase."[112] He rues the cause of his degeneracy, which he had been unable to resist: "And I find bitterer than death the woman, whose heart is snares and nets, and her hands as bands; whoever would be good before God will flee her."[113] His spite aside, the aged leader is shirking responsibility for his poor judgment, unwilling to accept the blame for his errors. Will a resentful Kohelet-Solomon never own up to his misdeeds or hold himself accountable?

Legacy – Every Leader's Litmus Test

Prophets of Israel sometimes doubled as scribes, inditing either their own works or, in the case of the early court prophets, the annals of Israel's monarchs (or, plausibly, both). As he had written of David, Nathan likewise wrote of Solomon, as do the subsequent prophets Ahiyah of Shiloh and Iddo (Yeddo) the seer.[114] The halcyon days of the Solomonic era dissipate, and Solomon's reign closes with his decease in 931 BCE. Having ruled over Israel from Jerusalem for 40 years, he is buried in the City of David and succeeded by his middle-aged son Rehoboam.[115]

The United Monarchy of Israel soon collapses and rives into two, often warring, polities. Weakened by division, the Israelite kingdoms are eventually conquered by mightier imperial powers (Assyria conquers Israel in 722 BCE; Babylonia conquers Judah in 586 BCE). Solomon failed to leave his realm on a strong footing, able to perdure in his absence. Scripture portrays Jeroboam as a divine instrument, but also reveals that the latter's rebellion succeeded due to the people's disaffection with Solomon's onerous corvée, as they explain to Rehoboam: "Your father laid a harsh yoke on us. But if you will lighten the harsh service we had to render your father and ease his heavy yoke that he put on us, we will serve you."[116] Rehoboam unwisely refuses, the kingdom splits, and when the obdurate king sends his loathed corvée overseer Adoniram/Adoram to conscript laborers from among the northern tribes of Israel, the latter is lapidated. Thus it transpires that Solomon ought to have sought volunteers to construct the Temple, as Moses had sought the Israelites' voluntarily assistance in constructing the Tabernacle, or at minimum should have employed paid laborers instead of relying on a compulsory service all too reminiscent of the Israelites' bondage in Egypt. Had Solomon done so, the United Monarchy's destiny, and Jewish history, might well have been very different indeed.

Centuries later, during the prophethood of the priestly Ezekiel ben Buzi in Babylonia (592–570 BCE),[117] it also transpires that Solomon committed other sins that rankled. By building his royal palace atop Mount Zion, adjacent to the Temple, Solomon had (perhaps inadvertently) equated deity and monarch, an act accounted as a presumptuous gesture of disrespect. Moreover, Ezekiel reveals that the Judahite kings' fornication and burial sites were unacceptably proximate to the holy sanctuary and offended God's dignity and sanctity: "And He said to me, 'Son of man, [this is] the place of My throne and [this is] the place of the soles of My feet where I shall dwell amidst the Children of Israel forever, and the House of Israel will no longer defile My Holy Name, they and their kings with their harlotry, and with the corpses of their kings in their high places. By placing their threshold with My threshold and their doorpost beside My doorpost, and the wall [was] between Me and them, and they defiled My Holy Name with their abominations which they committed, and I destroyed them with My wrath. Now they shall distance their harlotry and the corpses of their kings from Me, and I shall dwell among them forever.'"[118]

Solomon was a glorious king yet a flawed leader; in spite of his several major mistakes, however, he proves wise again in the end. Upon reflection, he concedes that "whoever keeps the commandment will know no evil, and a wise man's heart discerns time and judgment",[119] and adjures others to "revere God and keep His commandments; this is what being human is all about."[120] Kohelet's jaded, pessimistic Weltschmerz finally cedes to the original lyricism of the poet of *Song of Songs*, espousing a life-affirming outlook: "And the light is sweet, and it is good for the eyes to see the sun."[121]

About one thing did Solomon remain mistaken: "So I said to myself, 'If the same thing happens to the fool as to me, then what did I gain by being wise?', and I thought to myself, 'This too is pointless. For the wise man, like the fool, will not be long remembered, inasmuch as in the times to come, everything will long ago have been forgotten. The wise man, no less than the fool, must die.'"[122] Solomon was convinced that his legacy was forfeited, his posterity doomed. Not only would his scions be deprived of his dominion, but he himself would inevitably be disremembered: "the dead know nothing; there is no longer any reward for them, because all memory of them is lost."[123]

Not so. Solomon's life and times have resounded through the ages; from that day to this, his name has been synonymous with sagacity, his golden era recollected with longing.

Notes

1. *I Kings* 14:21. While Scripture does not explicitly call her Solomon's wife, Na'amah the Ammonitess, granddaughter of David's ally King Nahash of Ammon, was almost certainly a wife, and not merely a concubine, given that she was of royal lineage; that her son with Solomon, Rehoboam, eventually succeeded his father as king; and that Solomon had more than twice as many wives as concubines.
2. ibid. 11:3
3. ibid. 5:12; see also Rashi ad loc.
4. *Ecclesiastes* 12:9

5. *I Kings* 2:24-25
6. ibid. 2:26
7. ibid. 2:28-34
8. ibid. 2:46
9. ibid.
10. *Joshua* 10:12-14
11. *I Kings* 3:4; *II Chronicles* 1:2-3, 6
12. *I Kings* 3:5; *II Chronicles* 1:7
13. *I Kings* 3:9; closely paralleled in *II Chronicles* 1:10
14. *I Kings* 3:12-13; closely paralleled in *II Chronicles* 1:12
15. *I Kings* 3:28
16. ibid. 4:5
17. ibid. 4:7
18. ibid. 4:20
19. ibid. 5:4-5
20. ibid. 5:18
21. ibid. 10:27; *II Chronicles* 1:15, 9:27; Cf. *II Chronicles* 9:20
22. *I Kings* 5:9
23. *II Samuel* 8:15; almost verbatim in *I Chronicles* 18:14
24. *I Kings* 3:15
25. Phoenicians were seafaring Canaanites who referred to themselves according to their major cities, such as Tzidon (Sidon) or Tzur (Tyre). The Greeks called them "Phoenicians" because the latter were famous as Phoenix-colored (purple-red) dye producers.
26. ibid. 5:19; closely paralleled in *II Chronicles* 2:3-5
27. *I Kings* 5:25; *II Chronicles* 2:7, 9, 14
28. *I Kings* 5:23; *II Chronicles* 2:15
29. *I Kings* 5:27-28
30. *II Chronicles* 2:16
31. *I Kings* 5:29-30; *II Chronicles* 2:1, 17
32. *I Kings* 6:1, 38; *II Chronicles* 3:2
33. *I Kings* 7:48-50; *II Chronicles* 4:19-22
34. *I Kings* 6:23-35; *II Chronicles* 3:5, 7-14
35. *II Chronicles* 3:6; see Rashi ad loc.
36. *I Kings* 7:13-14; *II Chronicles* 2:12-13
37. *Proverbs* 22:29
38. *II Chronicles* 3:17
39. *I Kings* 7:13-45; *II Chronicles* 4:11-16
40. *I Kings* 7:46; *II Chronicles* 4:17
41. *I Kings* 7:51; *II Chronicles* 5:1
42. *I Kings* 8:65; *II Chronicles* 5:3
43. *I Kings* 8:65; almost verbatim in *II Chronicles* 7:8
44. *I Kings* 8:14-21; *II Chronicles* 6:3-11
45. *I Kings* 8:22-53; *II Chronicles* 6:12-42
46. *II Chronicles* 6:42

47. *I Kings* 8:54-61
48. ibid. 8:60
49. ibid. 8:63; *II Chronicles* 7:5
50. ibid. 7:1, 3
51. *I Kings* 8:1-11; *II Chronicles* 5:2-14, 7:1-2
52. *I Kings* 8:66; Cf. *II Chronicles* 7:9-10. See Rashi ad loc.
53. *I Kings* 7:2, 10:17; *II Chronicles* 9:16, 20; Cf. *Isaiah* 22:8
54. *I Kings* 7:1-8; the unnamed pharaoh is likely either Siamun (r. 986–967 BCE) or his immediate successor Psusennes II (r. 967–943 BCE), both members of the 21st Dynasty of Egypt.
55. ibid. 9:15
56. ibid. 9:16; see Rashi ad loc.
57. *II Chronicles* 8:4-6; *I Kings* 9:17-19
58. *I Kings* 9:20-21; *II Chronicles* 8:7-8
59. *I Kings* 9:22; *II Chronicles* 8:9
60. *II Chronicles* 8:10, and see Rashi ad loc.; *I Kings* 9:23, and see Rashi ad loc.
61. *I Kings* 9:3; almost verbatim in *II Chronicles* 7:12, 15-16
62. *Proverbs* 14:35
63. *II Chronicles* 8:14; Cf. *I Kings* 9:25
64. *I Kings* 9:25
65. *II Chronicles* 8:13
66. *Ecclesiastes* 2:4-10
67. *I Kings* 9:11-13; *II Chronicles* 8:2
68. *I Kings* 9:26-28; *II Chronicles* 8:17-18
69. *I Kings* 10:11-12, 22; *II Chronicles* 9:21
70. *I Kings* 10:1-5; *II Chronicles* 9:1-4
71. *I Kings* 10:6-9; almost verbatim in *II Chronicles* 9:5-8
72. *I Kings* 10:10; *II Chronicles* 9:9
73. *I Kings* 10:13; *II Chronicles* 9:12
74. *Song of Songs* 1:5-6
75. *I Kings* 10:14-17; *II Chronicles* 9:13-16
76. *I Kings* 10:18-20; *II Chronicles* 9:17-19
77. *I Kings* 10:20; *II Chronicles* 9:19
78. *I Kings* 10:23
79. *II Chronicles* 9:22-24; almost verbatim in *I Kings* 10:23-25
80. *I Kings* 5:6, 10:26; *II Chronicles* 1:14, 9:25
81. *I Kings* 10:28; *II Chronicles* 1:16, 9:28
82. *II Chronicles* 9:26; almost verbatim in *I Kings* 5:1
83. *Proverbs* 15:25
84. ibid. 15:33
85. *I Kings* 11:1-3
86. ibid. 11:2
87. *Proverbs* 22:14
88. *I Kings* 11:4
89. ibid. 11:5

90. *Proverbs* 20:26
91. *I Kings* 11:4
92. ibid. 11:6
93. ibid. 11:13, 32, 34, 36, 38
94. ibid. 11:12
95. ibid. 11:33
96. *I Samuel* 19:13-16
97. *I Kings* 11:7-8
98. ibid. 11:11-13
99. ibid. 11:26-28
100. *II Chronicles* 8:3-4
101. A pharaoh of the 21st Dynasty of Egypt, likely Amenemope, Osorkon the Elder, or Siamun.
102. *I Kings* 11:14-25
103. Sheshonk I, founder of the 22nd Dynasty of Egypt.
104. *I Kings* 14:25-26
105. *I Kings* 11:29-33
106. ibid. 11:40; to Pharaoh Shishak.
107. Ano, older sister of Shishak's wife Thekemina, according to the Septuagint, *I Kings* 12:24e
108. *Ecclesiastes* 3:12-13, 5:17, 8:15, 9:7
109. ibid. 4:13
110. ibid. 1:18
111. ibid. 7:23
112. ibid. 5:9
113. ibid. 7:26
114. *II Chronicles* 9:29
115. *I Kings* 11:42-43, 14:21; *II Chronicles* 9:30-31
116. *I Kings* 12:4
117. *Ezekiel* 1:2
118. ibid. 43:7-9
119. *Ecclesiastes* 8:5
120. ibid. 12:13
121. ibid. 11:7
122. ibid. 2:15-16
123. ibid. 9:5

Megiddo

Appendix 3

Maccabean Judea

Maccabean Judea

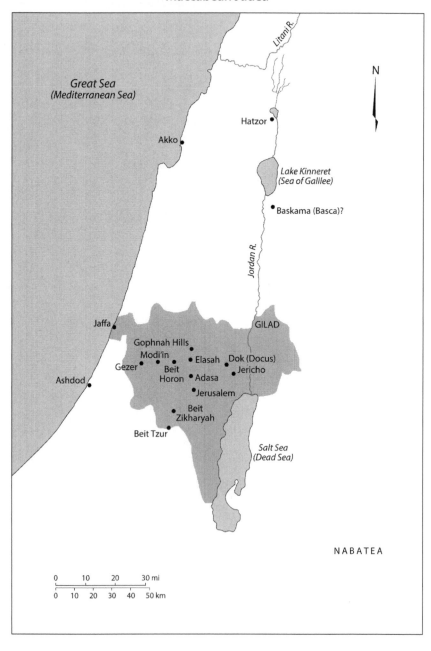

Originally indited in Hebrew but extant only in Greek translation, *I Maccabees* is both a history and a tripartite biography of Jewish leadership, covering more than 40 years of eventful affairs wherein courageous and tenacious rebels surmounted overwhelming odds and overthrew imperial occupiers who persecuted Jews and sought to suppress Judaism. The book was written by an unknown Judean author between 134 and 63 BCE, likely circa 100 BCE. As a religious history modeled on biblical histories, it limns a series of remarkable figures striving valiantly both for religious freedom and for national liberation – the Brothers Maccabee – especially Judah, Jonathan, and Shimon.

Rather than a continuation of *I Maccabees*, the independent *II Maccabees* is a partially parallel digest of the Maccabean Rebellion (167– 134 BCE), beginning and concluding its central narrative earlier than the former account and covering a period of about 15 years (corresponding to the first seven chapters of *I Maccabees*). Originally indited in Greek, it summarizes five books previously written by a certain Jason of Cyrene and its style is more Hellenistic. The work's target audience is Alexandrian Jewry, whose solidarity with the Jews of Judea it seeks to educe. Its date of composition is sometime after 124 BCE.

Initially, in response to the Hellenizing decrees and sacrilegious acts of Emperor Antiochus IV Epiphanes of Syria, the priestly Hasmonean patriarch Matityahu and his sons tore their garments, wore sackcloth, and mourned. Then they put away grief, vowing not to swerve from Judaism either to the right or to the left, come what may. They withdrew into the wilderness of the Gophnah Hills, dwelling amid the heights and within its caverns, eating wild plants, making their way secretly among Judean villages, rallying their kinsmen. Soon they recruited 6,000 loyalists and organized them into a trained and mobile guerrilla force. They attacked imperial Seleucid (Syrian-Greek) soldiers and Hellenist Jewish traitors abetting the enemy using surprise and the cover of night, capturing advantageous positions and inflicting numerous reverses on their foes.

On his deathbed, Matityahu singled out Shimon for his sound judgment and appointed him his successor, and also appointed Judah general owing to his might and bravery. Perhaps on Shimon's advice, Judah assumed command of the revolt and together the Maccabees, as they came to be known, "fought for Israel with a will."[1]

Following the example of their fervent father Matityahu, a zealot in the spirit of the high priest Pinhas and the prophet Elijah, the Brothers Maccabee devoted and even gave their lives in the cause of their ancestors and countrymen, resisting a pagan empire through intrepid leadership and willpower. Theirs were victories both martial and moral. Despite the occasional katabases, the Maccabees repeatedly proved resilient and resourceful. The following précis highlights their generational exploits as steadfast stalwarts in defense of tradition and homeland.

1. **Elazar (Avaran)** (d. 162 BCE) – The bold Elazar proved his mettle in the Battle of Beit Zikharyah, charging through the Seleucids' thick phalanx toward a royally caparisoned elephant that he presumed carried the young Emperor Antiochus V Eupator of Syria or else his regent Lysias. The elephant was taller than all the others arrayed by the Seleucids, and Elazar managed to scatter the enemy from before him in order to dart in beneath the beast and stab it fatally with his sword. But the pachyderm collapsed upon him, and Elazar died on the spot. He took a daring risk by attempting to target the enemy leadership, but ended up sacrificing himself in a hasty move that factored into the Judean battle loss. Elazar was the first Maccabee brother to fall.

2. **Judah (Yehudah/Maccabee)** (r. 166–160 BCE) – The mighty Judah overcame a series of Seleucid (Syrian-Greek) military commanders – Apollonius, Seron, Gorgias, Nicanor, Lysias – sent by Emperor Antiochus IV Epiphanes of Syria and his successors. He marshaled and exhorted his army to be strong, rousing them to courage, instilling in them the righteousness of "fighting for our lives and our laws."[2] Judah always led from the front. Like Moses, Judah organized and delegated leaders to oversee men by the thousand, hundred, fifty, and ten. He dismissed the fearful from his ranks. Undaunted, he inspired confidence in his fellows regarding their intimidating enemies, adjuring them to "not be afraid of their numbers" and to "not flinch at their attack."[3] He disciplined his men not to plunder when further battle urgently awaited them. At the first opportunity, Judah led his brothers and the entire army to Mount Zion (Temple Mount) to purify and to dedicate the sanctuary, which lay desecrated and partly ruined. He selected priests to remove the abomination of desolation (the pagan altar of Ba'al-Shamin), dismantle the profaned altar of sacrifice, and fashion a new altar and new sacred vessels. He did not usurp the authority of a high priest or a king but, in December 164 BCE, did institute the celebration of the rededication of the sacrificial altar and the Temple for eight days beginning annually on 25 Kislev – the Hanukah festival (in 160 BCE, he also instituted the short-lived Day of Nicanor holiday annually on 13 Adar, the day before the Day of

Mordekhai/Purim). He built high walls with towers round Mount Zion, stationed a garrison to protect the Temple, and fortified Beit Tzur to the south against the encroaching Idumeans. He rescued persecuted Jews in Gilad, rallying stragglers as they were brought into Judea. He sought alliance with Rome in order to consolidate his position. Abandoned by over two-thirds of his army before overwhelming enemy numbers, Judah fell in battle at Elasah (near Beit Horon), and "his memory is blessed forever and ever."[4]

3. **Yohanan/Joseph (Gaddi)** (d. 160) – The oldest brother, Yohanan commanded a division of fighters under Judah and later was sent by Jonathan to lead a convoy into Nabatea to solicit Nabatean Arab assistance, but he was ambushed, captured, and killed by the raiding sons of Jambri of Medeba.

4. **Jonathan (Yonatan/Apphus)** (r. 160–142 BCE) – Appointed by the Judeans, Jonathan succeeded Judah despite being the youngest brother. Whereas Judah was a masterful military strategist and tactician, Jonathan was politically astute and adroitly played one Syrian contender for the throne against another. After defeating the formidable Seleucid (Syrian-Greek) general Bacchides with Shimon's help, Jonathan negotiated peace terms and a prisoner exchange. He recovered Jewish hostages from the Seleucids, obtained the removal of foreign garrisons, and refortified Jerusalem. He was appointed high priest by Seleucid pretender Alexander Balas and was subsequently recognized in this role by Emperor Demetrius II Nicator of Syria and confirmed by Balas' young son, Emperor Antiochus VI Dionysus of Syria. He raised troops and manufactured arms in quantity, but was savvy enough to make a favourable impression upon Balas and Emperor Ptolemy VI Philometor of Egypt when they convened at Akko. With the help of military intelligence, he won an important victory over the forces of Demetrius II at Ashdod, and routed the Seleucids at Hatzor despite lacking timely military intelligence. He renewed the alliances with Rome and with Sparta. He not only enlarged the territory under Judean control but secured peace within its borders. Jonathan proved gullible, however, and was lured by a treacherous Diodotus Tryphon – a Seleucid usurper – into a trap at Akko, which cost him his freedom and the lives of 1,000 of his men. He was murdered and buried at Baskama (Basca) in Gilad, before being reinterred in the Hasmonean family tomb in Modi'in.

5. **Shimon (Thassi)** (r. 142–134 BCE) – Wise and patient, Shimon succeeded Jonathan and lent his support to Emperor Demetrius II

Nicator of Syria, who regained the Seleucid (Syrian-Greek) throne. Both Demetrius II and his successor, Emperor Antiochus VII Sidetes of Syria, recognized Shimon as high priest, military governor, and ethnarch of the Jews. With their political independence restored, the Judeans approved Shimon's titles and his hereditary rule was established. Shimon renewed the treaty with Rome and ushered in an era of stability and prosperity. He fortified and provisioned Judean fortresses, reconquered Jaffa, Beit Tzur, and Gezer, and expelled the die-hard holdouts from the Akra citadel in Jerusalem. "He established peace in the land, and Israel knew great joy. Each man sat under his own vine and fig tree, and there was none to make them afraid."[5] Tellingly, Rome and Sparta initiated the renewal of their treaties with Judea during Shimon's tenure. Like Jonathan before him, though, an aged Shimon proved credulous in his dealings with the mercurial Seleucids. Antiochus VII turned against the Jews, and Shimon's son-in-law Ptolemy ben Abubus, ambitious and currying favor, lured Shimon and two of his sons into a deadly banquet at the desert fortress of Dok (Docus/Dagon), overlooking the plain of Jericho. Only Shimon's son Yohanan Hyrcanus, who had not been present, survived to perpetuate Hasmonean rule.

I & II Maccabees make clear Judah's central concern for the welfare of the Jewish people and for the common good. In warfare, Judah could act preemptively and retributively: the hero known as The Hammerer struck mightily. Yet he was also inclined to diplomacy and during his campaign in Gilad he offered or accepted peace terms whenever reasonable opportunities presented themselves. He invoked God and frequently recalled Jewish history to his fighters to hearten them against the always daunting odds. Above all, Judah recurrently encouraged and exhorted his forces to remember all that they were fighting for, and to trust in divine favor. He was motivated as "a man who had devoted himself entirely, body and soul, to the service of his countrymen, and had always preserved the love he had felt even in youth for his people".[6]

Jonathan and Shimon evinced skill on the battlefield and deftness in the political realm; they conducted successful negotiations and assumed responsibilities while insisting on their national rights. They engaged in diplomacy when possible, waged war when necessary, and displayed loyalty according to their international treaties. Unlike Judah, however, Jonathan and Shimon did not maintain the separation of power between political ruler and religious leader; although the Hasmoneans were Jewish priests originally from Jerusalem, they did not descend from the Tzadokite dynasty from which the high priests had lineally derived for many generations, thus the Hasmonean brothers incurred criticism for arrogating the high priesthood in addition to their de facto kingship, similarly censured as a usurpation of the royal Davidic dynasty. Nonetheless, they rebuilt and refortified Judean sites and earned the enduring gratitude and fealty of the Jews – fighters and civilians alike – even above and beyond that which Judah had enjoyed.

Not all who would lead were of the same caliber as the Brothers Maccabee; even in their own day, there were would-be heroes "not of the same mould as those to whom the deliverance of Israel had been entrusted."[7] Likewise, not all rebels were equally zealous for the Torah and the ancestral ways: underlings who had accepted bribes from besieged adversaries were dealt with severely. Moreover, the popular Hassidean party (forerunners of the Pharisees) that had joined the Maccabean army were prematurely satisfied when religious freedom had been reclaimed, but the Maccabees understood that without their national sovereignty reestablished, Jewish freedoms would forever be subjected to the capricious whims of this or that foreign occupier.

When a hostile Emperor Antiochus VII Sidetes of Syria dispatched his envoy Athenobius to Jerusalem to reprimand Shimon Maccabee for supposedly occupying Jaffa, Gezer, and the Akra citadel in Jerusalem, threatening war unless these were surrendered or steep extortion payments were made for them, Shimon responded calmly with the wisdom for which his father Matityahu had commended him decades earlier: "It is not any foreign land that we have taken, nor any foreign property that we have seized, but the inheritance of our ancestors, for some time unjustly wrested from us by our enemies; now that we have a favorable opportunity, we are merely recovering the inheritance of our ancestors."[8]

During an epoch of deep mourning throughout Israel, when "the very land quaked for its inhabitants and the whole House of Jacob was clothed with shame",[9] the Brothers Maccabee arose to meet the challenge of their age and to uphold the faith of their forebears, each making the ultimate sacrifice in order to restore freedom of religion and national independence to the Jewish people.

Notes

1.   *I Maccabees* 3:2
2.   *I Maccabees* 3:21
3.   *I Maccabees* 4:8
4.   *I Maccabees* 3:7
5.   *I Maccabees* 14:11-12
6.   *II Maccabees* 15:30
7.   *I Maccabees* 5:62
8.   *I Maccabees* 15:33-34
9.   *I Maccabees* 1:28

Maccabean Tombs

Select Bibliography

Abramsky, Samuel. *Ancient Towns in Israel*. World Zionist Organization, 1963.

Aharoni, Yohanan. *The Land of the Bible: A Historical Geography*. Revised ed. Westminster Press, 1979.

Avi-Yonah, Michael. *The Holy Land: A Historical Geography from the Persian to the Arab Conquest, 536 B.C. to A.D. 640*. 2nd ed. Carta Jerusalem, 2002.

Avi-Yonah, Michael, and Emil G. Kraeling. *Our Living Bible*. McGraw-Hill, 1962.

Baly, Denis. *The Geography of the Bible: A Study in Historical Geography*. Revised ed. Fortress Press, 1974.

Barnavi, Eli. *A Historical Atlas of the Jewish People: From the Time of the Patriarchs to the Present*. Revised ed. Schocken, 2003.

Ben-Gurion, David, ed. *The Jews in Their Land*. Mordechai Nurock and Misha Louvish, trans. Revised ed. Aldus/Jupiter, 1974.

Bible Gateway, The Zondervan Corporation, 2010–2019, www.biblegateway.com.

Chabad, Chabad-Lubavitch Media Center, 1993–2019, www.chabad.org.

Elitzur, Yehuda, and Yehuda Keel. *The Daat Mikra Bible Atlas: A Comprehensive Guide to Biblical Geography and History*. Mosad HaRav Kook/Urim Publications, 2011.

Elitzur, Yoel. "Defining Biblical Israel by Geographical Regions". Rachel Rowens, trans. Bar-Ilan University, 2016, https://www1.biu.ac.il/indexE.php?id=17143&pt=1&pid=14620&level=0&cPath=43,14206,14376,14620,17143.

---. *Places in the Parasha: Biblical Geography and Its Meaning*. Daniel Landman, trans. Koren Publishers Jerusalem, 2020.

Encyclopedia Britannica, Encyclopedia Britannica, Inc., 2019, www.britannica.com.

Encyclopedia Judaica. 1st ed. Keter Publishing House, 1971.

---. 2nd ed. Macmillan Reference USA, 2007.

Finzi, Yaron, and Ina Ryvkin. "The Erosional Crater (Makhtesh) – A Rare but Diverse Phenomenon". Annual Meeting, Geologic Society of Israel, Mitzpeh Ramon, Israel, March 2017. Conference Presentation.

HaCohen, David Ben-Gad. "Solving the Problem of 'Kadesh in the Wilderness of Paran'". *TheTorah.com*, www.thetorah.com/solving-the-problem-of-kadesh-in-the-wilderness-of-paran/.

---. "Wadi Zered". *TheTorah.com*, www.thetorah.com/article/wadi-zered.

Har-El, Menashe. *Dwellers of the Mountain: The Geography of Jewish Habitation of Ancient Judea*. Carta Jerusalem, 1977.

---. *Understanding the Twelve Tribes: Boundaries & Surrounding Nations*. Carta Jerusalem, 2018.

Hillel, Daniel. *The Natural History of the Bible: An Environmental Exploration of the Hebrew Scriptures*. Columbia UP, 2007.

Israel Nature and Parks Authority, The Israel Nature and Parks Authority, 2017, www.parks.org.il/en/.

Israel: People/Land/State. Avigdor Shinan, ed. Yad Izhak Ben-Zvi, 2005.

JewishEncyclopedia.com, The Kopelman Foundation, 2002–2011, www.jewishencyclopedia.com.

Josephus, Flavius. *The Jewish War.* G.A. Williamson, trans. Penguin Books, 1959.

KKL-JNF, Keren Kayemet L'Yisrael-Jewish National Fund, www.kkl-jnf.org.

Leibtag, Menachem. "Masei: The Borders of the Land of Israel". Orthodox Union, 2019, www.ou.org/torah/parsha/rabbi-menachem-leibtag-on-parsha/masei-borders-land-israel/

Levin, Yigal. "Defining the Land of Canaan in Numbers 34". *TheTorah.com*, https://thetorah.com/defining-the-land-of-canaan-in-numbers-34/.

---. "The Three Biblical Maps of Israel: Small, Medium, and Large". *TheTorah.com*, https://thetorah.com/three-biblical-maps-of-israel-small-medium-and-large/.

Patai, Raphael. *Children of Noah: Jewish Seafaring in Ancient Times.* Princeton UP, 1998.

Sefaria, Sefaria, 2012, www.sefaria.org.

Shkolnik, Ya'akov, and Yadin Roman. *Hiking in Israel: 36 of Israel's Best Hiking Routes.* Toby Press, 2008.

Soncino Books of the Bible. A. Cohen, ed. The Soncino Press, 1973.

Tal, Alon. *All the Trees of the Forest: Israel's Woodlands from the Bible to the Present.* Yale UP, 2013.

The Society for the Protection of Nature in Israel, The Society for the Protection of Nature in Israel (SPNI), 2019, www.natureisrael.org.

Vilnay, Zev. *The New Israel Atlas: Bible to Present Day.* Israel Universities Press, 1968.

Further Reading

Alon, Azaria. *The Natural History of the Land of the Bible*. Hamlyn Publishing Group, 1969.

Elitzur, Yoel. *Ancient Place Names in the Holy Land: Preservation and History*. Eisenbrauns, 2004.

Har-El, Menashe. *Landscape, Nature, and Man in the Bible*. Carta Jerusalem, 2015.

---. *Understanding the Geography of the Bible: An Introductory Atlas*. Carta Jerusalem, 2015.

Kark, Ruth, ed. *The Land that Became Israel: Studies in Historical Geography*. Magnes Press/Yale UP, 1989/1990.

Smith, George Adam. *The Historical Geography of the Holy Land*. Hodder & Stoughton, 1894.

Strutin, Michal. *Discovering Natural Israel*. Jonathan David Publishers, 2001.

The River Jordan: An Illustrated Guide from Bible Days to the Present. Carta Jerusalem, 2015.

Tristram, Henry Baker. *The Land of Israel: A Journal of Travels in Palestine, Undertaken with Special Reference to Its Physical Character*. Cambridge UP, 2012.

Index